PREFACE

MUSICAL NOTATION is of necessity imprecise. It leaves much to the innate musicality of the performer, and much to his knowledge of the various conventions and usages of different periods. These last are often blandly ignored by performers—particularly those brought up in a mainly Romantic tradition—with the result that we hear Bach fugues played as though they were Brahms intermezzi, early rhythmic conventions ignored, and ornaments interpreted without any realization that they may mean entirely different things to different composers of even the same period.

The present anthology aims to point out a few of the more important of these problems of style and interpretation. It cannot in the nature of things be comprehensive, for the subject is as vast as the art of music itself; but if it helps to make some players aware that such problems exist and are worth trying to solve, much of its purpose will have been achieved. At the same time, Volumes 1 to 4 form a miniature history of music written for keyboard instruments (excluding the organ) from the mid-16th to the 19th century. The first two volumes together cover the two centuries from c. 1550 onwards, Volume 1 being devoted to composers from England and France, and Volume 2 to those from Germany and Italy. Since they deal with the same period, and with music written mainly for the virginals, the harpsichord or the clavichord, their Introductions are interdependent and should be read in conjunction with one another. Volumes 3 and 4 are both self-contained, and are devoted to, respectively, Classical piano music from Haydn to Schubert, and Romantic piano music from John Field to Brahms. Within the volumes, or sections of a volume, composers are arranged chronologically; and graded indexes are provided for the student who may wish to approach the pieces in order of technical difficulty.

The musical texts are printed as nearly as possible as the composers left them, the source of each being given on its title page. Where an autograph no longer exists, or is for some reason unavailable, either a contemporary manuscript copy or the earliest reliable printed edition has been used. No editorial phrasings, dynamics, pedallings or fingerings have been added. All these aspects of performance are, however, discussed in broad outline in the Introductions, and are often referred to in the Notes that appear before each individual piece. Editorial accidentals, rests, and notes are printed small, editorial slurs and ties are indicated thus: ‿ and other editorial additions are printed in square brackets.

With regard to phrasing, dynamics and pedalling: it is essential that the student should be able to see what a composer really did write, so far as this is possible, if he is ever going to learn how to interpret the existing marks correctly and supply the missing ones in an idiomatic and stylish way. It is also advisable that he should form an early habit of working out his own fingering; for though certain broad principles may be laid down, only the player himself can tell which of several possibilities is the best as far as he is concerned. From every point of view, therefore, it seems preferable to start with an unadulterated text. The student can then cultivate his musical imagination by learning to interpret it for himself.

A partial exception has been made concerning ornamentation. To avoid endless page-turning and reference to tables, a suggested realization of each ornament has been added above or below the stave at its first appearance in every piece.

The music in the various volumes was written for a variety of instruments—the virginals, harpsichord, lute-harpsichord, clavichord, fortepiano and modern piano. Anyone who has access to several of these will be lucky indeed; but even if the student is restricted to the piano alone he should not grieve unduly, for the important thing is that he should play and enjoy the works and others like them. In learning to do so in an idiomatic way he will be opening new fields of exploration and delight for himself, and at the same time enlarging and deepening his understanding of the music he already knows.

ACKNOWLEDGEMENTS

The majority of the pieces in the present volume have been taken from early editions, generally the first, owned by the British Museum. For the use of these, and for permission to publish, I should like to offer my warmest thanks to the Trustees. My thanks are also due to the Musée Mickiewicz, Paris, for permission to use a photograph of the autograph of Chopin's *Mazurka in A flat*; to the Deutsche Staatsbibliothek, Berlin, for a microfilm of the first edition of Liszt's *En Rêve;* and to the Internationale Felix-Mendelssohn-Gesellschaft, Basle, for a photograph of the first edition of Mendelssohn's *Fantasie in E.*

I am very grateful to my friend Mr. T. F. S. Scott for supplying a literal translation of the Salvator Rosa poem on p. 44; and to Mr. Oliver Davies of the Parry Room Library at the Royal College of Music for his help in unearthing 19th century Pianoforte Tutors.

Howard Ferguson
LONDON, 1963

INTRODUCTION

THOUGH the six composers included in the present volume were born in countries as widely separated as Ireland, Germany, Poland and Hungary, they form an unexpectedly interconnected group. John Field, the Irishman, was fifteen years older than Schubert; yet his gentle romanticism and his feeling for a new type of keyboard texture, in which widely-spaced broken chords where held together by a liberal use of the sustaining pedal, mark him out as the unassuming prophet of a whole school of piano writing. His European success as a pianist brought his works before a wide public; and slight though they were, they deeply influenced the composers of the next generation. Chopin gave his pupils the Nocturnes of Field to study, and himself profited by their example; Liszt later published them in an edition of his own; and their effect on Mendelssohn and Schumann, if more indirect, was scarcely less profound. The last link in this chain was provided in the following generation by Brahms, whose early admiration for the music of Mendelssohn was succeeded by a deeper and more lasting veneration for Schumann.

The Instrument and its Dynamics

The instrument for which these 19th century composers wrote was in process of changing its character, as we have already seen from the Introduction to Volume 3 of this anthology. (*Cf.* vol. 3, p. 6, *Fortepiano and Pianoforte*.) Field started his career in the late 1790s by demonstrating Clementi's *fortepianos*: instruments whose light and transparent tone was conditioned by their mainly wooden frames, thinnish, comparatively low-tensioned strings, small leather-covered hammers and shallow touch. But by the mid-19th century Liszt and Brahms were playing on what was virtually the modern *pianoforte*, with its all-iron frame, heavy high-tensioned strings, large, felt-covered hammers and comparatively deep touch, which produced a more powerful tone, but one that was also 'thicker' and less transparent than that of the earlier instrument. In the intervening period, Mendelssohn, Chopin and Schumann used pianos whose tone and touch lay between these two extremes.

The performer of today should always bear in mind the differences between these various instruments, for they are bound to affect his approach to the music itself. (*Cf.* vol. 3, p. 7, *The tone and touch of the Fortepiano*.)

The light touch and transparent tone of Field's fortepiano, coupled with its fairly restricted dynamic range, gives some indication of the type of sound required by his music. Dynamic contrasts should never be extreme, and the all-important melodic line should stand out effortlessly against an accompaniment which is sensitively moulded yet always discreet.

The pianos used by Mendelssohn, Chopin and Schumann were a quarter of a century nearer to our own, nevertheless they were still considerably less 'thick' and powerful than the modern instrument. Mendelssohn in particular must have preferred a touch and tone that was distinctly on the light side, for this would have suited the quick and delicate *pp* staccato effects of which he was so fond. He must also have been accustomed to a bass register that was transparent rather than powerful, otherwise he would never have written a passage such as the l.h. part of bb. 48-50 in his *Fantasie in E*, p.20. If these facts are not borne in mind when playing Mendelssohn today, the heavier quality of our pianos will continually distort his typically light and delicate texture.

With Chopin and Schumann the situation is less straightforward. Their music at times seems to reach out towards the weight and power of the modern pianoforte; yet it should never be forgotten that both composers wrote essentially for an intimate group of listeners in a *salon* or drawing-room, rather than for a more impersonal audience in a large concert hall. Hence, sensitiveness was of greater importance to them that sheer dynamic power. Chopin was delighted when Kalkbrenner mistakenly guessed from his playing that he had been a pupil of Field; and he preferred, as we know, a piano whose touch was much lighter than that used by many performers of his day. A. J. Hipkins of the firm of Broadwood, whose pianos Chopin used in England, wrote that his fortissimo was a full, pure tone without any suspicion of harshness or noise; that his nuances decreased to the faintest yet always distinct pianissimo; and that his singing legatissimo touch was specially remarkable. Schumann, even before he damaged one of his fingers, was not a pianist of the calibre of Chopin; but the intimate character of much of his music suggests that their outlook on performance cannot have been very dissimilar. We have, too, the delightful photograph of Clara Schumann seated at a small upright piano, with her husband gazing adoringly at her; and this suggests that the Schumanns, like Debussy three-quarters of a century later, may even have preferred the smaller type of instrument, at least in the home.

All in all, therefore, it would seem advisable for today's interpreter of Chopin and Schumann to moderate the power of his instrument somewhat. The impression of strength and weight of tone must often be there; but there should always be a reserve, to match not only both composers' preference for an intimate atmosphere, but also the 'inward' quality that is such an essential part of their music.

The full dynamic range of the modern piano was available to Liszt and Brahms. Brahms must have written for just such an instrument from a fairly early age. And though Liszt belonged to the previous generation, his music, like that of Beethoven, always demanded and anticipated every increase in power that the piano manufacturer could supply. Moreover, he outlived his contemporaries Chopin and Schumann by many years; so for

STYLE
AND
INTERPRETATION

An Anthology
of 16th-20th Century Keyboard Music

Edited with Introductions and Notes by
HOWARD FERGUSON

Volume 4: Romantic Piano Music

OXFORD UNIVERSITY PRESS
MUSIC DEPARTMENT
LONDON · NEW YORK · TORONTO

STYLE AND INTERPRETATION

FOREWORD

STUDENTS OF THE PIANO are often so pre-occupied with the acquisition of technical skill that they do not give enough thought to stylistic, textual and interpretative considerations. This is a great mistake, for technique is only a stepping-stone and remains meaningless until it is allied to musical understanding. Innate musicality is the first requisite; but this must be cultivated, not only through contact with a wide variety of music, but through a knowledge of the way in which style and interpretation changes from century to century and country to country. Such facts are quite as important as technical skill, and if a student ignores them, his playing, however brilliant superficially, will never penetrate to the core of the music.

In this anthology Dr. Ferguson has made an outstanding contribution to the clarification of these problems. His absorbing survey, written from the twin viewpoints of a composer and performer, is imaginative and lucid, and covers an extensive period in a way which has not, I believe, been attempted before. Everyone who is interested in keyboard music and its performance should find these volumes endlessly stimulating and instructive.

February 1963

MYRA HESS

Printed in Great Britain by Halstan & Co. Ltd., Amersham, Bucks.

much of his career he was able to play on the modern pianoforte itself.

Tempo: Metronome marks

Metronome marks would seem at first sight to solve every problem concerning the notation and interpretation of tempi; yet in practice they often pose almost as many questions as they answer.

The modern metronome was perfected in 1816 by a German mechanician named Johann Nepomuk Maelzel (1772-1838). Beethoven was at first greatly interested in the device. He had welcomed its immediate forerunner in 1812 with a short Canon ('Ta, ta, ta . . .', WoO 162 in Kinsky's catalogue), afterwards used as the opening theme of the Allegretto movement of the Eighth Symphony; and in 1817 and 1819 he issued two small booklets containing metronome markings for the eleven string quartets and eight symphonies that he had already published. He also included metronome marks in several subsequent works as they appeared, notably the 'Hammerklavier' Sonata, Op. 106, and the Ninth Symphony, Op. 125. Significantly enough, however, there are none in the last six string quartets and the last three piano sonatas—a fact which suggests that Beethoven, like Wagner a quarter of a century later, eventually lost faith in the usefulness of the metronome.

There are several possible reasons for such a change of attitude. Firstly, metronome marks may suggest to the performer that tempi are absolute, whereas experience shows that they depend to a certain extent on variable factors, such as acoustical conditions, the instrument used, etc. Secondly, a composer, unless he checks and re-checks his markings, can all too easily put down a figure that seriously misrepresents his true intentions, particularly if he attempts (as Beethoven must have done) to mark a large number of works in a short space of time. Thirdly, it is sometimes impossible to find a single metronome mark that makes sense of a whole movement, or even of a section of a movement. And lastly, metronomes in themselves are often inaccurate, even today: for example, two machines set at the same figure will rarely tick at the same speed; while even a single machine set at (say) 50 will hardly ever tick just half as slowly as when set at 100.

It seems likely that some or all of these reasons must have accounted not only for Beethoven's ultimate rejection of the metronome, but also for Brahms' complete avoidance of it. The remaining composers in the present volume were less consistent: sometimes they included metronome marks in their scores and sometimes not. When a figure is given, it *may* supply a valuable clue to the composer's intentions. On the other hand, it may equally well be totally misleading.

Schumann seems to have been particularly unreliable in this respect. In his *Kinderscenen*, Op. 15, for example, it is often quite impossible to reconcile the metronome marks with the moods implied by the titles. (There are no normal tempo indications.) Thus in the very first piece, 'Of Strange Lands and Peoples', the marking ♩ = 108 seems considerably too quick and matter-of-fact to convey the intended atmosphere of 'once-upon-a-time'; while 'A Curious Story', which follows, becomes flat-footed and humourless if played as slowly as Schumann's ♩ = 112. Two later markings are even more unconvincing. No. 7, 'Dreaming', would sound far from dream-like if played as quickly as ♩ = 100; and in No. 10, 'Almost too Serious', ♩ = 69 seems so absurdly fast as to make one think that it must be a misprint for ♪ = 69. Most of the remaining metronome marks in *Kinderscenen*, and many of those in Schumann's other works (*cf.* the *Romanze in F sharp*, p. 35), seem equally improbable. If they were consistently either too fast or too slow it would be less puzzling, for then one would assume that Schumann's machine had been wrongly regulated; but as we have already seen, this is not so. Such apparently capricious markings are hard to account for, unless the explanation of them is as simple as that given by a present-day composer concerning his own works. When asked about his somewhat unexpected metronome markings he replied, 'Are they wrong? I never thought of testing them with a machine.'

With this startling admission in mind, even if for no other reason, the student will understand that it is not *always* wise to follow metronome marks literally. What then should be done about them?

The safest rule is to assume that any metronome mark is worth noting, if the composer has put it there. It should always be tried out—not simply ignored, as so often happens. Then, if it is found to illuminate and make sense of the music, it should be accepted as an indication of the basic tempo of the movement or section of a movement, rather than as a speed from which the player may never deviate by a hair's-breadth. On the other hand, if the music sounds persistently 'wrong' or uncomfortable at the speed indicated, the player must feel free to experiment with different tempi: slightly slower or faster in the first instance, to allow for small differences between metronomes; then, if need be, at tempi that are considerably faster or slower, to allow for Schumann-like quirks. At some point in this process, the player will find that the rhythmic detail of the music suddenly slips into focus with its mood; and when this happens, he may feel tolerably certain that he has found the correct basic tempo of the movement or section concerned.

Metronomic rhythm is rarely an ideal to be aimed at in performance, except in certain cases such as quick dances and marches. Almost every other kind of music—and romantic music in particular—'breathes' in a way that is altogether foreign to a machine. In spite of this, the metronome can be exceedingly useful at times for purposes of practice. It may never allow the player sufficient time for the *rits.* and more subtle kinds of rubato that he would normally make; but it will show him, generally to his pain and surprise, that he often unconsciously hurries a crescendo, drags a diminuendo, clips the ends of runs, and so on. Not all of these tendencies are invariably out of place; but the player should be aware of them, and only indulge them when he intends to do so, otherwise his performance will become flaccid and uncontrolled.

It need hardly be added that editorial metronome marks—including those given in the Notes to the pieces of the present anthology—have no textual authority whatever. They are merely the expression of an editor's opinion, which may or may not be helpful to the player.

Tempo: Unmarked sectional changes

Broadly speaking, there are two kinds of unmarked variation of tempo in music of all periods: small local changes, including *rubato* which will be discussed later; and broader though less ubiquitous *sectional changes*.

Examples of the latter in early keyboard music are found in the different tempi required in ricercars, canzonas, capriccios, variations and toccatas. (*Cf.* vol. 1, top of p. 10, under *Tempo*; and vol. 2, p. 11, under *Italy: Ornamentation*.) Since the tempo indications of today were little known at that period, the correct interpretation of these works depended, as we have already seen, on the combined knowledge and instinct of the performer.

In classical music this is less likely to be the case; not only because tempo indications were customary, but also because the typical large-scale forms of the period—the various movements of Sonata or Symphony—were generally conceived in a uniform basic tempo throughout. Thus, in the opening *Allegro con brio* of Beethoven's 'Waldstein' Sonata, Op. 53, small local variations of tempo may be in place, but the slowing down of its second subject (b. 35) to what Tovey dubs an *Andante religioso* is not. Nor is it either musical or logical to play the opening of the 'Appassionata' Sonata, Op. 57, at an entirely different speed from its recapitulation (b. 135), merely because the latter happens to have an added quaver accompaniment.

A basically uniform tempo—or at least the *impression* of a uniform tempo—should therefore be aimed at in classical music. Exceptions to the rule are occasionally found, however, and the student should be on the look-out for those that are unmarked. They are most likely to occur in sets of variations, since these are in themselves sectional and at times contain abrupt changes of mood. An isolated minor variation in a major context, for instance, may imply so great an emotional contrast that it must be accommodated by some relaxation of tempo; and similar adjustments may be required elsewhere.

A subtle and unexpected type of tempo change is needed in certain rhythmically cumulative variations. In the slow movement of the 'Appassionata' Sonata, for example, where the theme is mainly in crotchets and the three variations are successively in quavers, semiquavers and demi-semiquavers, it will be found that no single tempo fits both theme and third variation. This is not because of the difficulty experienced in virginal music of playing sixteen demi-semiquavers in the time of one crotchet, it is for precisely the opposite reason: here there is too much time for the demi-semiquavers, for a curious aural illusion at times makes slow music sound less slow, and quick music less quick, than it is in fact being played. Hence if we want to give the *impression* of a uniform tempo in this movement, we must increase the speed very slightly with each succeeding variation—much as an ancient Greek architect made the lines of his buildings slightly curved in order to give an effect of straightness. Such progressive tempo changes are by no means always necessary in cumulative variations: they are, indeed, only likely to occur when the theme itself is on the slow side.

Some of Schubert's sonata-form movements, unlike those of Beethoven and earlier classical composers, require different tempi to suit the sharply contrasted moods of their themes. In the *Sonata in A minor*, Op. 42 (D.845), it is impossible to find one tempo that makes sense of both the opening subject and its pendant (b. 26), for either the first will sound too fast or the second too slow. Here, and throughout the movement, two slightly different tempi seem to be intended. It is up to the player, therefore, to preserve the sense of continuity by making the changes as unobtrusive as possible. Where a musical link exists, a gradual transition can often be made from one tempo to the other, as in bb. 10-20, where a slight accelerando will carry the listener imperceptibly from the relaxed mood of the opening to the more urgent mood of b. 26. If there are no links, as in the last dozen bars of the exposition, the changes will perforce be abrupt.

With the advent of romantic music tempi in general become more fluid than before. Sectional changes are more usual and local changes more exaggerated, and the two types even merge at times. Luckily for the performer, the sectional changes are generally clearly marked. Exceptions do occur, however; particularly in the Chopin Mazurkas, whose rhythmic freedom is a legacy of their prototype, the Polish folksong-cum-dance. Some of the Mazurkas, like the Schubert A minor Sonata, require two distinct tempi; but here the difference between the two is likely to be greater than in the earlier work. As before, the player will generally find that the presence of a musical link implies a gradual transition from one tempo to the other, while the absence of a link implies an abrupt change. Examples of both will be found in the *Mazurka in C sharp minor*, p. 28. The Note to this piece also draws attention to an interesting combination of tempo-change and rubato, very typical of Chopin. In it, there is a gradual change from the slower to the quicker of two tempi, followed by a gradual return to the original speed, the whole forming what might be called a 'rhythmic arch' (*cf.* bb. 9-16).

Not all of Chopin's Mazurkas require sectional tempo changes. The *Mazurka in A flat*, p. 26, is one of the many that has a single basic tempo throughout; though small local variations are of course still essential to the life of the music.

Tempo: Rubato

During the earlier part of the present century the true nature of rubato was hotly disputed: did it, through an exact balance of *rit.* and *accel.*, leave the basic pulse unchanged in the long run? or did it radically disrupt the pulse? The answer is that it does both, for there are two different kinds of rubato: melodic and structural.

In *melodic rubato* the accompaniment keeps strict time, while the melody follows the freer dictates of 'vocal' expressiveness. The two rhythms coincide at structurally important points in the bar or phrase, and thus the basic pulse remains intact.

Early examples of one type of this rubato are found in the *Notes inégales* of the French harpsichordists (*cf.* vol. 1, p. 18). And Mozart later referred to another aspect of it when he wrote to his Father in October 1777:

> Everyone is amazed that I can always keep strict time. What these people cannot grasp is that in tempo rubato in an Adagio, the left hand should go on playing in

strict time. With them the left hand always follows suit. [Emily Anderson's translation.]

Occasionally Mozart even systematized one form of melodic rubato by including it in his notation. A particularly interesting instance of this is the passage of descending thirds seven bars before the end of the Adagio of the *Sonata in F*, K.332. In the autograph it is written straight-forwardly, thus:

Then, sometime between the composition of the work and its publication six years later, Mozart must have decided that the final appearance of the phrase required a more wayward expressiveness, for in the first edition of 1784 it is printed:

This is a broader and more regular version of melodic rubato than would normally be added by a performer; nevertheless it shows one aspect of what was in Mozart's mind when he wrote to his Father.

Descriptions of melodic rubato (though under different names) appear in treatises from the early 18th century onwards, including those of Couperin (1717), Tosi (1723), Quantz (1752), C. P. E. Bach (1753) and Leopold Mozart (1756). In the 19th century it was taught by Chopin, who told his pupils that the singing hand may deviate, but the accompaniment must keep time. And today it is heard continually in the melodic anticipations and delays of jazz musicians. It is, indeed, so natural a part of any music founded on a vocal style, that it is likely to have been used, if not defined, long before the 18th century.

In *structural rubato*, the second of our two types, melody and accompaniment deviate from strict tempo simultaneously. This means that no exact balance of *rit.* and *accel.* is needed to keep the hands together; and since such a balance is unlikely to be achieved by accident, there is almost bound to be a change in the basic pulse.

This type of rubato will be much more familiar to the student than the other, for he uses it whenever he obeys a composer's direction *rit. - - - a tempo*, or makes the smallest unmarked *rit.* or *accel.* on his own initiative. It was equally familiar to early writers, one of the first to mention it being Frescobaldi in the prefaces to his Toccatas and Partitas (1614-15) and Capriccios and Canzonas (1624). (*Cf.* vol. 2, p. 11, under *Italy: Ornamentation.*) It too is such a natural part of any music founded on a vocal style that we can safely assume it was known and practised from the earliest times.

How, then, should the player of today use these two different types of rubato in his interpretation of music of different periods? No detailed answer can be given to this question, for the convincing use of rubato depends more on feeling and instinct than on rule. Nevertheless, the following hints may provide some rough guidance for the student:

1. Rubato of one kind or another is natural to most music, except when its appeal is predominantly rhythmic (marches, quick dances, etc.).

2. Melodic rubato, in which the rhythm of the accompaniment is strictly maintained while the melody deviates from it, is a type of 'vocal' expressiveness. Only very small rhythmic deviations are involved—generally much smaller and more irregular than those of the Mozart example quoted above—and it is more likely to be needed in slow music than in fast.

3. Structural rubato, in which melody and accompaniment together deviate from strict tempo, is characteristic of almost all types of music, except the purely rhythmical. It is used not only for its expressive value, but also at times to help define phrasing and structure. (*Cf.* vol. 1, p. 10-11, under *Phrasing.*) It can be anything from a scarcely perceptible delay to a broad *rit.* or *accel.*, or *rit.* and *accel.* combined.

4. The *degree* of rubato used contributes more than anything else to the rightness or wrongness of its effect.

5. Romantic types of music require more pronounced rubato than classical. Hence music of the 19th century is likely on the whole to require greater rhythmic freedom than that of the 18th.

6. Within this broad classification, a romantically minded composer will require a more pronounced rubato than one who is classically minded. Thus, moving backwards in time, Schumann requires more freedom than Brahms, Chopin more than Mendelssohn, Schubert more than Beethoven, W. F. Bach more than his brother Johann Christian, and Froberger more than Couperin.

7. The freer forms are likely to require a corresponding freedom of rhythm, while the stricter forms generally (but not invariably) require less freedom. (*Cf.* vol. 1, top of p. 10, under *Tempo.*)

8. No matter how extreme a rubato is used, the player must always take the greatest care never to lose sight of the basic structure of the music.

Pedalling

The romantic period in piano writing might almost be called the Era of the Sustaining Pedal. This will be apparent if a comparison is made between the music contained in the present volume and in the preceding one. In Volume 3, *Classical Piano Music*, it would be perfectly possible, though hardly comfortable, to give a musical performance of almost every piece without touching the pedals. (The sole exception is the Beethoven *Bagatelle in E flat*.) In the present volume, on the other hand, the musical effect and meaning of every piece depends at one point or another, and sometimes throughout, on the use of the sustaining pedal.

The fundamental cause of this change was the gradually increasing sonority of the piano itself. (*Cf. The Instrument and its Dynamics*, p. 6.) With the greatly enriched harmonics of the newer instruments, 'close-position' chords in the bass, whether broken or unbroken, no longer sounded tolerable. Composers therefore opened out the chords, played their notes successively instead of simultaneously, and used the pedal to sustain what could not be stretched by a single hand. This was only a development of an age-old device, for broken chords had been used from an early time to provide both rhythmic interest and a sustaining effect in keyboard music (*cf. The Short Mesure off My Lady Wynkfylds Rownde*, vol. 1, p. 22, bb. 13-14, etc.). What was new was the realisation that the pedal permitted spacings which were not only beyond the reach of a single hand, but also peculiarly suited to the evanescent tone of the piano. A new and beautiful type of keyboard texture was thus evolved, whose immense potentialities were developed continuously up to the time of Debussy and beyond.

All the composers in the present volume use some form of this characteristic romantic piano texture, of which two basic types may be distinguished. In the first, the chord is spread out in single notes, as seen in the Field *Nocturne*, p. 17, where

And in the second, the chord is divided into smaller chords, or a combination of smaller chords and single notes, such as are found in the Chopin *Mazurka in C sharp minor*, p. 28, where

It is important that such lay-outs, and any combination of them, should be recognized by the student, for though they depend entirely on the r.h. pedal for their effect, the composer (as can be seen from the first example) does not always bother to mark the necessary pedal changes in his score. When there are no marks, the safest way to determine the pedalling is to reduce the open-textured 'chords' to their closed position, as shown in the 2nd half of the above examples. The pedalling will then generally be found to coincide with the changes of harmony. At times, of course, other factors must be taken into consideration. In the Brahms *Capriccio*, p. 52, for example, the first three bars contain only two basic harmonies each; yet three pedals per bar will probably be required—on the 1st, 5th and 9th quavers—otherwise the middle of each bar may sound over-thick. But notice that the second pedal-change, on the 5th quaver, never involves the loss of the

true bass, for the 5th note is always just an octave higher than the 1st. In bb. 49-50, on the contrary, the pedal could not be changed on the 5th quavers, as this would mean losing the true bass. Instead, the passage must be pedalled thus:

Another possible reason for modifying 'harmonic' pedalling may be the complexity of the r.h. part. The lesser sustaining power of the treble as compared with the bass will generally take care of this. But at times the sound must be thinned out by means of the kind of half-pedalling that leaves the more resonant bass notes still partly audible; and in extreme cases the bass must be abandoned altogether and left to the surprisingly co-operative imagination of the listener.

In the Brahms example above, the editorial marks in brackets indicate legato-pedalling, the type most frequently used nowadays. In it, the pedal is depressed immediately *after* a note has been struck. and released simultaneously with the attack on a note; with the result that the second note is joined to the first in a perfect legato, and without the slightest trace of 'fuzz' or carry-over in sound from one to the other. An earlier method, now less common, is sometimes known as rhythmic-pedalling. Here the pedal is depressed *simultaneously* with the attack, and released just before a note is struck. The legato obtained thus may be slightly less perfect; but the notes acquire a sort of 'bloom', due to the sympathetic vibration of the other undamped strings, which can be extremely beautiful in a slow cantabile. A third type of pedalling, related to the last, can only be used after a silence. In it, the pedal is depressed *before* the note is struck, with results very similar to those achieved by rhythmic-pedalling.

The editorial pedal-marks shown above, and several other types found in 20th century editions, can give absolutely precise indications of pedalling. Unfortunately, the same cannot be said of the normal 19th century marks, ℘ and ✳. Not only are these far too large to be exact, but they were often written and printed very haphazardly. Generally this was due to sheer carelessness; but at times it was because there was not enough space in either the MS or the engraving to place the signs correctly. This is particularly true of the bulky *Ped.* sign, which often gets pushed to one side by the ledger-lines of the bass note to which it is meant to apply. (*Cf.* the Note to Schumann's *Abschied*, p. 38.)

These various facts, coupled with the previously mentioned difference in sonority between old and modern instruments, all suggest that pedal indications in romantic music, as in classical, should be interpreted with discretion rather than followed blindly. The student should do his best to divine what effect the composer was aiming at in each instance. He should then strive to reproduce that effect as closely as possible with the means at his disposal.

One other notational peculiarity connected with the sustaining pedal must be mentioned. As can be seen from the Chopin example quoted above, composers sometimes use staccato marks in combination with pedal signs. At first sight this would appear to be a contradiction in terms. What is meant, however, is not that the player should attempt an impossible shortening of the notes concerned, but that he should play them with the same touch and attack as he would use for a staccato; for this, as experiment will show, produces a slightly different tone from playing the same notes legato and with pedal.

The l.h. 'soft' pedal (Italian, *una corda*; German, *Verschiebung*) is completely in keeping with the style of the period, though it is indicated less frequently than one might expect. When the student is considering its use in works where it is not marked, he should remember the advice given on p. 14 of the Introduction to vol. 1:

> Since it [the l.h. pedal] effects nothing but the tone, it can be used for long or short periods as required. The player must, however, be on his guard against relying on its help every time he wants to produce a quiet sound; otherwise he will inevitably halve the number of colours at his disposal, and (worse still) become incapable of appreciating and producing subtle tonal differences by means of his fingers alone.

Fingering

Widely spaced basses, such as those shown in the last example of the previous section, led to a new 'Brahmsian' way of fingering broken chords. It consisted in dividing an arpeggio into complete handfuls, instead of part-handfuls, and relying on the pedal to mask the inevitable breaks in legato between 5th finger and thumb. The method will be clear when normal classical fingering is added above the stave and the Brahmsian kind below:

Here the classical fingering uses the thumb as a pivot to achieve a legato independent of the pedal; whereas the Brahmsian type depends on the pedal to supply the legato between the 2nd and third quavers of each bar.

In this particular passage there is little to choose between the two methods, since pedal must in any case be used. Elsewhere, the Brahmsian type of fingering may be essential to the musical effect, the following passage from the Brahms *Rhapsody in E flat*, Op. 119, being a case in point. The downward crotchet-stems suggest not only that the arpeggio should be fingered in four-note handfuls, but also that a slight accent is required on the first note of each group:

If this arpeggio were fingered in the normal classical way— that is, as a recurrent three-note pattern of 421—pedal-changes might take care of the sustaining effect of the

crotchets, but the hand-movements would be going clean against the implied accents. With the Brahmsian method, shown in brackets, both sustaining effect and accents are achieved automatically.

The student should bear in mind this type of fingering, as it is often required in Brahms, even when no hints such as separate crotchet-stems are included in the score.

Ornamentation

During the 19th century the use of graphic signs for ornaments continued to decrease. Apart from shakes and arpeggios, it became more and more usual to write out ornaments in full, either in normal-sized notes as an integral part of the rhythmic scheme, extra-rhythmically in small notes, or in a mixture of small and normal-sized notes. The first of these methods presents no problems; but the exact interpretation of the other two can at times be puzzling.

In contrast to 18th century practice, shakes now begin with the main note instead of the upper auxiliary, as can be seen from the Pianoforte Schools of Johann Nepomuk Hummel (1828) and Carl Czerny (1839). (John Field may be an exception in this respect, for he was born a good deal earlier than the other composers in the present volume, and was moreover a pupil of Clementi, who followed the 18th century rule. Nevertheless, at least one of his shakes— in b. 29 of the 11th Nocturne in E flat— sounds wrong if begun on the upper auxiliary. Some of the rest seem to require a start on the main note, while others need the auxiliary; so the player should make his choice according to the context.) Another 19th century innovation is that the small crossed quaver ($\flat$) no longer represents an alternative way of writing a semiquaver, but is now a sign in its own right meaning a short appoggiatura.

The ornaments most frequently encountered are listed below, together with hints for their interpretation. 19th century treatises were no exception in being somewhat behind the times; so it has been necessary to deduce certain features of contemporary practice from the works of composers themselves. The sign for the Beat (*Mordent*) is rarely used, and will not be found in the present volume of pieces, but it has been added here for the sake of completeness.

1. The Shake (*Triller*): tr, ᴡ.

(a) short ♩ = ♫♪. or ♫♩ (on the beat);

(b) long ♩ = (long trill notation) or (trill notation) (on the beat).

Sign (a) no longer implies more than a three-note shake, sometimes called an inverted- or upper-mordent. Occasionally, if it occurs on a very short note, it must even be reduced to a single short appoggiatura, ♪♩ . Note that when the ornament is part of a chord, it still must be played on the beat: (notation) = (notation)

The *tr* sign can also occasionally mean the same as sign (a) if it appears on a short, or a very short note. But generally it implies a shake with a greater number of repercussions, beginning on the main note and on the beat, lasting as long as the written value of the note, and ending on the main note.

Long shakes are often preceded by one or more small notes. These are generally (but not invariably) played on the beat and included as part of the ornament. If the main note and the small one immediately before it are the same, as often happens in Chopin, the shake proper should start with the auxiliary; for the contiguous notes of a shake and its prefix should always differ.

Closing-notes must sometimes be added to shakes when unmarked, but as a rule they are only required when included in the text, either as small notes or as an integral part of the rhythmic scheme.

2. The Beat (*Mordent*): ♠ .

♠ = or (on the beat).

This ornament is generally written out in full in 19th century music, either as part of the rhythmic scheme in large notes, or else in small notes: . In the latter case it is also played on the beat.

3. The Turn (*Doppelschlag*): ∾ .

(a) on the note = or (on the beat)

(b) after the note = or (off the note = or the beat)

or some rhythmic variation of the same notes.
Both (a) and (b) are often written out in full, in large or small notes. In the latter case the ornament is played in one of the ways suggested above.

4. The Short Appoggiatura (*kurzer Vorschlag*): ♪ , ♪ , ♪ , etc.

In 19th century music long appoggiaturas are almost invariably written out in normal sized notes as part of the rhythmic scheme, while small notes (of whatever denomination) are reserved for short appoggiaturas. Contemporary books of instruction all agree that the short appoggiatura should be played *on* the beat; but the music itself suggests that there must be many exceptions to the rule, and that they are likely to increase in number as the century progresses. The explanation is probably two-fold. Firstly, there is always a time-lag between theory and practice. And secondly, as composers and performers moved away from the period in which the old ornament signs were in constant use, they tended to forget their correct interpretation, and to accept the graphic position of the substituted small-note ornaments as an accurate indication of their rhythmic position. So much so, that the normal 20th century practice is to play all grace-notes before the beat, unless the composer directs otherwise, as Ravel did in *Le Tombeau de Couperin* (1917) when imitating an earlier style.

At times, 19th century composers indicated anticipatory appoggiaturas by placing them before the barline if they occurred on a first beat. (*Cf.* Schumann's *Abschied*, p. 38,

b. 48.) But unfortunately for us, appoggiaturas are not restricted to first beats, nor are composers always consistent, even in their own works; so we are often left in doubt as to what was intended. It seems certain, however, that a single-note appoggiatura always anticipates the beat when it is identical with the following note, whether this be large or small. (*Cf.* section 6, *Arpeggio.*) And it is probable that anticipation is also intended with many bass appoggiaturas that are followed by a leap to a higher note or chord, as these are merely a kind of pedal indication. (*Cf.* Schumann's *Abschied*, p. 38, b. 45, where the poignancy of the discord on the first beat would be lost if the r.h. C and the l.h. B flat were not played simultaneously.) Other cases are more uncertain, so each must be judged on its own merits.

By the mid-19th century it seems likely that appoggiaturas come before the beat as a rule rather than as an exception. This can be deduced from a passage such as the fortissimo version of the march theme in Liszt's *Ballade No.* 1 (1848):

Here the l.h. appoggiaturas must be played as anticipations, otherwise the three-note chords that follow lose all their power through failing to coincide with the beats of the r.h. Moreover, the single r.h. appoggiatura must also be intended as an anticipation; for had Liszt meant it to be different from the rest, he would have drawn attention to the fact by using some such notation as

The Brahms *Ballade*, p. 48, provides further confirmation of this new practice. Admittedly it would be possible throughout the piece to play the grace-notes on the beat, with the l.h. following the pattern . But if that were done, it would be necessary to play the r.h. first beat of b. 64 as ; and this seems improbable, since it introduces the interval of a ninth, which has never hitherto appeared in the theme.

5. Groups of small notes.
As was pointed out in the Introduction to vol. 3, it is not possible to give hard and fast rules for the rhythmic placing of groups of small notes. Nevertheless it is often helpful to remember that they may be realisations, or part-realisations, of an old ornament. If, therefore, there is a resemblance between the outline of the small-note group and the realisation of one of the older ornament-signs (*cf.* Germany: Ornamentation, vol. 2, p. 9), the small notes should probably be interpreted in the same way

rhythmically as the ornament. Hence:

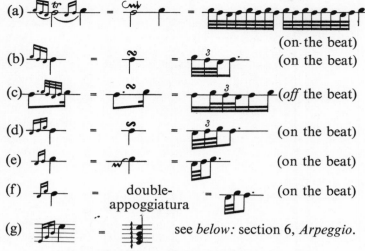

or some rhythmic variation of the same notes.
If both (b), on the beat, and (c), off the beat, are possible interpretations of a three-note group, as in:

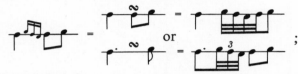

the version that sounds the more musical in its context should be chosen.

Small-note groups containing more than four notes are likely to come before the beat, subtracting their value from the previous note.

Helpful as the above comparisons may be at times, it should be remembered that they are less consistently valid for the 19th century than for the 18th. For it seems likely, as pointed out in the last section, that anticipated grace-notes become more common as the 19th century advances. For example, in the Liszt *Piano Concerto No. 2 in A*, 10 bars after letter C, the cellos and violas have the following figure: [music]. At an earlier date these grace-notes would have been played on the beat; but here we know they should be played before, for Liszt contrasts the two kinds of notation in the piano part throughout the previous 10 bars, thus:

and there would be no point in doing this unless the second beat meant something different from the third.

6. *Arpeggio:* ‖ and (.

Both these signs show that the chord should be broken upwards, either quickly or slowly as the context suggests. In theory the arpeggio should begin on the beat, and it generally does so if it occurs in the r.h. alone. When in the l.h. alone it often comes before the beat, its top note coinciding with the beat itself. An arpeggio sign extending over both staves implies that the chord should be broken continuously from the lowest to the highest note. If each hand has a separate sign, the hands should generally begin simultaneously, or with one hand (generally the r.h.) starting slightly after the other, the main consideration being to avoid a thin tonal effect.

When grace-notes are combined with arpeggios, the grace-note (or -notes) should be interpolated immediately before the note nearest to which it stands:

This ornament must not be confused with the long-appoggiatura-plus-arpeggio of the Baroque period (*cf.* vol. 2, p. 10), where [music].

Note the following unusual notation in Chopin's *Nocturne in F sharp minor*, Op. 48, No. 2, and several other of his works, where the apparent slur is really a curved arpeggio sign:

Arpeggios written out in small notes follow the same rules, at least in theory. Chopin certainly intended r.h. small-note arpeggios to be played on the beat, for he drew the following dotted lines in a pupil's copy of the Nocturnes:

Nocturne, Op. 15, No. 1   *Nocturne, Op. 37, No. 1*   *Nocturne, Op. 48, No. 2*

In an ornament such as [music] the first small D would also come on the beat. But if the first D were written separately, as in b. 5 of the *Nocturne in G minor:* [music], the beat would coincide with the *second* small D; for, as we have seen in section 4, *above*, a single appoggiatura anticipates the beat when it is identical with the following note.

Other Romantic composers would appear to be less strict about starting small-note arpeggios on the beat. In Mendelssohn's *Song Without Words*, Op. 62, No. 6

(the famous 'Spring Song') the small-note broken chords almost certainly anticipate the beat throughout; likewise in his 'Venetian Gondola Song', Op. 62, No. 5:

 . In Schumann's *Etudes*

Symphoniques, Op. 13, the small-note downward arpeggios

in the r.h. of Etude IX

would also seem to require anticipation, otherwise the rhythmic bite of the descending scale of the theme is lost.

From these examples it will be seen that no binding rule can be given concerning the placing of these ornaments. So once more, and for the last of many times in this anthology, the student is advised to follow his instinct and play the version that sounds the most musical in its context.

Editions: Urtexts and others

In the Prefaces to these volumes it has been stated that the musical texts are here printed *as nearly as possible* as the composers left them. By way of Epilogue it would be as well to consider why any such reservation is necessary, and exactly what it implies both in general and in relation to the present edition.

One might think that a composer's autograph, if it exists, could be printed virtually as it stands. But this is rarely true. Composers are fallible, like other human beings; and in addition some are careless, while others are plain muddle-headed. The story goes that a present-day copyist was puzzled by a passage in a new orchestral work, and wrote to ask the eminent composer whether it was intended for a B flat or an A clarinet—which sound a semitone apart. A postcard came in reply: 'Can't make head or tail of it. Better leave it out altogether.'

As we move backwards in time from the mid-19th century the difficulties multiply, for changes in notational practice, both small and large, make it less and less possible to print an autograph as it stands. The player of today might be only momentarily worried by the way in which composers as unexotic as Mozart, Beethoven, Schubert and even Chopin may or may not expect an accidental to carry over into subsequent bars (*cf.* the Note on Chopin's *Mazurka in A flat*, p. 26, bb. 2-4); but he is likely to be less at ease with Bach's soprano, alto and tenor clefs; and would probably be altogether foxed by the virginalists' stave of six or more lines, with its G, F and C clefs placed on whichever line happens to be convenient, its irregular barring, haphazard accidentals, and baffling disregard for the correct alignment of notes.

Often, too, a work exists in more than a single source. There may be several differing autographs, in which case it must be decided which one contains the composer's final version. Or an autograph may exist together with a contemporary printed edition or MS copy in another hand, or several of each; and if this is so, it is not necessarily the autograph that provides the definitive text: for the composer may have made alterations at the proof stage (*cf.* the two Mozart quotations on p. 9, under *Tempo: Rubato*); or a MS may be a copy of a later autograph version that has since disappeared.

Finally, no autograph whatever may have survived, in which case a modern edition must rely on any early editions or MS copies that may be available.

In all of these cases an editor's intervention is obviously required, both for the major task of establishing the text itself, and for the minor one of making the original notation reasonably readable for the player of today. A conscientious editor will always make perfectly clear the extent of his intervention in matters of textual importance. But however anxious he may be to present an authentic text, he would find it unpractical to specify every minor deviation from the original.

In the present volumes, for example, treble and bass clefs have as usual been substituted for the less familiar clefs used by early composers. Yet even as simple an alteration as this often necessitates a new distribution of notes between the two staves. Other changes of lay-out may result from an editor's decision not to reproduce certain features of earlier MSS, such as writing both hands on a single stave whenever they play in the same register, giving a separate stem to each note of a chord, or shifting a single part from stave to stave in order to avoid the use of ledger-lines. Such alterations are textually unimportant, and it would be pointless as well as impossibly cumbersome to list them in detail.

Though a definitive text should take account of all the available sources, it has not been possible to follow this rule with every piece included in the present volumes. Practical considerations have in some cases limited the editor's choice to one of several possible sources, notably with certain of the English virginal pieces in vol. 1, with the Bach *Prelude*, *Tempo di Gavotta* and *Fugue* in vol. 2, and the Beethoven *Bagatelle in E flat* in vol. 3.

None of the pieces in vols. 1 and 2 exists in autograph, with the exception of an early version of the Bach *Tempo di Gavotta* from the Partita in E minor that appears in the Anna Magdalena Book. All the works in these two volumes have therefore been taken from contemporary MS copies or printed editions. More autographs of the classical period have survived, so it has been possible to use the composer's own manuscript for more than half of the pieces in vol. 3. First editions again become of prime importance in the 19th century, for composers were by then beginning to correct their own proofs with care, which they had rarely been given a chance to do at an earlier period. Hence, all the pieces in vol. 4, except one, take the first edition for their source.

Publishers have only comparatively recently begun to realise that reprints of older music should aim to give an unencumbered picture of the composer's text. In the second half of the 19th century, when most of the standard German popular editions of the classics were first produced, it was usual to invite a famous virtuoso or teacher to act as editor. This he would do by smothering the unfortunate classic with countless additional marks of phrasing, dynamics and fingering, none of which were in any way distinguishable from the original. (An honourable exception was Dr. Hans Bischoff, whose Steingräber edition of the keyboard works of Bach, published in the

1880s, clearly differentiated between Bach and Bischoff, and ingeniously managed at the same time to include all the variant readings that were then known.)

In reaction to this approach, and as a corrective to some of the inadequately edited volumes of the great Collected Editions of Breitkopf & Härtel, the Berlin Academy of Arts began in the 1890s to issue a series of 'Urtexts' (original texts) of some of the keyboard works of J. S. Bach, C. P. E. Bach, Mozart (including his Violin Sonatas), Beethoven and Chopin. Their aim, not always successfully realised, was to present a composer's un-adulterated text, as it appeared in the most reliable autograph or edition. Other German publishers slowly followed this lead, with the result that more and more 'Urtexts' appeared from the 1930s onwards. Sometimes the description was merited, and sometimes it was not. One normally reputable publisher even fell as low as adding a new cover and title-page, prominently labelled *Urtext*, to a grossly over-edited volume that had been in his list for years. Luckily, however, this sort of thing was the exception rather than the rule; and in recent years firms have on the whole tackled with increasing seriousness the problem of providing reliable musical texts. The Henle Verlag of Munich, the Bärenreiter Verlag of Kassel and the *Musica Britannica* series of London are notable examples of this trend, and others will be found mentioned in the Notes to the individual pieces in the present volumes.

In spite of this gradual improvement, bad editions of every description still clutter the market. For this reason, the student should take careful thought before laying the all-important foundations of his working library, other-wise much of his money may be wasted. He might find that Beethoven's views on the dynamics of Bach, as reported in Czerny's edition of *The Forty-Eight Preludes and Fugues*, have a certain interest of their own; but they do not provide a very satisfactory foundation on which to try and build an authentic interpretation. Nor do many of the other editions that are swamped in editorial markings.

If he keeps his eyes open, the student will gradually learn to recognise the outward signs of a good or a bad edition. Until he can do this, he may find it helpful to remember the following points:—

1. In an edition of music of an earlier period, the source or sources of the reprint should always be stated.

2. There should be some form of editorial commentary, however short, which presents the relevant facts concerning the work and its editing.

3. Editorial marks should be differentiated typographically from those of the original.

4. Significant editorial alterations of the text should be noted.

5. When editorial realizations of ornaments or rhythmic conventions have been added, they should *not* be incorporated in the text, but printed separately above or below the stave, or at the foot of the page.

The fulfilment of these conditions is no guarantee of the quality of the editing itself; but they are the minimum requirement that should be expected of any modern edition of a classic that claims to be worthy of serious consideration.

ADDENDUM

After the text of the Chopin *Mazurka in C sharp minor*, p. 28, was prepared for the press, the editor has learnt from Mr. Arthur Hedley that the most reliable early Chopin editions were generally those published in Paris, as these were usually engraved from the composer's autograph, whereas the Austrian/German and the English editions frequently relied on MS copies. In the case of the C sharp minor Mazurka the differences between the Paris and Vienna editions are small, and concern virtually nothing beyond details of phrasing and dynamics. Anyone interested in comparing the two will find the Paris edition reproduced in *The Oxford Original Edition of Frédérick Chopin*, vol. 3, p. 92; ed. Edouard Ganche: Oxford University Press, London 1932.

SUGGESTIONS FOR FURTHER READING

Edward Dannreuther, *Musical Ornamentation:* Novello, London [n.d.].

Thurston Dart, *The Interpretation of Music:* Hutchinson, London 1954.

John Petrie Dunn, *Ornamentation in the works of Frederick Chopin:* Novello, London [n.d.].

Walter Emery, *Editions and Musicians; a survey of the duties of Practical Musicians and Editors towards the classics:* Novello, London 1957.

Grove's Dictionary of Music and Musicians, 5th edition: Macmillan, London 1954: especially the article 'Pianoforte'.

Rosamund E. M. Harding, *Origins of Musical Time and Expression:* Oxford University Press, London 1938.

Rosamund E. M. Harding, *The Pianoforte:* Cambridge University Press, Cambridge 1933.

Reimar Riefling, *Piano Pedalling:* Oxford University Press, London 1962

Curt Sachs, *Rhythm and Tempo:* Dent, London 1953.

Erwin Stein, *Form and Performance:* Faber, London 1962.

Donald Francis Tovey, *Essays in Musical Analysis: Chamber Music:* Oxford University Press, London 1944.

Nocturne No. 5

Source: *Cinquième Notturno:*
Charles Lissner, St. Petersbourg [c. 1816-17]

JOHN FIELD
(1782-1837)

John Field was born in Dublin in 1782, worked as a boy with Clementi in London, toured with him on the continent to demonstrate his pianos, and eventually settled in Russia in 1803. He became a highly successful performer and teacher, and again toured Europe extensively during the early 1830s. Later he returned to Russia broken in health, and died there at the age of 55. Field's music had a far-reaching influence during the first half of the 19th century, yet it is rarely heard today. Three of his four Piano Sonatas are available in an admirably straightforward Augener edition, and all eighteen Nocturnes (over-edited by Louis Koehler) in a single volume issued by Peters; and recently three of the four Piano Concertos have been brought out as Vol. 7 of Musica Britannica.

The present reprint of the 5th Nocturne is taken from the 1st Russian edition of c. 1816. Though the music is so sparsely marked, it is not difficult to sense that its main requirement is a r.h. cantabile of the utmost beauty of tone and subtlety of inflection. The l.h. part, as is usual with such accompaniments, should be somewhat less prominent. In itself it consists of two elements: the lowest note of each harmonic group, which may be imagined as representing the quietly sustained cellos and double-basses of an orchestra; and the remaining notes, which fulfil the more neutral function of 'background' clarinets or violas.

The varied elements of the texture are held together by the r.h. pedal, which as a rule is changed with each change of harmony. (Note that the grouping of the l.h. quavers often indicates the pedalling: e.g. in bb. 8 & 9, though *not* in bb. 33-36.) The r.h. 'sighing' quavers in bb. 8 & 30 and the two short semiquaver figures in b. 36 are not parts of the tune, but intensifications of the accompaniment. The semiquavers in bb. 24 & 28, on the other hand, are melodic decorations, and require the same slight rubato that would be made instinctively by a sensitive singer. In the continuous quaver chords of bb. 18-21 & 38-41 the 'accompanist' comes into his own. On Field's piano these passages could have been played with the pedal left down for a bar at a time. On the resonant modern instrument more frequent changes are required, possibly one with every quaver. There is no tempo indication in the original, but a speed of about ♩. = 58 will be found to reconcile the gently reflective mood of the melody with the unhurried flow of the accompaniment. (Spohr wrote suggestively of the 'dreamy melancholy' of Field's playing.) In b. 22 the *fz*s must not disrupt the atmosphere that has been created. They should be treated as quiet stresses rather than violent accents.

[1] E, not C, in the original edition; but *cf.* bb. 11 & 25

Reproduced by kind permission of the British Museum.

[2] The turn in b. 14 is above the dotted crotchet C in the original edition. In the parallel passage in b. 36, however, it comes after the note, which is the more likely position musically.

[3] The sixth l.h. note is B (without a natural) in the original. G seems more probable, as it preserves the pattern of the figure.

[4] In the original edition the last five high B flats in the l.h. of bb. 38 and 40 are missing; but the cresc. suggests that bb. 18 and 20 give the correct version.

Fantasie in E, Op. 16, No. 3

Source: *3 Fantaises ou Caprices:*
Pietro Mechetti, Vienne 1831

FELIX MENDELSSOHN
(1809-47)

The Three Fantasies, Op. 16, were written in 1829, the year before *The Hebrides* overture. (Mendelssohn's piano works are published complete by Augener and Peters.) The present reprint is taken from the 1st edition, published in Vienna in 1831. An English edition, in which this third piece was entitled *The Rivulet*, appeared a year later.† Its phrasing is slightly different, if equally capricious; but it has the same unexpected and unmarked five beats in b. 35.

Apart from the many obvious phrasing mistakes, due either to careless engraving or to the ambiguity of Mendelssohn's MS, it will be noticed that the phrases often follow the old convention of stopping at a barline. (*Cf.* vol. 3, p. 11, *Phrasing & Articulation: Slurs.*) Hence the sextuplets in bb. 21-26 should be treated as one long phrase, not broken up into bar-lengths; and similarly with the crotchets in bb. 31-33.

The pedal marks are not always reliable, as can be seen from the absence of *Ped.* signs to correspond with the release-stars in bb. 50 & 53. In addition, it should be remembered that Mendelssohn's *sempre Ped.* probably means 'continue to use the pedal' rather than 'keep the pedal down unchanged'. Thus a new pedal is certainly now required (and probably would also have been required in Mendelssohn's day) at the beginning of bb. 22, 23, 24 & 25, followed by flutter-pedalling during b. 26 to clarify the diminuendo.

The difference in the resonance of Mendelssohn's piano and the instrument of today must influence our interpretation not only of the pedalling but also of the l.h. part in bb. 48 & 50. Here the upper notes of the thirds should be played much more lightly than the lower notes, otherwise the passage will sound unpleasantly thick.

In the l.h. part of b. 56 it is best to use the 5th finger on both the E and B of the 1st beat and the two Bs of the 3rd beat. The tempo should be about ♩ = 80.

† In fact the English edition was earlier, for it was entered at Stationers Hall on 1 December 1830. (Information kindly supplied by Mr. Alan Tyson.)

[1]The last top note in b. 16 is G in the original. F is more probable as it avoids consecutive octaves and matches the figure in bb. 18 and 19.

[2] bb. 34-35 are printed thus in the original edition, and in the earliest English edition (c. 1832), but without any change of time-signature. Later editions regularize the barring by omitting the 1st beat of b. 34 and shifting the barline to after the 1st beat of b. 35.

3 b. 42 r.h. 3rd beat is G in the original, not E; but *cf.* b. 7. E in the English edition.

4b. 57 r.h. 2nd beat is $_E^G$ in original, which does not fit the bass. $_D^F$ in the English edition.

Mazurka in A flat (1834)

Source: Autograph (photo),
Musée Mickiewicz, Paris

FRÉDÉRIC CHOPIN
(1810-49)

Though Chopin's fifty-eight Mazurkas contain some of his finest and most characteristic music, they are probably the least known of his compositions; two of them have therefore been chosen to represent him in the present volume. (Chopin's complete works are published by The Fryderyk Chopin Institute, Warsaw, with very comprehensive editorial notes in English and other languages. The Mazurkas appear in Vol. 10.)

The *Mazurka in A flat* is even less familiar than the rest, for it was not published until 1930. Like Beethoven's *Klavierstück in B flat* (*cf.* vol. 3, p.52), the autograph is part of an album that belonged originally to the Polish pianist Maria Szymanowska (1789-1831), a pupil of John Field and a friend of Goethe. The composer headed the MS *Mazur* and added the date Paris 1834. As this was three years after the death of Maria Szymanowska, it seems likely that the piece was written for her daughter Celina, who came to Paris in July 1834 to marry Chopin's friend, the poet Adam Mickiewicz.

The 1st edition of 1930 and the new Warsaw edition both reproduce facsimiles of the autograph; yet oddly enough, neither prints the work quite correctly. In the autograph Chopin has indicated the join to the coda by means of the misleading sign ⫶‖⫶ . Both editors have taken this to be a repeat, shifted it to the end of b. 20, removed the dots on the right-hand side, and indicated a return to the beginning of b. 5. This reading cannot be correct, however, for if a repeat were intended, it would lead back to a 3rd not a 1st beat, and no 3rd beat is musically possible. Furthermore, there are no repeat-dots at the beginning of b. 5 in the autograph, nor are there any later ones to correspond with the dots of the r.h. side of Chopin's mark in b. 20. Another curious mistake in both editions is that the first D in b. 38 is printed with a natural in place of the perfectly clear flat shown in the autograph. With regard to the present editorial accidentals in bb. 2-4: it seems likely that the D naturals were intended, for accidentals in MSS were often assumed to carry over to the following bar or bars, unless contradicted.

Though there is no tempo indication in the original, this would seem to be one of the brisk Mazurkas with a single basic speed, say about ♩ = 160. (*Cf.* p. 28 for a Mazurka that requires two contrasted tempi.) There are, of course, small local variations, such as in b. 12, where a fraction of extra time is needed to accommodate the strong 2nd beat accent so characteristic of a Mazurka, and to 'round the corner' into the ornamented version of the main theme. And again in the descending chromatic scales of bb. 26-28, where a slight rubato is required either at the top or the bottom of the scale (the player can choose which he prefers) in order to swing the music back to b. 5. A slight stress on the 3rd beat of bb. 6, 8, 14 & 16 makes a good contrast to the 2nd beat accents in bb. 10 & 18, and is also typical of Mazurka rhythm. At the very end of the piece, a *rit.* in b. 40 will help to underline both the diminuendo and the resolution of the D flat on to the 4th quaver C.

[Fine: to Coda
2nd time]

Dal segno al
fine, e poi

[Coda]

Mazurka in C sharp minor, Op. 50, No. 3

Source: *Trois Mazourkas, Op. 50:*
Pietro Mechetti, Vienne [1842]

FRÉDÉRIC CHOPIN

The majority of Chopin's works were published, soon after they were written, by three different firms in Paris, Vienna (or Leipzig) and London. The earliest issue of the Three Mazurkas, Op. 50, was the Viennese edition, which appeared in September 1842. It has been used for the present reprint. An autograph of the C sharp minor Mazurka is preserved in the Jagilloński Library, Cracow; but it has not been used here as it is of a slightly shorter, earlier version of the work.[1]

We are so accustomed to seeing Chopin's music buried under a mass of editorial marks that it comes as a surprise to find how comparatively few indications there were in either the autographs (*cf.* the *Mazurka in A flat*, p. 24) or the early editions. Admittedly the texts pose many problems for editors, for manuscripts (if they exist) often differ from one another, and invariably disagree with the equally divergent early printed editions. (The variants are noted in the excellent edition of The Fryderyk Chopin Institute, Warsaw, mentioned in the Note to the *Mazurka in A flat*.) Nevertheless, the student may find it both interesting and instructive to see, for once in a way, what one of these early editions looked like. The present Mazurka has therefore been reprinted almost exactly as it appears in the Viennese edition, and no attempt has been made to reconcile its inconsistencies of phrasing, many of which were probably due to the difficulty of deciding where the slurs in the MS began and ended. Any editorial additions are, as usual, distinguished typographically.

In many of the Mazurkas two basic tempi are required, though only one indication appears in the score. (Experiment shows that no single tempo will make musical sense of the contrasting moods of such pieces.) Here the main theme should be roughly ♩ = 112 at each of its appearances, including the long coda from b. 157. The remaining subjects, beginning in bb. 17, 25, 61 & 141, require considerably more movement, say about ♩ = 144. Some of the latter, such as the theme in A major, b. 17, pick up the quicker tempo abruptly and keep to it fairly strictly; while others, for example the long *mezza voce* phrase starting in b. 45, slide into it more gradually and also remain flexible within themselves. The contrasting phrase of the opening section, bb. 9-16, requires a type of rubato that is very common in the Mazurkas: it starts at the slower of the two tempi, gradually quickens until it reaches the faster tempo (say at b. 13), then gradually slows down again to where it started. In this particular Mazurka every return to the opening theme and tempo is gradual, as there is always a musical link. Where there are no links the changes of tempo are generally abrupt.

Two small textual points may be noted. The chord on the 1st beat of b. 9 is more correctly notated at its return in b. 101, from which it will be seen that the r.h. should play the top three notes and shorten them to a quaver. In b. 67, etc., the short slur is not intended as a tie, but shows that the two chords are to be played legato, with the first of each pair slightly stressed.

The pedal marks are less carelessly printed than in many early Chopin editions. Nevertheless it should always be remembered that, even when accurate, they were intended for a much less resonant instrument than the piano of today, and may therefore require modification.

Unlike the classical and baroque composers, Chopin generally intended a *piano* when he put no dynamic mark at the beginning of a piece.

[1] See p. 15 for an Addendum on early Chopin editions.

Reproduced by kind permission of the British Museum.

29

[1] The natural to the l.h. 3rd beat G appears in the French edition only.

Romanze in F sharp, Op. 28, No. 2

Source: *Drei Romanzen, Op. 28:*
Breitkopf & Härtel, Leipzig [1840]

ROBERT SCHUMANN
(1810-1856)

The Three Romances, Op. 28, were written in 1839, a year later than the better-known *Kreisleriana*, Op. 16, dedicated to Chopin. (Schumann's piano works are available in several editions. The Henle is the best, though as yet incomplete.) The present reprint follows the accurate original edition of 1840.

The full tonal beauty of this *Romanze* will best be realised if the thumb melody in the r.h. is slightly more prominent than that of the l.h. (Avoid any suspicion of a bump on the demi-semiquavers in b. 2, etc.) The semiquaver accompaniment should float quietly and evenly in the background. The general indication *Pedal* shows that the texture is held together by a liberal use of the r.h. pedal, which should be changed with each change of harmony: e.g. four times in b. 1 and thrice in b. 2. A completely new colour appears in b. 9, where the melodic interest shifts to the treble, with the l.h. slurs in bb. 10 & 12 drawing attention to the half-imitations in the bass. In b. 13 there is yet another change of colour, brought about by the three-bar canon between treble and bass. In b. 17 we find an example of Schumann's idiosyncratic notation of a *rit.*, which often assumes an *a tempo* either at the end of the ------ mark, or at the beginning of a new phrase or bar. After the pause in b. 24 the music has a slightly freer and more improvisatory character, particularly in the middle of b. 26 (an interrupted cadence) and the second half of b. 30 (main cadence), until the opening tempo is resumed in b. 31. (Note that in b. 26 the r.h. 2nd semiquaver B sharp leads to the C sharp quaver in the l.h., not the r.h.) The metronome mark ♪ = 100 seems on the quick side for such a reflective piece; but Schumann's metronome markings are often puzzling (*cf. Tempo: Metronome Marks*, p. 7). A quaver movement of about 80 is perhaps more in keeping with the mood.

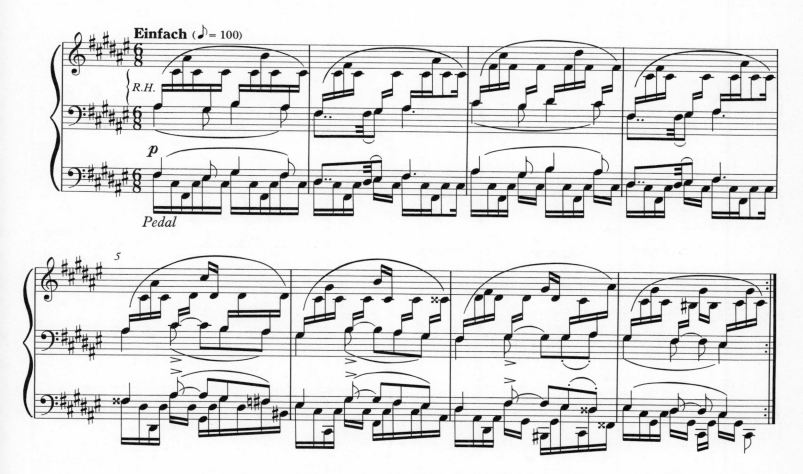

Reproduced by kind permission of the British Museum.

36

[grace-notes
before the beat]

Abschied

(Waldscenen, Op. 82)

Source: *Waldscenen, Op. 82:*
Barthold Senff, Leipzig [1851]

ROBERT SCHUMANN

The set of nine pieces entitled *Waldscenen (Woodland Scenes)*, of which *Abschied (Farewell)* is the last, was written in 1848-49, shortly before the 3rd Symphony. (See the Note on the *Romanze* for an edition of Schumann's piano works.) The 1st edition is carefully engraved and has been used for the present reprint.

Like many of Schumann's piano pieces, *Abschied* has much of the character of a song. The double-bar near the beginning suggests that the opening two bars form a short introduction for the 'accompanist', after which the 'solo voice' enters in b. 3. Similarly, bb. 11-12 form an interlude. The double-bar in b. 28, on the other hand, serves only to separate one 'verse' from the next at a point where there is no interlude. The 'solo' finishes on the 1st beat of b. 49, and the remaining bars provide the 'accompanist's' epilogue. The importance of recognising this structure is shown in b. 48, where the 'soloist' needs a fairly large *rit.* (unmarked) to conclude his phrase, before the 'accompanist' picks up the tempo again on the 1st beat of b. 49.

A typical feature of Schumann's piano texture is the emergence every now and again of wisps of counter-melody, sometimes clearly indicated and sometimes half-concealed. In b. 13, for example, the main interest lies in the l.h. melody beginning on tenor C, which in the following bar is carried up to the r.h. minim C by means of a slur. In the next pair of bars, however, matters are less clearly defined, for the inner phrase seems to peter out in the middle of b. 16. Yet the passage makes perfect musical sense if we realise that in the course of b. 16 the top part becomes increasingly important. (An added 'hairpin' crescendo over beats 3 & 4 will carry the listener's attention towards the treble theme on the 1st beat of b. 17.)

At times Schumann's notation may even hinder our understanding of his intentions. In b. 30 the shape of the inner melody, G, G, A flat, B flat, would be far clearer if the 1st beat G in the alto were a crotchet, with the triplet stems of the treble turned upwards. But though this passage looks obscure to the eye, it must not sound so to the listener's ear. Nor must the hidden tenor melody in bb. 39-40, D, D, F, E flat, D, be allowed to disappear.

Even in carefully engraved music, such as this, the pedal indications are sometimes found in the wrong place, generally because there was insufficient room to write them accurately in the original MS. It is more than likely, for example, that Schumann intended the *Ped.* signs in bb. 5, 7, 23 & 25 to be below the first quaver of the bar, so that the bass would be sustained; but he probably found that the lowness of the note concerned prevented him from putting it there. The player should, of course, correct this point.

In b. 19, as in most such cases, the equal-valued unison pair (the 4th beat A) should be played by the melodically more important part, which is here the r.h.

Reproduced by kind permission of the British Museum.

[1] It is hard to say whether the grace-notes in this piece should come on the beat or before it. Possibly just before, with the one in b. 48 rather more pointedly and melodically so. (*Cf. Ornamentation* Appoggiaturas, p. 12.)

En Rêve
Nocturne

Source: *En Rêve:*
Em. Wetzler, Wien [1888]

FRANZ LISZT
(1811-86)

This magical and little-known piece was written by Liszt not long before he died, and was dedicated to his young pupil August Stradal (1860-1930). Its impressionistic mood and inconclusive ending are typical of the composer's later works, in which he appears to be more intent on exploring his own fancy than on satisfying the demands of the public. The present reprint follows the 1st edition, which was published two years after the composer's death. (No complete edition of Liszt's works is at present available. The more familiar pieces are obtainable in many editions, while some of the less familiar have been issued in several volumes by Schott on behalf of the Liszt Society in England.)

Though there are almost no slurs, the r.h. part is clearly a legato cantabile which begins with an 'upbeat' bar. (In b. 6 ff. the pedalling should continue as before.) At the second appearance of the theme, bb. 21-28, the new 'thumb' counterpoint mounting in the l.h. needs to be brought out slightly more prominently than the more static opening version, the pedal F sharps remaining secondary in both cases. In b. 29 the l.h. interest moves to the lower line (the 1st, 3rd & 5th quavers of each bar) which now defines the shifting harmony.

If the player finds it more convenient, the r.h. G sharps in bb. 39-42 can be taken with the l.h. 2nd finger, as the top of the arpeggios. Likewise in b. 45, players with small hands could play the r.h. F sharp with the l.h. thumb.

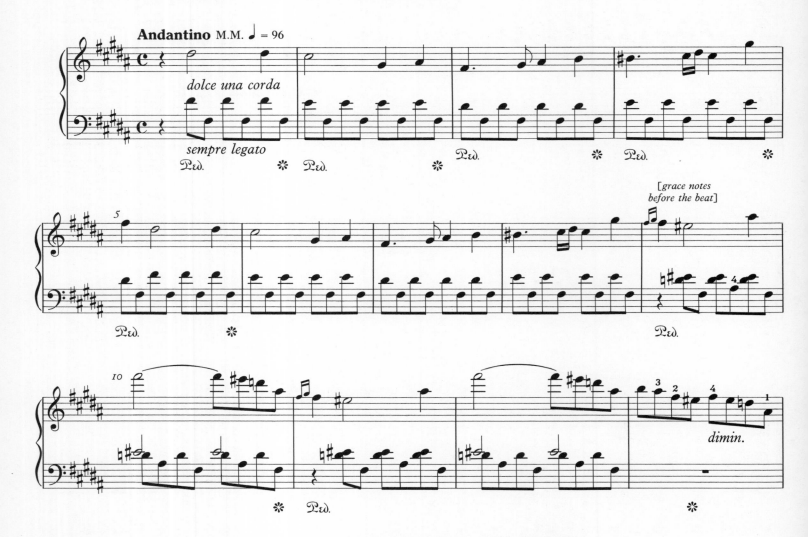

Reproduced by kind permission of the Deutsche Staatsbibliothek, Berlin.

In bb. 29 & 31 the thumb is marked on the fifth l.h. quaver in the original edition. Judging both by convenience and by b. 30 this was probably a misprint.

Canzonetta del Salvator Rosa

(Années de Pélerinage: Italie)

Source: *Années de Pélerinage, Deuxième*
Année: Italie; B. Schott, Mayence [1858]

FRANZ LISZT

The song on which this piece is based was first printed in Charles Burney's *A General History of Music*, 1789, from a MS in his own collection. It has since been shown that the song is not in fact by Salvator Rosa, but by some unknown composer working in the second half of the 17th century. (*Cf.* Frank Walker, 'Salvator Rosa and Music', *Monthly Musical Record*, Oct. 1949 & Jan. 1950.) Liszt's delightful version was written in 1849, and first published nine years later in the second of three sets of pieces entitled *Années de Pélerinages*. (*Cf.* the Note to *En Rêve* for available reprints of Liszt's piano works.) The 1st edition is followed in the present reprint.

The tempo indication *Andante marziale* may suggest too slow a speed unless it is realised that it here means literally 'like a military march', i.e. ♩ = 120-126. As in Schumann's *Abschied*, p.38, the interludes of the 'accompaniment' should be clearly differentiated from the 'vocal' passages, particularly when they are identical in pitch and texture, as in bb. 7-8. (Note that the vocal line belongs to the l.h. in bb. 27-28 & 31-32.) The phrasing in b. 7, etc., suggests that the crotchet should always be slurred to the following quaver wherever this figure appears. In bb. 23-24 & 66-67 the dovetailed phrases, though unmarked, must be made clear to the listener: i.e., a new phrase begins on the lower r.h. A on the 1st beat of b. 23 and the 3rd beat of b. 24. The semibreve chord in b. 20 must be sustained with the r.h. pedal, with the help of a half-pedal at the middle of the bar. (The third pedal had not been invented when this piece was written.) The *rall.* in b. 34 carries on until the end of b. 36. The *a tempo* which starts on the 1st beat of b. 37 may be a fraction below the true tempo, in order to underline the *espressivo* character of the following seven bars. *Tempo I* then returns with b. 44. The general mood of the piece may be gathered from the following free translation of the words:-

> Though I may change my dwelling-place
> I cannot change desire.
> Passion will always burn my heart
> And I must feed its fire.

Reproduced by kind permission of the British Museum.

¹The second r.h. top note of b. 32 is D, not C, in the original edition. B. 28 confirms that this was a misprint.

Ballade in D minor, Op. 10, No. 1

(After the Scottish Ballad 'Edward', in Herder's 'Stimmen der Völker')

Source: *Balladen, Op. 10:*
Breitkopf & Härtel, Leipzig [1856]

JOHANNES BRAHMS
(1833-97)

The four Ballads, Op. 10, were written in 1854 when Brahms was 21. They are contemporary with the *Variations on a Theme by Schumann*, Op. 9, dedicated to Schumann's wife Clara, and a year later than the Piano Sonata in F minor. (Brahms' piano works are available in several editions. The Breitkopf & Härtel and the Henle— the latter not yet completed— are both admirably edited.) The present reprint follows the 1st edition of 1856.

One version of the Scottish ballad 'Edward', on which this piece is founded, is printed in *The Oxford Book of English Verse* (1st line: 'Why does your brand sae drop wi' blude'). The music follows the poem in outline rather than in detail. In bb. 1-26 two alternating themes and tempi set the scene of question and answer between mother and blood-stained son. The music then expands into a single tremendous arch (bb. 27-59) followed by a *sotto voce* return of the opening theme, together representing the son's confession to the murder of his father and the curse he lays on his mother.

One point should be noted about the tempo indications. In order to give sufficient contrast to the two themes of the opening, the *Andante* should be about ♩ = 76 and the *Poco piu mosso* about ♩ = 100. At first sight it would then appear that the later *Allegro* should immediately be quicker still. In practice, however, it will be found that the qualifying *(ma non troppo)* is of overriding importance, for the new triplet-figure already supplies sufficient extra momentum. This section should in fact begin at about ♩ = 92, and gradually move on, with the mounting tension and dynamics, to about ♩ = 108.

In the two *Poco più moto* sections the slightly breathless ⁵⁄₄ phrasing should be stressed. The word *sostenuto*, with which they end, implies (as always in Brahms) a holding back of the tempo. At the beginning of the *Allegro* the r.h. triplets should be fairly light, so that the l.h. comes through easily— note the alternating importance of the lower-line and the thumb-line in the l.h. part. Between bb. 31 & 35 the middle part must sound absolutely continuous, with no false accents or changes of colour when one hand takes over from the other. The triplets in the top part gradually gain in importance, until by b. 36 they have assumed the main thematic interest.

The grace-notes throughout should anticipate the beat.

Reproduced by kind permission of the British Museum.

[1] The hairpin crescendo, missing from the original edition, was added by Brahms in his own copy.

Capriccio in C, Op. 76, No. 8

Source: *Clavierstücke, Op. 76*:
N. Simrock, Berlin 1879

JOHANNES BRAHMS

The eight Piano Pieces, Op. 76 were written around 1878, at about the same time as the Violin Concerto, and published in two volumes a year later. (See the Note on the *Ballade* for editions of Brahms' piano works.) The present reprint follows the 1st edition of 1879, except that bb. 19 & 56 incorporate emendations taken from Brahms' own copy of the work.

Though there are no pedal indications in the *Capriccio*, Brahms, like Field, Chopin and the rest, is continually relying on the pedal to make sense of his widely-spaced l.h. part. The student will find that the pedalling depends largely on the harmonic changes, and that a fresh pedal is generally needed on the lowest note of each broken chord, accompanied by a slight dynamic stress.

The indication *Anmutig lebhaft* at the beginning, meaning *graceful and lively*, suggests a tempo of about ♩ = 144. The constant pull between two-in-a-bar ($\frac{6}{4}$) and three-in-a-bar ($\frac{3}{2}$) is of great rhythmic importance; for though the time-signature shows that there are basically two accents in a bar, the ubiquitous r.h. figure tends continually to fall into a three-in-a-bar pattern. The player must always be aware of this tendency, yet contrive at the same time to preserve the hint of a secondary accent on the 4th crotchet of the bar. For example, bb. 1 & 2 would lose much of their flavour if treated as a perfectly straightforward $\frac{3}{2}$, though this would be quite appropriate for the differently grouped quavers of b. 3.

As already noted, a *sostenuto* in Brahms means a slight holding back of the tempo (*cf.* bb. 8 & 54), somewhat less marked than a *rit.* An *a tempo* is understood either where the ----- marks stop, or at the beginning of a new bar or phrase. The dovetailed phrases at the end of b. 4 require a smaller *sost.* (unmarked) than the one shown in b. 8. Likewise, the bar-long phrase beginning on the 2nd crotchet of b. 52 requires a less noticeable version of the *sost.* marked in b. 54.

Grace-notes (bb. 52 & 54) and arpeggios (bb. 48, 66 & 67) should come before the beat, the arpeggio in b. 48 demanding, as so often in Brahms, a slight lengthening of the beat on which it occurs.

Stress slightly the unmarked tenor line in b. 17, etc., foreshadowing in inverted form the new r.h. subject in b. 20; and allow the hidden tenor part of this new subject to emerge clearly, as it moves downwards from B flat in contrary motion to the r.h. The *cresc.* in b. 32 should carry right through to the *f* in b. 37, the intervening hairpins being local variations within the crescendo. With regard to the unison Cs and E flats in bb. 16, 18, 24 & 26: it is easiest to play them with the r.h. rather than the l.h., in accordance with the rule that unisons of unequal value should be played by the hand which has the longer note. In b. 38 the three accented chords must exactly match the three chords in the preceding bar, with no change of colour as one hand takes over from the other.

It will be found that the two *f* chords in bb. 66-67 require a touch of pedal, in spite of their staccato marks, otherwise they will sound unpleasantly hard and abrupt. The r.h. chords should coincide with the top note of the l.h. arpeggios. At the join of bb. 61 & 62 the pause is on the barline, not on the preceding note. Brahms makes this distinction elsewhere, implying that the pause should be a silence.

Grazioso ed un poco vivace

Anmutig lebhaft

[1] The fourth l.h. quaver is F in the original edition. Brahms later changed it to G.

² The original edition reads  . In his own copy Brahms made the alterations shown in the text.

MONTE BANCA CRT FIAT
LLO DI RIVOLI

the Collection

CHARTA

Catalogue

Graphic Coordination
Gabriele Nason

Editorial Coordination
Emanuela Belloni

Press Office
Silvia Palombi Arte & Mostre, Milan

Editing
Ready-made, Milan

Production
Amilcare Pizzi Arti grafiche, Cinisello Balsamo, Milan

© 1995
Castello di Rivoli Museo d'Arte contemporanea
© 1995
Edizioni Charta, Milan

ISBN 88-8158-007-1

Regione Piemonte
Banca CRT
FIAT

Chairman
Clara Palmas

Director
Ida Gianelli

Management Consultant
Massimo Melotti

Press Office
Massimo Melotti
Roberta Aghemo

Administration
Gabriella Traschetti

Architectural Conservation Manager
Andrea Bruno

Maintenance and Systems
Gianfranco Gritella

Exhibition Office
Antonella Russo
Giorgio Verzotti
Franca Terlevic

Education Department
Anna Pironti
Paola Zanini

Secretary
Manuela Vasco

Technical Department
Mariano Boggia
Giorgio Carli
Fulvio Castelli
Filippo Di Giovanni

Insurance Consultancy
Pulsar P & I Insurance Brokers srl, Turin

Catalogue graphics and design
Gabriella Bocchio e Giulio Palmieri
(Segno e Progetto srl, Turin)
Pietro Palladino
(Studio Badriotto & Palladino, Turin)

Photographs
Paolo Pellion, Turin

Bruna Biamino, Turin
(cover and page 12)

Attilio Maranzano, Rome
(page 131)

Giorgio Mussa, Turin
(page 109)

English translation
Juliet Haydock, London

*T*he Castello di Rivoli has changed its status from a derelict barracks to International Museum in a few short years.

Yet it was no easy decision to turn this former residence of the Savoys into a museum of any kind, let alone a Museum of Contemporary Art.

When the Piedmont Regional Authorities began restoration work in 1978, contemporary art certainly did not top its list of cultural priorities. The decision to turn such a prestigious building from an historical and architectural stand point into a museum aroused lively debate and many arguments ensued.

Ten years on, we can now see that the decision was justified.

The imposing solemnity of the castle provides a perfect backdrop for all the works of art the collection has acquired since our inaugural "Ouverture" exhibition.

Some may say that it certainly took an act of courage, rare among public authorities, to decide to undertake this collection, and particularly to collect contemporary art. Personally, I prefer to consider it a display of great sensitivity and far-sightedness.

Today we are able to visit great museums because in the past someone dared to collect works of art that may have been unknown at the time or at least unsupported by critical favour. Sadly, if the critics do not like a work, the consensus of opinion will go against the piece and it will be doomed to failure.

The Castello di Rivoli Museum of Contemporary Art is also an example of cooperation between public and private organisations. The results of this joint enterprise are tangible and encouraging.

This gelling of effort around a new, some would say risky, project, has been a very important experience for the Region. It has introduced a new way of creating a museum not merely from an artistic point of view, but also in terms of activities, management and international consensus.

Giampiero Leo
Head of Cultural Affairs for the Region of Piedmont

Friends of the Museum

Antonella Altissimo, Turin
Sergio Bertola, Genoa
Anna Boglione Pecco, Turin
Marco Bosca, Turin
Geda Canale, Borgaro T.se
Bianca Catalano, Turin
Paolo Catalano, Turin
Maria Cattaneo, Turin
Sergio Cembrano, Turin
Alvise Chevallard, Turin
Gail Cochrane, Turin
Nicoletta Cornaglia, Turin
Anna Rosa Cotroneo Bidolli, Naples
Tommaso Cotroneo, Naples
Cristina Crotti, Scandiano
Leonardo Cuttica, Turin
Antonio Destefanis, Turin
Enrica Dorna Metzger, Turin
Marina Ferrero Ventimiglia, Turin
Giorgio Ferrino, Turin
Renato Fiorentini, Milan
Carlo Formica, Genoa
Cesare Furno, Turin
Marco Garbero, Turin
Giuseppe Gasparrini, Milan
Paola Genti, Turin
Claudia Gian Ferrari, Milan
Maurizio Giordano, Turin
Eliana Guglielmi, Turin
Marinella Guglielmi, Turin
Giorgia Ilotte, Turin
Franco Koelliker, Turin
Carola Lattes, Turin
Giulio Lattes, Turin
Frida Levi, Turin
Marcello Levi, Turin
Gloria Levoni, Castellucchio
Wilmer Malinverni, Turin

Enrico Mambretti, Turin
Rocco Mangia, Milan
Silvia Marchesi, Turin
Cen Massobrio Maciotta, Turin
Silvano Mastragostino, Genoa
Luisa Mensi, Turin
Giuliana Migliardi, Turin
Rosaria Mondino, Turin
Lucetta Morino Dogliotti, Turin
Renata Novarese, Turin
Gian Luca Onorato, Turin
Luca Paveri Fontana, Turin
Roberta Pellegrini, Turin
Giorgio Persano, Turin
Cristiano Picco, Turin
Mario Pieroni, Rome
Fabio Pierotti Cei, Milan
Giorgia Pininfarina, Turin
Magda Poddighe, Milan
Agostino Re Rebaudengo, Turin
Patrizia Re Rebaudengo, Turin
Sandra Reberschak Furlotti, Turin
Gianna Recchi, Turin
Alessandro Riscossa, Turin
Alberto Rolla, Turin
Emilia Sandretto, Turin
Massimo Sandretto, Turin
Tommaso Setari, Milano
Carlo Silvera, Rome
Federica Simone De Dominicis, Turin
Delfina Testa, Turin
Gemma Testa, Turin
Laura Trinchero Naddei, San Mauro T.se
Antonio Tucci Russo, Torre Pellice
Emanuela Vallarino Gancia, Turin
Franco Vallini, Barone Canavese
Filiberto Vercellino, Turin
Michele Vietti, Turin

It is with a sense of appreciation and, dare we say, complacency, that we look back on the role we have played in the first ten years of the Castello di Rivoli.

The Museum has grown and made a name for itself against all odds, exactly as we hoped. Despite the status it has achieved, the enterprise has never lost the pioneering spirit of adventure generated by its small diligent staff of founders. The feeling has always been of forging ahead at the leading edge of contemporary art where the pages of tomorrow's history are written.

An ever-present sense of commitment has prevented the enterprise from flagging, and kept the project moving ahead. We have carried out research, kept abreast of cultural tendencies, maintained contact with a concerned public and established close links between research and communication, particularly on the international scene, which is where contemporary art belongs nowadays. The creation of a new Museum has been an innovative and unusual departure for the companies who have decided to become involved. Our own involvement in the Castello di Rivoli project has been not merely a satisfying experience, but also a stimulating one because we have been granted the opportunity to play a part in museum management and not simply to offer financial support.

For this, all praise is due to the Piedmont Regional Authorities, which not only launched the project and provided financial backing, but also continued to believe in its objectives and were responsible for offering private companies an opportunity to become involved in promotion and management.

The fact that public and private organizations have contributed equally to a project within the field of culture constitutes a inuque experience for Italy. We are proud to have played a part in this project and hope that the future will prove to be even more rewarding.

Cesare Annibaldi
FIAT S.p.A. Vice-President External Relations and Communication

Andrea Comba
Chairman of CRT Cassa di Risparmio di Torino Foundation

Marco Rivetti
Chairman GFT S.p.A.

Contents

An Indiscriminate, All-Embracing Passion

Ida Gianelli

The Museum's passion for its collection is 'indiscriminate' in the sense that it embraces all possible artistic differences and affinities. All it seeks to exclude is mystification and superficiality.

We make no claim to avoid all ambiguity and assert no infallibility. Our aim is rather to surprise and provoke; to enjoy the thrill of the hunt and ultimate discovery. Once it has discovered a work, the Museum finds out whether it can live with that work before declaring its passion, which can only ever be indiscriminate because no individual constraints can operate in this public arena. The Museum begins by focusing attention on a newly discovered opus until it gains acceptance and then seeks to acquire the work. Thus, appealingly, our collection has grown out of a transparent web of contacts, dialogues and encounters. The artists and their work erupt into the Museum's open spaces, where they are forced to engage with the museum's own identity and history. Thus another piece is fitted into the jigsaw puzzle, another artistic love story is consummated.

Each encounter with a new artist creates a new relationship, and every new love story disturbs the former equilibrium: the indiscriminate passion proliferates as it feeds on the infinity of possibilities offered by our burgeoning collection.

Every Museum director is indiscriminate and all-embracing in his or her desire to collect artistic encounters of one sort or another. Every Museum director leaves his or her mark on the works and the artists that ultimately come to be associated with the Museum.

The life story of the Castello di Rivoli Museum of Contemporary Art has been short albeit eventful. We pride ourselves that the encounters (past, present and future) we have arranged between opus and institution and between artist and director make ours an organisation of sensitivity and historical relevance.

Between 1984 and 1994, the Museum's creative emphasis shifted from Art to the arts: from the specificity of sculpture and painting to the inspecificity of other creative languages. It is now our declared intention to work within all fields of image-making, including photography and film as well as architecture and music. In expanding our range, we do not seek to reconcile diverse forms but simply expand the possibilities for encounter and contact in a way that adds new appeal to the enigma of creating art. The premisses underlying the museum's collection have therefore also changed: the unexpected has been added to the expected; the unknown projected onto the neutral and the obvious. Our own acquisitions have been swelled by generous donations. The pursuit has been exciting, demanding and sometimes exhausting. This convergence of forces and energies has produced a magnetic pole of attraction. The most important constituent forces are those generated by the artists themselves as they move between the personal and the social planes, constructing the story of their images. Around them, peripheral forces are generated by all those who come to love artists' work and strive to make it known to the world.

The collection owned by the Castello di Rivoli Museum of Contemporary Art reveals the intensity of these relationships. The overall picture is one of extreme richness and reveals both Italian and international influences. At the castle, history meets the present-day in a dizzying, spectacular display. All our dreams and hopes are combined in a fantastic dimension with pretensions to a permanent place in history. If we succeed despite all the reckless disorderliness of our indiscriminate, all-embracing passion, we will have set a new precedent and the Museum's love affair with art will go on.

Pontus Hulten, a Collector

Interview by Ida Gianelli

I first met Pontus Hulten at a Venice Biennale some twenty years ago. He had just been appointed Director of the Pompidou Centre in Paris, which was still under construction. Creator of some of the finest exhibitions of the previous thirty years and museums that have set their mark on the history of modern art, Hulten was the great director I longed to work with.

I never imagined my wish would come true a few years later or that we would enjoy a close working relationship during which I came to appreciate his extraordinary professional qualities as well as his outstanding sensibilities. Meeting him today is as much of a pleasure as ever and we take up our conversation as if it had only just broken off.

I. G.

Ida Gianelli. Pontus, I'd like to take up a subject we have often discussed over the years: collecting. When and how do you think the idea of forming a collection emerges?

Pontus Hulten. I think it may date back to the *Wunderkammer* (Chamber of Marvels). These chambers first emerged in Protestant cities like Basel and Copenhagen and were originally intended as private collections, though soon opened to the public. In Copenhagen a certain Ole Worns amassed a huge collection of at least 1,800 items, some of which are now on display in the Kunsthalle in Bonn. The Hapsburg family did the same sort of thing at much the same time, first in Vienna, then in Prague. Their intention was to create a museum with a great collection of artifacts and paintings. The Emperor Rudolph commissioned Arcimboldi, the famous Milanese painter, to create a sort of introduction to the collection in the form of a hall with a fountain at the centre and portraits of the imperial family representing the elements and the seasons on the walls around it. Today, we would call it political propaganda because it certainly seemed to be claiming that those people represented the world. It's an interesting point that when the portraits were finished, first in Vienna and then in Prague when the court moved to that city, copies were immediately made and sent to Madrid where the Hapsburgs also ruled. So it really was a political project: the museum as propaganda. No one remembers it because it was never finished: Rudolph fell ill and forgot all about his original plan. So Arcimboldo went back to Milan and his solid silver fountain was simply melted down.

So that's where I think the modern concept of the collection really began. Let's not forget that the original *Wunderkammer* was an actual chest with lots of drawers and compartments. In other words it was a real little portable museum, just like what Marcel Duchamp was to create very much later.

Ida Gianelli. You mentioned the Kunsthalle in Bonn, where you've been director since 1990 and where there is currently a *Wunderkammer* exhibition. I get the impression that you are still working on the collection concept.

I'd like to run through the history of your own "collections", beginning with your first directorship at the Moderna Museet in Stockholm in 1959-73.

Pontus Hulten. In the late Fifties, the Stockholm National Museum decided that it ought not to neglect modern art and opened a small contemporary art museum. That museum inherited a collection of works by Swedish artists as well as major paintings donated by collectors like Rolf De Maré, the Director of the Ballets Suedois in Paris. De Maré had been a friend of artists like Picasso, Leger, Duchamp and had bought some of their works. Collecting wasn't the first thought in my mind, since we had no funds for purchases. So I began by putting on temporary exhibitions, some of which, like *Art and Movement* in 1961 and *Four Americans* in 1962, were a great success.

It was a real pity we couldn't buy any of the works exhibited: they were extraordinary and very cheap as well. I remember one man who kept coming back to gaze at the painting by Jasper John. He was absolutely fascinated by it, so much so that he eventually asked me how he should approach the artist in order to buy the painting. I gave him John's telephone number and he did buy the picture for less than a thousand dollars. That was sad for us, but it did make us think about the need to own a permanent collection. It also led us to examine what people in our business call the "gaps" in our collection. There were times when "gaps" were almost all we had and it was obviously going to take a major operation to rectify the situation. That was when I had the idea of organising an exhibition entitled *Le musée de vos désirs*. The plan was very simple: we would exhibit the Picassos, Braques, Picabias and so on in our collection and when we lacked an example from a particular period we would borrow it from the artist's family or a private gallery. In the end, we were able to exhibit some two hundred works. In the magnificent collection we created, our own paintings were enhanced by the loans and vice versa. The then-current Minister of Culture used to visit the museum and hated some of our things as much as he adored others. He came to the exhibition and a miracle occurred.

The Ministry granted us five million dollars for purchases. That was an enormous sum at a time when paintings cost far less than they do today. The Ministry asked me to do the job and granted me total autonomy, so we set up a small purchasing committee. One oddity of that period was that all major works had a set price of 200,000 francs, whoever they were by. So we bought about twenty-eight paintings and sculptures at that price. The one exception was a metaphysical painting by Giorgio de Chirico: *Le cerveau de l'enfant*. We already owned one of his horse paintings but I wanted a really good metaphysical picture and the most important one still in private hands was *Le cerveau de l'enfant*, which belonged to André Breton. It was an ambitious plan, but Arturo Schwarz, Ulf Linde and above all Marcel Duchamp helped me to arrange a meeting with Breton in his Rue Fontaine studio in Paris.

I was extremely tense. Breton was the most prestigious figure in Parisian cultural circles at the time. Sartre was a celebrity too, but Breton meant much more to me.

Finally I entered the famous studio, crammed with thousands of objects and paintings. Among the most splendid, I remember Salvador Dali's *Le grand masturbateur*, Mirò's *La tache rouge* as well as a truly impressive hoard of ethnographic artifacts and thousands of books.

I'm sure André Breton knew what I was there for. His willingness to enter negotiations was due to several concomitant factors. That was the time of the OAS, the Algerian secret army, a genuine terrorist organisation. They had already set their sights on the Surrealists so André Breton was a target as well. In fact, they'd tried to set fire to his studio by pouring petrol outside the door. The fire was quickly put out, but the gas meter was right outside the door, so there could have been a real tragedy. Marcel Duchamp had also often told Breton it wasn't fair to keep such an important painting in a private house, that the proper place for it was a museum, a public place. At a certain point in our conversation Breton asked me how much money I had to spend on the purchase and I answered, "I can offer you the equivalent of the Nobel Prize". He thought that was very funny since he knew as well as I did that the ultra-conservative Stockholm Committee was never going to give him the Nobel Prize. Perhaps, anyway, it was the price he had in mind: about 550,000 French francs. Today Nobel Prize winners get much more than that, but I think 550,000 francs was the figure at the time. We went on talking for a long time after that. Breton noticed my interest in the paintings around me, especially a stupendous Miró called *La tache rouge*. He said I could buy that too if I liked and I got it for 200,000 francs.

Breton really hated parting with the de Chirico painting. He told me he had come across it by pure accident when he saw it in an antique shop window while riding on a bus. He also said he had found the essence of Surrealism in that painting.

The de Chirico painting became a sort of beacon for our museum, and it helped us to get major loans from other institutions.

Ida Gianelli. What was the museum's acquisition strategy? Did you decide to go on simply plugging the "gaps" or did you opt to concentrate on representing certain specific artists well?

Pontus Hulten. I have always fought against the sort of collection that represents every artist you can think of by a single work. I have always wanted a living, breathing collection, so rather than "plugging gaps" I tried to build on what we already had. This meant accepting the fact that we lacked some major works that we simply couldn't afford to buy. I think it's wrong to try to form a perfect, comprehensive collection. For one thing, it would lack personality and would end up as a collection of names rather than works of art. The Stockholm National Museum also possesses major collections of certain artists like the painter Papazot, or Eva Aeppli (the museum owns eighty of her works, some donated by Eva herself), or Niki de Saint Phalle and Marcel Duchamp.

I organised several small exhibitions of Duchamp's work, and when I was planning my "Art in Movement" exhibition in 1961 it was obvious that Calder and Man Ray and Tinguely and Duchamp absolutely had to be represented. The perfect Duchamp for our exhibition would have been his *Large Glass*, but that was impossible: it can't be moved from the museum in Philadelphia because the glass has cracked. So I thought up the idea of making a copy. I talked it over at great length with Marcel, who was then living in New York. Then one day when we were trying to choose the colours over the telephone and the whole thing was turning into a nightmare I heard him say "Mais, je viendrai". He did come and he liked both the concept of the exhibition and the works we had selected. So we eventually finished the *Large Glass*, and Duchamp signed it as a "certified true copy". After that we tried to find more of his work from around the world. I remember the trouble we had with the sketch for *Etant Donnés*, his final masterpiece constructed in the Philadelphia museum. It belonged to a woman who lived in Brazil and had no intention of selling it. When she died, the Duchamp was inherited by a daughter who didn't want to sell it either. I kept in touch with the family and when her daughter, who had moved to Tripoli, also died, the heirs decided to sell the Duchamp. Unfortunately, the museum had no money for purchases at the time, so I persuaded a Swedish collector to buy it on a temporary basis together with another drawing for *Etant Donnés*. Subsequently, other collectors chipped in, and both the drawing and the sketch ended up in the museum's collection. This is why the museum now possesses a rare collection which may not be compared to the Duchamp collection in Philadelphia but is nevertheless of importance.

Lastly, I should like to emphasise the fact that the Moderna Museet was and remains a national museum. This means it has a duty to Swedish artists, a duty to establish a major collection representative of Swedish art over the years. Naturally there is a temptation to collect internationally famous names. For example, the Moderna Museet has a nice collection of Oyvind Fahlstrom's work. Still, as I said, a national museum has an obligation to represent even those national artists who may never change the course of art history.

Ida Gianelli. So the Stockholm adventure ended and another even more exciting adventure began with the construction of the Pompidou Centre in Paris. France's national museum of modern art opened in 1977 with a big Duchamp exhibition, but your work there began earlier, in 1973 with the design and construction of the building itself.

Pontus Hulten. I moved to Paris to take on the Musée national d'art moderne Pompidou

Centre and was captivated by the task. Paris, unlike Stockholm, had plenty of money to go around, and it was made available to the museum as soon as they decided to move out of the old building and transfer to the Beaubourg site. On the other hand, the collections were modest to say the least, far more modest than you can imagine. Even the many paintings of the *École de Paris*, for which the museum was renowned, were of modest quality. Some of the paintings were fine: the Picassos (donated by the artist), a few Matisses, a Dalì painting, a minor Giacometti. Surrealism, arguably the most representative Parisian cultural movement, was not even represented. It was a real shock, but since we had a huge budget we could go for a really ambitious programme.

I was working with a committee of twelve people, some of whom were staff and some outsiders. Matters were further complicated by red tape. Still, as chairman of the committee I was able to introduce an unanimity rule. In other words, a work of art could be purchased only if everyone was in favour. I didn't want to buy a painting when seven committee members had voted for it and five against. The unanimity rule worked out quite well. Though I remember on one occasion I wanted to buy a Magritte painting but was prevented from doing so because one of my staff voted against it. I gave in but was furious because it was a wonderful Magritte. In any case, I proposed the same painting again the following year and that time we bought it.

I have no idea why our budget kept getting bigger and bigger. I do know we bought thousands of art works and built up the biggest European collection of art of the present century in just a few years. Perhaps the politicians had recognised the importance of the enterprise. There is no doubt that the state's generosity should be recognised as should Georges Pompidou's simple yet brilliant idea of allowing artists' or collectors' heirs to donate works of art to the state in lieu of death duties.

In order to avoid interminable red tape, the value attributed to a work for tax purposes may only be discussed twice. After that, either the heirs pay death duties or the works of art pass into the hands of the state - or, in the case of twentieth-century works, to the Musée national d'art moderne. This is how the Pompidou Centre acquired its great Picasso and Matisse collections.

We should not forget that both Georges Pompidou and his wife Claude had always been interested in poetry and later in art, and their engagements always included visits to Paris galleries. This went on even when Pompidou was President of the Republic. Subsequently he and his wife launched their own highly distinctive collection that included drawings by Rodin, as well as paintings by Picabia, the *École de Paris* and Yves Klein. I think it was the first time any Head of State created a collection of modern art.

What they call "the Pompidou effect" signalled the end of the divide between society and creative work.

Ida Gianelli. I have always been impressed by the number and quality of the donations to the Musée national d'art moderne. I'm thinking of the Kandinsky collection, the Brancusi studio reconstruction. How did you manage it?

Pontus Hulten. When I took over as director, complex negotiations were already under way with Madame Kandinsky, who owned about a hundred of her husband's paintings. This beautifully designed collection covered all the various periods of his output. Talks had been held between the museum and Nina Kandinsky, but things didn't look too promising. Luckily, I knew Nina well because I had shown her collection at the Moderna Museet years earlier. She had loved Stockholm, she'd appeared on Television there and we had remained good friends. So I went to see her and suggested she sell some of her paintings to the museum. She was, however, very old by then and was less interested in selling than in finding the ideal home for the work of the great painter. Nina had already given Georges Pompidou Kandinsky's sketches. They had the idea of using them as frescoes to decorate all four walls of a windowless room with two doors. Nina and Pompidou thought of creating that room for the opening of the Pompidou Centre. I was intrigued by this idea, dating from the early Twenties, of a room entirely taken over by a single pictorial composition. With great difficulty I managed to recreate that room for the official opening and very slowly our friendship developed. Nina, however, just would not make up her mind. I think she was having a lot of fun being flattered and wooed by all the museums in the world. I also knew the German government had conferred an important honour upon her, and since Munich already owned a major Kandinsky collection, there was a very real risk of our losing Nina's collection. I therefore decided to play my hand. I invited Nina to dinner in one of Paris' best restaurants, La Serre in Avenue Montaigne. In this marvellous place, the roof opens to leave you sitting in a magnificent dining room in the open air as night darkens the Paris sky above you. It was a delectable evening with the chestnut trees in blossom. Paris was as indescribably beautiful as it can be in spring and Nina was won over. She said the collection must stay in Paris. So she immediately made a will leaving us all her paintings and furniture as well as the Kandinsky library. She also set up an association to protect the rights to her husband's works. Now this "Société Kandinsky" is using the royalties from those works to fund regular publication of a Kandinsky catalogue.

Ida Gianelli. And the Brancusi studio?

Pontus Hulten. Yes, the Brancusi studio was another important determining factor in the design and construction of the Pompidou Centre. Brancusi spent his entire life trying to create a permanent home for his work but never succeeded. To some extent, he achieved his dream in Romania, in the famous park where he erected his *Infinite Column*. In Paris he tried more than once to find a place for his ideal environment but always failed. So gradually he transformed his own studio into a place where every sculpture had its own particular place. When one piece was sold, it was quickly replaced by a plaster cast or another casting or a bronze. Over the years, as sculptures and furniture were assigned their ideal positions, the studio acquired an incredible beauty of its own and became a sort of temple. It had no symmetry but displayed that subtle harmony between masses that only infinite time can create. As they were slowly shifted, inch by inch over the years, those masses achieved a perfect harmony that showed each sculpture to its very best advantage. Ultimately Brancusi used not simply his own sculptures but also large boulders and what remained of his casts to create this unique environment. At last he finally succeeded in creating the environment he desired. Sadly, it was ahead of its time and misunderstood. Government response was cool when Brancusi made a desperate effort to preserve it by donating it to France's old Musée national d'art moderne in the Palais de Tokyo. His Romanian nationality was cited as one reason for this refusal, so he even acquired French nationality in an attempt to save his studio. The odd thing was that once the agreement was signed, the museum lost all interest in the Brancusi studio. It was left to Madame Istrati, Brancusi's heir, Jean Tinguely and myself to look after the building as best we could. Branches from nearby trees fell on the roof, breaking the skylights; rain poured in causing considerable damage and nobody did anything about it. Eventually, the contents of the studio were moved to a new site, but even then the museum took not the slightest interest. Original glass photographic plates got broken. The *Infinite Column* was too tall for its new site and sawn up. As a token gesture towards respecting the instructions in Brancusi's will, a tiny part of the former studio was reconstructed in what it would be generous to call an approximate fashion.

The museum project was well under way when I arrived in Paris to take charge of the Pompidou Centre. Then suddenly President Pompidou died. This was the sign for all and sundry to fall on the project like so many Furies. Many donors, including Brancusi's heirs, decided that they no longer wanted their gifts moved into the new Piano and Rogers building. In the end I succeeded in convincing everybody that the studio would have to be rebuilt exactly as it was during Brancusi's lifetime. The same materials would have to be used and the light would have to enter at the same angle. This is the story of how we rebuilt Brancusi's little studio, outside the museum, in Place Beaubourg, where it still stands today. It was no easy task. People couldn't understand why I was doing it and dreadful City Council meetings were held with everybody shouting at everybody else. Wild statements were made, such as: "What if every Romanian sculptor thinks he can expect a studio in a Paris square?" Still, in the end we did get the atelier built – although it seemed like a miracle. This is the reason why a modest little building made out of scrap materials stands beside the sleek, high-tech Pompidou Centre today.

I believe it will be preserved, although it has had its ups and downs. It has been neglected. My successors did not share my views. However, Renzo Piano, the architect responsible for designing the great building, is now working on the restoration of the Brancusi atelier.

Ida Gianelli. In 1981, your French life ended and your American adventure began. Again your task was to create a new museum of contemporary art, this time in Los Angeles.

Pontus Hulten. Los Angeles was something else again. For one thing, there was absolutely nothing there. We decided to concentrate on the building first and choose an architect before thinking about the collection. Our real problem was that we had absolutely no money. So we had to go out and work for it, to find sponsors for the entire project. I set out on yet another hunt for donations and had started to achieve some results. Then we started talks with Giuseppe Panza di Biumo. We wanted all his amazing collection, and we did manage to rake up enough money to buy part of it, the historically significant part. That way we acquired paintings by Rothko, Franz Kline and Fautrier as well as some of Rauschenberg's very best work. We had a hard time negotiating the purchase because Americans see any collection strictly in terms of price and monetary value. For them, art is merchandise first and foremost. Whereas a European museum belongs to a state, city or region and collections can never be sold, American museums are private property, and so the museum directors can sell off their merchandise (the art works) at will. In an attempt to expand the collection in the run-up to the opening of the museum and in order to improve our financial position, we tried to trade works by Californian artists for the same number of works by Polish artists. We then presented our trophies in an exhibition held at the Musée d'Art Moderne de la Ville de Paris. Sadly, the Californians showed not the slightest interest in Polish art, so we had to console ourselves with the Polish's admiration for Californian art. In another attempt to collect funds we asked Californian artists to make and donate large engravings, etchings, lithographs and silk-screen prints. Our of these works we created a portfolio. But it was all terribly hard going. Nevertheless, by the time I left Los Angeles in 1985 we had enough of a collection to open the museum.

Ida Gianelli. Your next ports of call after Los Angeles were the Palazzo Grassi in Venice (1985-89) and the Kunsthalle in Bonn (since 1990). Neither of those museums had collections either.

Pontus Hulten. This was the sad truth. It is a great shame, especially in the case of the Palazzo Grassi. However, I'm also working as director of the future Jean Tinguely Museum in Basle, where there is already a great collection of works donated by the artist's widow, Niki de Saint Phalle. The company Hoffman Laroche is making a special building, designed by Mario Botta, to house the collection. The collection will be entirely devoted to the works of Jean Tinguely, and we are now buying additional works to illustrate his entire artistic career from 1955 until his death.

Ida Gianelli. So far we have only talked about public collections. Have you ever created a collection for a private individual?

Pontus Hulten. No, not really. That's a real minefield, I think. Because of my position, collectors think they can hire me to get them art-works on the cheap. Then if I suggest young artists, they're disappointed. Another problem not to be under-estimated is that these are almost always rich people of "divorceable" age. If a divorce occurs, any collection you build up gets broken up by the new wife, who either takes no interest in art or thinks she knows better than me.

Ida Gianelli. Perhaps we should end by discussing the collection of Pontus Hulten himself.

Pontus Hulten. Well, you know, I've never really done any collecting as such. I have things I like that I consider souvenirs. I possess nothing that isn't linked to some aspect of my life, nothing that doesn't have some personal reference. The things I own are essentially "documents" of my generation. Now I have settled down happily in my big house, surrounded by my books and the things I love after a life of roaming. But I get bombarded with requests for loans, so now at last I realise why it was always so hard to obtain works of art for exhibitions.

Paris, November 18, 1994

Note

Acknowledgement

Research and editing: Elena Gigli

History. Milestone dates in each museum's history are given: foundation, refurbishment, new sites and expansion projects. This information is obtained from systematic catalogues, guide books and correspondence conducted by the present management.

Collections. The main stages in the history of the Twentieth-century art exhibited at the museum are recorded, together with information on donations and acquisitions.

Management. The main managers are given. These may have brought continuity to the museum or engineered a change in direction.

Exhibitions. Periodic exhibitions are described where these have been held. Exhibitions are often held as a matter of museum policy. Refurbishment and exhibition design are also described.

Catalogues. The series of catalogues dating from the museum's foundation to the present day are described. If no systematic catalogue is available, the reader is directed to exhibition catalogues or specific publications.

Fin de siècle. An attempt has been made to outline the history of this last decade of the Twentieth-century and suggest prospects for the future. A questionnaire was sent to museum managements with the aim of identifying certain key points: current management and main collaborators/list of exhibitions during the nineties/teaching activities/main acquisitions of the nineties/forecasts for the immediate future. The information provided by those kind enough to return the questionnaires is given here.

Fifty-five large and small museums have been included in this *fin de siècle* report, in addition to public and private collections managed by organisations and institutes. The author asks to be excused for any collections overlooked (though this is only the beginning of the survey).

The author of this text and her assistants would like to thank the following for the information provided (and particularly for their patience and prompt response): Adele Auregli, Paolo Barbaro, Gabriella Belli, Maria Teresa Bettarini, Gloria Bianchino, Gaia Bindi, Giovanna Bonasegale, Nicoletta Boschiero, Beatrice Buscaroli Fabbri, Andrea Buzzoni, Angela Cipriani, Ester Coen, Pier Giovanni Castagnoli, Bruno Corà, Giorgio Cortenova, Gian Alberto Dell'Acqua, Bianca Maria Dell'Acqua, Lucia Dell'Orto, Gloria Fazia, Mario Ferrazza, Luigi Ficacci, Maria Teresa Fiorio, Stefano Fugazza, Clara Gelao, Maria Flora Giubilei, Flaminio Gualdoni, Mario Guderzo, Giulio Masobrio, Maria Masau Dan, Lucia Matino, Vittorio Mezzomonaco, Gianfranco Monaca, Anna Maria Montaldo, Antonio Natali, Mario Nibbi, Giorgio Pacifico, Riccardo Passoni, Michele Polverari, Antonella Purpora, Mario Quesada, Isabella Reale, Valerio Rivosecchi, Maria Cristina Rodeschini, Patrizia Rosazza, Antonella Russo, Gabriella Sarelli, Chiara Sarteanesi, Carlo Sisi, Antonella Soldaini, Nicola Spinosa, Angela Tassinari, Angela Tecce, Marcello Toffanello, Anna Ugliano, Mariella Utili, Silvio Zanella.

Public Collections of Modern Art in Italy at the End of the Twentieth-century: their Past, Present and Future

Maurizio Fagiolo dell'Arco

Modern and Contemporary art is about to complete its first century (assuming its birth dates back to 1900-1905, the period between the Paris Exposition Universelle and the explosion of Cubism). Modern art museums also date back to much the same period.

When I accepted Ida Gianelli's invitation to write something for the catalogue devoted to the first ten years in the life of the Castello di Rivoli, it seemed a good opportunity to review the history of Italy's museums. An individual section on each institution gives details of foundation and development; collection contents; new acquisitions; exhibitions and teaching activities; successive directors; catalogues and other publications. As we approach the end of the century, one final section is devoted to the last decade: achievements of the Nineties and prospects for the immediate future.

Survey report (provisional)

So many Modern Art museums these days seem to be best described as clinics or rest-homes, mortuarys or madhouses. The ancient idea of a Museum as a home for the Muses has been lost. Italy is full of cavernous barracks, more or less adequately equipped, the resting place not just of innumerable art works but primarily of countless opportunities lost, pitiful silences and unexpected banning orders. And yet we still go on visiting these mausoleums, still dutifully attend the sick and the dead.

We go out of pity, perhaps, certainly not out of any vital interest. The poor visitor, the unfortunate historian, is not wholly to blame: the state and local authorities do their best to strew obstacles in the path of anyone who wishes to appreciate the present and the past, or gain an understanding of the future of human society.

Italian museums reflect an Italy that is only apparently united, an Italy that actually still functions at municipal level. Power is already split between the municipal and regional authorities and now the promise (or threat) of "federalism" seems likely to bring more hungry guests to the table. Too many cooks are spoiling the broth in the name of "autonomy"! The fragmented, irresponsible management is overly subject to individual whim and the dictates of various boards of internal and external auditors.

Individual town museums, on the other hand, are often slaves to local contingencies.

Topography and typology

There is no lack of permanent and temporary homes for modern art in Italy. There are many different types of museum, reflecting great differences in origins and growth (usually a somewhat haphazard process). The only efficient state-owned institution is the National Modern Art Gallery in Rome. Other collections are medium-sized (Modena), tiny (Naples) or consist purely of donations (the Pinacoteca di Brera in Milan).

Then there are the municipal museums, where modern art is often mixed up with works from earlier centuries and even with archaeological collections. As one would expect, the biggest, most active museums are to be found in Turin and Milan. These museums house major collections and run efficient exhibition and educational programmes. Piedmont can offer museums in Alessandria and Asti. Lombardy has museums in Bergamo, Brescia and Gallarate. Liguria has its Genoa-Nervi museum. In the Veneto, we find museums in Bassano del Grappa, Trieste, Udine, Venice and Verona. Tuscany can offer the Arezzo and Pistoia galleries. Emilia offers museums in Bologna, Ferrara and Modena. Rome itself owns a Municipal Museum that has been forgotten for fifty years. In the South, we find museums in Bari, Foggia and Palermo. Last but not least, there is a museum in Cagliari, Sardinia.

Scattered all over Italy, we also find collections built up by certain institutions (the Quirinale Presidential Palace or the Montecitorio Chamber of Deputies, for example) or by Foundations (set up by the art historian Roberto Longhi or the artist Alberto Burri, for example). Next, there are semi-public collections owned by banks and insurance companies (Banca Toscana, Banca di Roma, BNL, Caricalu, Carima, Assitalia). There are University collections (Parma) and collections held in museums of other types (Accademia di San Luca, the Gabinetto delle Stampe print collection, the Uffizi collection of self-portraits). There are occasional local oddities like the Mario Rimoldi collection in Cortina and several attempts – like the Della Ragione collection in Florence – to create a municipal museum, as well as company collections that have been converted into public galleries as in Piacenza.

The institutions created in the semi-autonomous regions (Aosta, Trento) come under a slightly different heading, as do the ones established on a mixed public-private sector basis (Rivoli, Prato). The bizarre collection in the Vatican has its own unique status, since in historical terms it is not in Italy at all.

Key points

The sections on individual museums reveal all the usual disagreements and reluctance to accept change. I make no excuses for mentioning them here, because any museum director, director, librarian or lecturer would say the same thing.

Exhibitions. Originally organised only as an occasional activity, peripheral to the main museum collection, exhibitions have become practically the only event museums organize these days. At least they give the newspapers something to talk about.

Donations. All private collections are ultimately destined for public museums. However, the process of acquiring individual works or collections has become increasingly haphazard. We all know about the unfortunate saga of the Jucker donation in Milan, while other donations have been turned into museums in their own right (the Della Ragione collection in Florence). One exemplary case was the De Fornaris bequest to Turin. De Fornaris left the city not just his collection but also a large amount of money, and this money has been carefully managed and used to enrich the city's Galleria Civica with innumerable art works in recent years.

Structures. Education departments are becoming very popular these days. New methods are being applied in certain cases, while guided tours and workshops are offered in most Italian museums nowadays. Libraries, photographic libraries and archives are often present, though all too often they are considered no more than ancillary services.

Opening hours. This issue has become a national scandal in Italy, where any sizeable museum employs more people than the Prado yet is still shut half the time. Often you arrive at a museum to find that it is closed for alterations. Even more infuriatingly, parts of the permanent collection are often closed down to make room for a temporary exhibition. (I must confess that I too have had to take down a Klimt to make room for a Lo Savio.)

Private-sector management. This is increasingly the plea of all those collections that have run out of ideas. However, it does present an extremely delicate problem. As a number of irresponsibly run museums have shown, it is no easy task to harmonise a scholarly approach with crowd-pleasing, conservation with exhibitionism, quality with popular appeal.

I wish to thank all those musums which responded to my questions, often providing me with exhaustive information. I learnt a lot about Italy's various museums during the years I struggled to find out more about Italian art (usually by visiting exhibitions). On such occasions, I rediscovered collections that had been unknown or hidden from view. (Happily many of them are now documented in catalogues.) I also learned to appreciate the far-sighted acquisition policy in operation throughout the pre-war period. I shared the bright hopes that flourished among directors not all that long ago, although those hopes are now somewhat tarnished.

Finally, I wish to make it clear that the descriptions of each museum's historical background and any opinions expressed about management and programmes are mine alone and that I take full responsibility for them.

Alessandria - Museo e Pinacoteca Civica (Civic Museum and Art Gallery)

History. The Modern Art Gallery was created as an annex to the Museum soon after World War I with the aid of local artists (Carlo Carrà, Leonardo Bistolfi). Following a 1922 exhibition of Sardinian and Piedmontese art, the town acquired its first "modern" paintings: *Le Maschere* by Felice Casorati and a self-portrait by Francesco Menzio. Activities were supported by the local Savings Bank. In the Thirties, Director Arturo Mensi developed a plan for expansion of the collection through acquisitions at the Venice Biennale and other exhibitions with the emphasis on work of local interest. Since World War II, the collection has acquired new works through the "Premio Città di Alessandria" competition, under the terms of which prize-winning entries are purchased by the gallery. Another acquisition campaign in 1968 was relaunched in 1972. A report by Giovanni Romano (1986) recounts the opportunities offered the museum. It was able to grasp them quickly with the aid of bank sponsorship.

Collections. Pia Vivarelli's register (1968) described the constitution of the Museum. The collection includes works by Divisionist painters (Morbelli, Pellizza da Volpedo) and local painters (Pietro Morando); a few Twentieth-century works up to the post-war period; and then the latest trends in new figurative art and Italian Pop Art.

Exhibitions. With the assistance of Marisa Vescovo, the gallery has put on almost a hundred exhibitions since 1972. Most of them have been one-man shows: by Piero Guccione, Mario Ceroli, Lucio del Pezzo, Vasco Bendini and others (almost all of whom have donated a work to the town).

Catalogues. *Il Museo e la Pinacoteca di Alessandria* by C. Spantigati with a preface by G. Romano, Alessandria 1986.

Fin de siècle. The gallery is currently closed to the public. Its present director (Giulio Massobrio) is planning its reorganisation and transfer to new premises. A selection of Twentieth-century works was exhibited in the modern art room at the Palazzo Guasco in late 1994.

Arezzo - Galleria Comunale d'Arte Contemporanea (Municipal Gallery of Contemporary Art)

This gallery has only existed for thirty years and its permanent collection is not open to the public. It owns about three hundred works, mostly from the post-war period. All of these were exhibited in an exhibition entitled *Mostra antologica della Galleria Comunale* in 1992-3. Exhibitions are held in the Sala di Sant'Ignazio (several in recent years). The gallery has no director, but Enrico Crispolti acts as consultant.

Asti - Pinacoteca Civica (Civic Art Gallery)

Exhibitions are organised by the gallery and the Assessorato alla cultura (local Council cultural department). Vittoria Villani has been director since 1978. I remember two exhibitions, *George Grosz* (1992) and *Piero Ruggeri* (1993). An annual "Maestro per il Palio" exhibition has contributed new works to the collection, which has also received several gifts.

Aosta - Assessorato, Ufficio mostre (Town Council, Exhibitions Office)

This autonomous region has been extremely active for many years and owns several exhibition sites such as the Centro Saint-Benin and the Tour Fromage. Directed since 1986 by Jeanus and Anna Ugliano, the Exhibitions Office has produced a splendid series of exhibitions (albeit of a somewhat spasmodic nature) that have ranged from historical painters (*Arturo Nathan*, 1992; *Alberto Savinio, pittore di teatro*, 1991) to international celebrities (*Joe Tilson*, 1991) and young painters (*Giuseppe Modica*, 1991). The office also publishes books and a newspaper and runs a specialised library. Various exhibitions held in recent years have enriched the office with nearly two hundred works. These are destined for the new Val d'Aosta Art Gallery currently under development.

Bari - Pinacoteca Provinciale, Galleria d'Arte Moderna (Provincial Portrait Gallery and Modern Art Gallery)

History. Opened in 1967 as an annex to a Portrait Gallery set up thirty years earlier with a gift of forty mediocre to poor paintings. Under the directorship of Pina Belli d'Elia, it was expanded by the Grieco donation in 1987.

Collections. Somewhat random, given the way the gallery was established. Roman School, the occasional Twentieth-century master, a great many works by minor Tuscan artists.

Catalogues: *Per Una Galleria d'Arte Moderna*, Bari 1966. *La Collezione Grieco. Cinquanta Dipinti da Fattori a Morandi*, by C. Farese Sperken, Bari 1987.

Fin de siècle. For the immediate future, the director (Clara Gelao) plans an exhibition of the Simone Estate and a review of Twentieth-century art in private Apulian collections arranged by L. De Venere. The gallery has an Education Department and in recent years has put on several exhibitions including some retrospectives (I remember the one devoted to *Wols*, 1992) and some photographic exhibitions (*Luigi Ghirri*, 1993). Its most recent exhibition was *Così lontano così vicino - Iconografie di inizio e fine millennio*.

Bassano del Grappa - Museo Civico (Civic Museum)

The Museum owns some modern works. Its director, Mario Guderzo, organises exhibitions in collaboration with the Palazzo Agostinelli Committee. Among the most recent: *Guido Balsamo Stella incisore* in 1993 and *Disegni della Resistenza* in 1994.

Bergamo - Galleria d'Arte Moderna e Contemporanea (Modern and Contemporary Art Gallery)

Recently (November 1991) established as an annex to the town's School of Fine Arts, the Gallery is directed by Vittorio Fagone. Its permanent collection ranges from early Twentieth-century art to the *Informel* and is now being reorganised and expanded. The Gallery has organised many exhibitions, some devoted to photography and film. I remember a recent retrospective exhibition entitled *Gli anni del Premio Bergamo 1939-1942*.

Fin de siècle. The Gallery is planning an anthological exhibition of Emilio Vedova's work, a Vincenzo Angetti retrospective, a Carlo Carrà exhibition (organised jointly with the National Gallery of Modern Art), an analysis of the work of Gianni and Joe Colombo and a review of the "pittura-pittura" movement dating from the early Seventies.

Bologna - Galleria d'Arte Moderna (Modern Art Gallery)

History. Left to the city in the hope that "the sight of beauty will lift the spirits of its inhabitants", Villa delle Rose became the home of the Gallery in 1930. Its collection was expanded with the aid of purchases from exhibitions and legacies. The Gallery was relaunched in 1961, largely due to the efforts of Francesco Arcangeli. It has now acquired over two thousand works, some stored in the Town Hall offices.

The Modern Art Gallery was refounded in 1974 and can therefore boast twenty years of acquisitions and exhibitions. Its present home is a modern building at the "Fiera", although this is now too small to house the many legacies and purchases amassed over the years. In 1993, the Morandi Museum was opened in the Town Hall to house new donations.

Today, exhibitions are held both at the "Fiera" and in Villa delle Rose. In recent years the Gallery has acquired a great deal of contemporary art, partly through acquisitions made at the "Arte Fiera" exhibition with the help of enlightened sponsors.

Collections. The gallery's acquisitions policy has mostly given preference to the Twentieth-century Emilian School. Its collection ranges from painters of the Roman Secession (Alfredo Protti, Guglielmo Pizzirani, Grazia Fioresi, Giovanni Romagnoli, Carlo Corsi) to the great Giorgio Morandi. Romagnoli, who won the Pittsburgh Prize in 1924, is a special case and a painter whose work is yet to be properly assessed. In the Twenties, the gallery acquired works by artists who revolved around the "Francesco Francia" painters' society while in the Thirties works by artists connected to *L'Orto* magazine were bought. Then came Bruno Saetti and Mario Pozzati. The post-war period is represented by new movements instigated by artists whom Francesco Arcangeli has described as "the last naturalists": Pompilio Mandelli, Sergio Vacchi, Bruno Romiti and Carlo Corsi. The collections also pay due attention to the Sixties and the latest trends.

Directors. Following Francesco Arcangeli's brief interlude at Villa delle Rose, Franco Solmi was appointed director to the new museum. He put on a great many exhibitions and undertook a major acquisitions campaign. Since 1987, the director has been Pier Giovanni Castagnoli. He is rearranging the institution and has put on some outstanding exhibitions. The Morandi Museum is directed by Marilena Pasquali, and Adele Auregli curates the Villa delle Rose exhibitions.

Exhibitions. The Museum opened with a Giorgio Morandi exhibition arranged by Lamberto Vitali, and Morandi has remained its core concern. A major exhibition *Morandi e il suo tempo* (Life and times of Morandi) was organised in 1985-86 and various exhibitions promoted abroad. So far the Museum has organised two hundred and forty-eight exhibitions including one-man shows, retrospectives and experimental projects.

One outstanding exhibition during the Seventies was devoted to *Renzo Vespignani* (1975). Other exhibitions of photography were devoted to artists such as *Irving Penn* (1975) and *Sergio Romiti* (1976). Another was entitled *Il liberty a Bologna e Emilia Romagna* (1977), followed by Franco Solmi's *Metafisica del Quotidiano* in 1978 and *Giuseppe Pagano fotografo* in 1979. A patchy but impressive exhibition entitled *La Metafisica - gli anni Venti* was arranged by Franco Solmi and Renato Barilli in 1980. The Eighties also saw a lively series of exhibitions under the umbrella title *Esercizi di lettura*. I remember those devoted to Mattia Moreni, Renato Guttuso, Mimmo Paladino, Emilio Vedova and Mario Merz. Forays were made into bordering territories, including one devoted to Design of Italian Fashion in 1982. The museum has also organised retrospective exhibitions. One entitled *L'Informale in Italia* (1983) curated by Renato Barilli and Franco Solmi and dedicated to Francesco Arcangeli.

The museum's exhibition activities appear to be extremely well planned (about a dozen shows a year). Even more important, they are of excellent quality as we can see from the gallery's own catalogues and publications.

Catalogues. The Gallery is not systematically catalogued but its files are open to academics. The Morandi Museum does have a catalogue edited by M. Pasquali (Charta, Milan 1993).

Fin de siècle. Pier Giovanni Castagnoli will remain in charge until 1995 and will then be faced by the difficult task of organising the move from the Gallery's present inadequate home to new premises in the former Tobacco Factory. There is also talk of a temporary move to the Palazzo di Re Enzo in Piazza Maggiore in spring 1995.

Among exhibitions of recent years, I remember *Giulio Paolini* (1990), *Acquerelli di Morandi* (Morandi water-colours) (1990-91), one-man exhibitions on *Piero Dorazio* and *Concetto Pozzati* (1991), *Arte a Bologna 1990-1960*, an exhibition featuring works owned by the Gallery (1992), and a Gianfranco Ferroni exhibition in 1994.

The Gallery is currently preparing exhibitions on Bernard Schulze (January 1995) and Nunzio (at Villa delle Rose in February 1995).

In February 1995, the new Salara exhibition centre will open with a display of works by Jannis Kounellis especially created for this site. In other words, this is an active, well-run museum, although currently in the throes of growing pains.

Alberto Burri, former Tobacco Drying Plant, 1991
(Photo by Lionello Fabbri)

Brescia - Civica Galleria d'Arte Moderna e Contemporanea (Civic Gallery of Modern and Contemporary Art)

History. It became apparent that Brescia needed a modern art collection when the Tosio-Martinengo Portrait Gallery opened a modern art section in 1964. However the project was not approved until 1982.

The original home of the museum was the Monastery of Santa Giulia and its display centred on the privately owned Cavallini collection (subsequently withdrawn), which included a memorable selection of abstract-concrete, abstract and *Informel* works by Italian, European and American artists. The city now mourns this lost opportunity – the second in its history because it also failed to make proper use of the Pietro Feroldi collection which originally introduced Brescia to the European scene. A committee was set up to examine prospects for a new museum, and in 1989 a controversial exhibition was put on entitled *Proposte per una civica Galleria d'arte moderna e contemporanea* (Proposal for a civic modern and contemporary art gallery).

Collections. An interesting Nineteenth-century collection: from Neoclassicism to Lombard Romanticism. The Gallery also owns a substantial body of work (purchased in 1963) by the Brescian artist Romolo Romani, an undercover Symbolist and Futurist artist. Other Futurist works come from the collection of Anton Giulio Bragaglia which formed part of an exhibition entitled *Dopo Boccioni* (After Boccioni) held in the Medusa Gallery, a model museum in its day. The Gallery also acquired several early Twentieth-century works with the Scalvini bequest in 1985.

Catalogues. Dai neoclassici ai futuristi e oltre - Proposte per una civica galleria d'arte moderna e contemporanea exhibition catalogue by R. Stradiotti with contributions by B. Passamani, R. Bossaglia, M. Mondini, V. Terraroli, R. Stradiotti, and U. Spini, Brescia 1989.

Fin de siècle. Director: Bruno Passamani. No exhibits were organized until the Gallery collections were exhibited in 1989.

Cagliari - Galleria Comunale d'Arte (Municipal Art Gallery)

Anna Maria Montaldo has been director since 1987 and has presented a dozen exhibitions in recent years, most of them devoted to the local art scene and Educational in intention. A selection of the Gallery's collections was shown in the exhibition entitled *Gli artisti sardi nelle collezioni civiche del '900* (1990) and subsequent exhibitions.

Città di Castello - Collezione Burri (The Burri Collection)

History. On December 12, 1981, the restored Palazzo Albizzini opened with works donated by Alberto Burri to the Palazzo Albizzini Foundation. On that occasion Cesare Brandi delivered the inaugural, stating: " Città del Castello is Burri and Burri is Città del Castello". The works are clearly displayed in roomy surroundings and include masterpieces from Burri's various periods: constructions in sacking, iron, timber, "combustions", plastic and cellotex. The gallery was designed by the architects Zanmatti and Sarteanesi. Nearly a decade later, a new collection of monumental works was opened in the ex Seccatoi Tabacco (former Tobacco Drying Plant): these eleven sheds form the perfect background to Burri's last great series from *Il Viaggio* (The Journey) to *Orsanmichele* and from *Sestante* (Sextant) to *Annottarsi* (Growing dark).

Catalogues. Collezione Burri, Fondazione Palazzo Albizzini, Città di Castello, 1986. *Collezione Burri*, by N. Sarteanesi, ex Seccatoi Tabacco, Città di Castello, 1992.

Fin de siècle. Under the directorship of Nemo Sarteanesi the collection has recently been expanded by the addition of new Burri cycles: *Metamorfotex* (1991) and *Il Nero e l'Oro* (The black and the gold) (1993). It has held conferences and workshops ("Educare con l'arte - Un laboratorio per il museo" ("Educate with art - a museum workshop") (1993) as well as courses of lectures. One recent acquisition was a series of sixteen small-scale works formerly owned by J.J. Sweeney. The Burri Collection is currently organising a "Contemporary Art Project European study tours".

Cortina - Galleria d'Arte Moderna Mario Rimoldi (Mario Rimoldi Modern Art Gallery)

History. The collection of Mario Rimoldi, owner of the famous Hotel Corona, went on public display in the winter of 1941. Reorganised in its new "Regole d'Ampezzo" home in 1983, the gallery now owns three hundred and sixty-four works of art. Among the most significant we find a group of paintings by Filippo de Pisis as well as works by *Novecento* painters (two major works by Savinio) and some from the Roman School, but also post-war works such as Renato Gattuso's *La Zolfara*. Recent exhibitions devoted to Twentieth-century art have often drawn on the gallery's own collection.

The gallery's first catalogue was for its inaugural exhibition (Cortina 1941); its latest is the *Catalogo della Galleria d'Arte Moderna Mario Rimoldi* by L. Magagnato and S. Zanotto, Venice 1983.

Cosenza - Collezione della Cassa di Risparmio (Cassa di Risparmio Collection)

In addition to its collection of Southern Baroque, the bank has also acquired some good modern work: from Umberto Boccioni to Alberto Savinio. For the works exhibited in 1986, a catalogue was produced by R. Monti and E. Mattucci (De Luca, Rome 1986).

Ferrara - Musei Civici - Galleria d'Arte Moderna e Contemporanea (Civic Museum Gallery of Modern and Contemporary Art)

History. The museum was started with a donation of paintings by Giovanni Boldini (1932) and has been housed in Palazzo dei Diamanti, Palazzo Massari and Palazzina dei Cavalieri di Malta. There have been periodic exhibitions since an initial one-man show of Boldini's works was held in Casa Romei.

Collections. A recent exhibition *Opere dell'Ottocento e del Novecento nelle collezioni della Civica Galleria d'Arte Moderna e Contemporanea* (Works of the Nineteenth and Twentieth-century in the Civic Modern and Contemporary Art collection) displayed the gallery's possessions. They range from a large body of works by Giovanni Boldini (a museum within the museum) to groups of paintings by the Ferrari Divisionist painters (Giovanni Previati, Giuseppe Mentessi) and the Parafuturists (Aroldo Bonzagni). Magnificent rooms are also devoted to two other great Ferrara artists, Roberto Melli and Filippo de Pisis.

Catalogues. The Gallery has not published a catalogue, but a newsletter edited by B. Buscaroli and M. Toffanello: *Un museo in mostra*, 1994.

Fin de siècle. Exhibitions have been held at all the Gallery's various sites over recent years. I remember the Visual Arts Centre in Palazzo dei Diamanti conducted a valuable examination of historical realism under the title of *Painting and Reality* (1993), curated by Fabrizio d'Amico, Flaminio Gualdoni, and Andrea Buzzoni. Other exhibitions have been devoted to *Ennio Morlotti* (1994) and *Lucio Fontana* (1994-5). Palazzo Massari will continue to offer exhibitions of contemporary art. Other noteworthy shows were devoted to *Mimmo Rotella* (1991), *Artisti di Corrente* (1992) and *Bepi Romagnoni* (1994).

The museum is very concerned to offer educational guidance for schools and the general public. Educational themes have included leading Ferrara artists of the Twentieth century and also young contemporary artists in general. Palazzo Massari used to contain a "Metaphysical museum", which was set up for teaching purposes. This was Francesco Farina's idea, but has now been dismantled. The gallery's recent acquisitions include several good paintings by Previati and De Pisis.

The present director, Andrea Buzzoni (appointed in 1994), plans conservative restoration work on both buildings and art works. This project will also involve a photographic survey and systematic cataloguing. A series of exhibitions on great post-war artists is currently being prepared.

Florence - Galleria d'Arte Moderna di Palazzo Pitti (Palazzo Pitti Modern Art Gallery)

History. The question of endowing Florence with a Modern Art Gallery dates back to the nineteenth century when Palazzo Vecchio's Eleanora area were identified as an appropriate site (the Diego Martelli donation was the start of this collection). However, the first real museum was not opened until 1909 in Palazzina delle Cascine with Ugo Ojetti as director. The turning point for the museum came in 1913 when the municipal authorities transferred the property to the Italian state and the collection moved to a few rooms in the Accademia. In 1920 The Friends of the Modern Art Gallery chose Palazzo Pitti as a site, but the new Gallery was not actually opened until 1924. Between the wars, the Gallery bought major works from exhibitions held at institutions or directly from the artists. The Gallery stagnated somewhat after World War II until the mid-Fifties when Licia Collobi Ragghianti was able to establish the urgency of the problem. During this period, acquisitions from Fiorino Prize exhibitions added major works of the past and present to the gallery's collection and it also received the Leone Ambron donation. Yet Florence still remained the city of the Thirteenth century and the Macchiaioli.

It was not until Sandra Pinto took over as director in the Seventies that the collections were finally reorganised. In 1979, thirty exactly arranged rooms were opened with over two thousand works on show (all researched, rediscovered and restored). Nevertheless, the collection still refused to venture into the Twentieth century.

The task of beginning to reorganise the gallery's Twentieth-century works (about eight hundred) was left to the next director, and a large selection (hundred and twenty works) were presented in an exhibition held in 1986.

Collections. The Tuscan School is extremely well represented, from the early days of Galileo Chini and Giovanni Costetti to masters of the Twentieth century (Ardengo Soffici, Ottone Rosai, Giovanni Colacicchi). A vast number of items are stored in the Accademia dell Arti del Disegno while its impressive graphics collection has been stored in the Uffizi Gabinetto dei Disegni e Stampe degli Uffizi. The Gallery also owns a few major works by early Twentieth-century artists; I remember de Chirico and Savinio, Gino Severini, Felice Casorati, Antonio Donghi.

Directors. Giuseppe Marchini was director in the Fifties. In the Seventies a lot of work was done under Sandra Pinto. She was followed by Ettore Spalletti, and the present director is Carlo Sisi.

Catalogues. Le collezioni del Novecento 1915-1945 - Presentazione antologica, by E. Spalletti, Florence, 1986. Because a museum catalogue has not been published, we have only an exhibition catalogue listing just one hundred and twenty works out of a total of eight hundred, as a reference.

Fin de siècle. Only the first three rooms (28-30) on the second floor of the Pitti display modern works. Florence has rejected modernism yet again. In the past few years, the occasional exhibition has been put on (*Giannino Marchig*, 1994) and more has been done on the educational side in conjunction with the Superintendent's Office.

The purchasing side has done rather better, with one hundred works (gifts and purchases) entering the collection in the past few years. They include Colacicchi's masterpiece *Fine d'estate*, and the nineteen Rosai paintings of the Simeone collection. Sisi now plans to open a few of the thirteen rooms that will be devoted to Twentieth-century art.

Florence - Collezione della Banca Toscana (The Bank of Tuscany Collection)

"A bank can be a place of memories" writes the Banca Toscana Chairman in his introduction to the bank's collection of some two hundred works, mostly by Italian artists of the *Novecento*. The collection has expanded dramatically in recent years and now includes several masterpieces, while still retaining its own distinctive character. I remember a group of drawings by Carlo Carrà, *La scuola* by Felice Carena, as well as Donghis, Morandis, Rossis (*Giocatori di Toppa*), the Italiens de Paris group, (Severini's painting of Maison Rosenberg, Tozzi, de Pisis, de Chirico), and even a seminal work by Alberto Burri.

The collection was reviewed recently in the catalogue for the exhibition *Da Fattori a Burri. Collezione della Banca Toscana* produced by S. Bietoletti, R. Campana, and S. Lucchesi, with a preface by C. Sisi, Florence, 1993.

Florence - Fondazione Roberto Longhi (The Roberto Longhi Collection)

The art historian's villa outside Florence houses works by the Twentieth-century artists he supported. Mina Gregori's work entitled *La Fondazione Roberto Longhi a Firenze* (Milan 1980) systematically catalogues the works of Carlo Carrà and Giorgio Morandi, Filippo de Pisis and Mario Mafai, Renato Guttuso and Alberto Ziveri. Another work purchased at the same time was Mario Cavaglieri's masterpiece (1920).

Florence - Gabinetto Disegni e Stampe degli Uffizi (Uffizi Gallery Drawing and Print Room)

Italy's finest collection of graphic art includes a large number of Twentieth-century works. Among its earliest acquisitions I remember a Savinio purchased in 1934. Subsequent purchases are documented in two catalogues *Acquisizioni 1944-1974*, Florence 1974; *Dieci anni di acquisizioni 1974-1984*, Florence 1985. These describe all the latest trends from Lucio Fontana to Fausto Melotti and Emilio Vedova to Gianfranco Ferroni. A major collection of works by Giorgio Morandi is included.

Florence - Galleria degli Uffizi. Corridoio degli Autoritratti. (The Uffizi Gallery Self-Portraits Corridor)

This annex to the Medici collection was begun in 1981 to celebrate the Uffizi's four hundredth anniversary. This expanding collection of contemporary self-portraits already includes paintings by Giacomo Balla (*Autocaffè*), Virgilio Guidi, Renato Guttuso, Alberto Ziveri and others: nearly two hundred faces of Twentieth-century artists. The Uffizi has also benefited from substantial donations such as Corrado Cagli's *Battaglia di San Martino* and a huge *Cellotex* by Alberto Burri. The director is Antonio Natali.

Florence - Museo Marino Marini (The Marino Marini Museum)

Opened in 1988 in the Albertian complex of San Pancrazio, this museum also organises exhibitions and lectures. The Foundation owns nearly two hundred works donated by the artist's wife, Marina, which are arranged in subject groups rather than chronological order. It has held several exhibitions in recent years (*Giovanni Colacicchi*, 1992) and arranged seminars with a critic and an artist, and exhibitions of some of the works. The museum is described in a catalogue (Milan, 1988) and a guidebook written by Carlo Pirovano (Milan, 1990).

Florence - Raccolta d'Arte Contemporanea Alberto Della Ragione (Alberto Della Ragione Collection of Contemporary Art)

This collection was the first donation made to the museum of contemporary art by Carlo L. Ragghianti following the floods of 1966. (Other donations in search of a home are those of Alberto Magnelli, Mirko e Cagli, Bruno Saetti). The collection is currently housed in the Cassa di Risparmio bank on Piazza della Signoria. In 1970 Alberto Della Ragione, an engineer from Sorrento who worked in Genoa, donated a further two hundred and forty-one works. His collection was first exhibited in Turin in 1938 (Galleria La Zecca). Oscar Kokoschka painted his wife in 1933; he provided a home for Guttuso and the Mufais during the war; he was in touch with Birolli, Guttuso, and Santomaso; he was the protector of Manzù and Marini. Della Ragione's collection includes masterpieces by futurist painters (Fortunato Depero, Enrico Prampolini), and the occasional *Novecento* master (Morandi, de Pisis, de Chirico), as well as works by the Roman School (Donghi, Melli, seventeen Mafais, three Scipiones) and even some by *Corrente* artists.

Foggia - Museo Civico e Palazzo dell'Arte (Civic Museum and Palace of the Arts)

The modern section of Foggia's picture gallery, directed by Gloria Fazia, is mainly devoted to the postwar period. The Palazzetto dell'Arte directed by Mariano Vitale has held numerous exhibitions devoted to contemporary local artists in recent years and educational activity is carried out continuously.

Forlì - Galleria d'Arte Moderna e Contemporanea (Gallery of Modern and Contemporary Art)

This somewhat obscure museum is slightly off the beaten track but owns a collection that casts an intriguing light on the Italian cultural scene at a particular point in time. I refer to the collection of Giuseppe Verzocchi, a manufacturer of fire-bricks who in 1949 commissioned a series of paintings by seventy two artists on the theme of work. He also required them to put one of his own firebricks beside their signature. Giorgio de Chirico interpreted the subject in his own particular way in a painting entitled *La Fucina di Vulcano*. The collection also includes works by the surviving Futurists, Gino Severini, Fortunato Depero, Enrico Prampolini, as well as a few representatives of the *Novecento* (Carlo Carrà, Achille Funi), the Roman School (Antonio Donghi, Fausto Pirandello), the Realists (Renato Guttuso) and the abstract-art artists (Giuseppe Capogrossi, Renato Birolli, Afro). The Gallery's first catalogue, *Il lavoro nella pittura italiana d'oggi*, was published in Milan in 1950. More recently (Milan, 1984) M. de Micheli produced a catalogue for another exhibition of paintings most of which was stolen. All but one of the stolen pictures were later recovered and presented in an exhibition entitled *Il ritorno*. According to the present director, Vittorio Mezzomonaco, the museum now concentrates on local talents and has made several purchases, including plaster casts by Ercole Drei.

Gallarate - Civica Galleria d'Arte Moderna (Civic Gallery of Modern Art)

This much-expanded gallery was opened in 1966 under the directorship of Silvio Zanella, who still remains in charge. It all started with the donation of some one hundred works obtained through the Gallarate Prize. Since then, the gallery has accumulated nearly two thousand works of art. Today its twenty rooms cover all the various movements of the post-war period. It holds periodic exhibitions (I remember one curated by Luciano Caramel in 1984 on the *Arte Concreta* movement) and does some educational activity. The museum is now to move to new premises.

Genoa - Galleria d'Arte Moderna, Villa Serra, Nervi (Villa Serra Modern Art Gallery, Villa Serra, Nervi)

History. Opened in Villa Serra in 1928, the gallery owns an extensive collection of Nineteenth-century works and a fair number from our own century as well. Sculpture is well-represented, with works from the Genoese school to Arturo Martini (*La Convalescente*). The Twentieth-century works were mostly acquired at exhibitions. Artists represented include Ferruccio Ferrazzi and Antonio Donghi, Filippo de Pisis, and Felice Casorati. Ligurian artists are also well represented by Oscar Saccorotti.

Fin de siècle. The present director, Maria Flora Giubilei, hopes she will be able to reopen the Museum. It has been closed to the public since July 1989 and lacks staff or attendants.

In December 1994, she plans an exhibition entitled *Materiali per un progetto di recupero di Villa Serra*, which will outline plans for the restoration of Villa Serra, In 1995, the gallery will also help put on an exhibition of Ligurian painters from the past one hundred years (*I pittori liguri alle Biennali 1985-1995*) to be held at the Frugone Collection in Villa Grimaldi Fasso in Nervi. This exhibition will include some three hundred Nineteenth and Twentieth-century works ranging from Boldini to Segantini and Michetti.

Macerata - Collezione della Cassa di Risparmio (Savings Bank Collection)

The collection belonging to the Cassa di Risparmio bank is housed in the historic Pallazzo Ricci and ranges from Futurist artists (Gino Severini) to *Novecento* artists such as De Pisis and Carrà. The Roman School is the most extensively represented movement with the best of Scipione's work as well as works by Mario Mafai and Fausto Pirandello. Examples of other recent trends can also be seen. A succinct catalogue was produced by Giorgio Mascherpa (Milan, 1983). Over the past decade, the Bank has organised some splendid one-man exhibitions ranging from Scipione in 1985 to Mario Mafai, Luigi Bartolini, Mino Maccari, Roberto Melli, Amerigo Bartoli, and Fausto Pirandello. This is an exemplary case of a private sponsor creating a semi-public collection.

Milan - Civico Museo d'Arte Moderna - CIMAC (Civic Museum of Modern Art)

History. Milan began to consider the idea of a Modern Art Museum at the end of the last century. In 1903, the Galleria d'Arte Moderna opened in a few rooms of the Castello Sforzesco. In 1921 it moved to a new home in Villa Belgioioso, a residence recently transferred to the Municipality by the Italian government. Before long, however, the building (designed by Pollak) proved too small for the museum's requirements as it accumulated more and more donations and acquisitions. In 1934, for example, the Ausonio Canavese donation added a great many works to the collection, including a major group by Umberto Boccioni. Works purchased at the Venice Biennale, the Rome Quadrienniale and exhibitions put on by the worker unions, the GUF and the Cremona Prize were added to the haul. A catalogue produced by Giorgio Nicodemi and Mario Bezzola in the Thirties listed nearly 4,000 works.

After World War II, Milan had to find more room for contemporary art and found a suitable building in the Villa Reale. This was redesigned as a museum by Ignazio Gardella in the years between 1948 and 1954 and opened with a Georges Rouault exhibition. In 1956, it acquired the Carlo Grassi collection, which was donated by his widow in memory of their son who died in battle in North Africa. This impressive collection included several works by French Impressionists and Post-Impressionists. A new wing of Villa Reale, designed by Gardella, opened in 1958.

In 1974, the museum acquired the collection of Antonio and Marieda Boschi; nearly 2,000 works accumulated by the wealthy rubber manufacturer in Milan and Paris over a period of forty years. It included a splendid set of Italian *Novecento* paintings as well as examples by the post-war abstract expressionist and *Gesto* movements (forty two by Lucio Fontana, six by Manzoni).

1979 saw the reopening of PAC (The Contemporary Art Pavilion), which put on a splendid albeit somewhat patchy series of exhibitions. In 1984 CIMAC moved into the second floor of the Palazzo Reale. Recent acquisitions include donations from Marino Marini (1973), Fausto Melotti and Atanasio Soldati.

Collections. As we have seen, collections and exhibitions form an integral part of the gallery's expansion. It all began with an outstanding group of Italian and foreign paintings that ranged from the Impressionists to Modigliani. The Lombard Divisionist movement is particularly well represented, as the equally important Milanese Futurist movement. As early as 1934, the museum acquired a huge Umberto Boccioni collection. Almost all subsequent donations have featured many Giacomo Balla canvases from every period. Naturally pride of place is reserved for the Italian *Novecento* of which Milan was the epicentre with Gussoni, Sarfatti and Barbaroux. It has therefore been gallery policy in recent years to purchase any major works from this period that appear in exhibitions: examples include Giorgio de Chirico, Carlo Carrà, Giorgio Morandi, Felice Casorati, Filippo de Pisis, Mario Sironi, Arturo Martini, and Giacomo Manzù. The Roman School is represented in Milan by several masterpieces by Scipione and Mafai, Donghi and Guidi, Pirandello and Fazzini. The Boschi collection endowed the gallery with a number of important items such as Giorgio de Chirico's great painting *Gladiators* for the Maison Rosenberg, which was bought from the heirs of Léonce Rosenberg in Paris.

Abstract art and Futurism are represented by major works by Fortunato Depero, Enrico Prampolini, Osvaldo Licini, Mario Soldati, and Alberto Magnelli. All the really important artists are represented by major works and in substantial quantity: the Boschi collection features a great many *Spazialisti* works and reveals a particular interest in *Nuclearism* and the *New Dada*.

The museum owns important collections of abstract art and *Informel* works (Piero Dorazio, Tancredi) as well as many of the new imagist and neo figurative artists of the Sixties (Giulio Paolini, Jannis Kounellis) while more recent trends are represented by artists like Enzo Cucchi. The catalogue of the collection, produced by Luciano Caramel and Carlo Pirovano in 1973-4, lists 1,123 works (not including the Boschi and Grassi donations). Today CIMAC is said to own nearly 3,000 works of art.

The catalogue for the exhibition *Arte Contemporanea per un museo. 10 anni di acquisizioni delle Raccolte d'Arte di Milano* (1989) lists nearly two hundred works: from Giacomo Balla to Fausto Melotti, from the *Informel* to the latest trends. Most recently, the museum acquired the important Riccardo Jucker collection (which had been assigned to the Brera and then withdrawn). This includes several major Futurist works (four Ballas, Boccioni's *Elasticità*) several Metaphysical paintings (Giorgio Morandi, Carlo Carrà) and a few European masterpieces (Mondriaan, Picasso and Matisse).

Exhibitions. Between 1979 and 1989 the Contemporary Art Pavilion presented a series of exhibitions: some important, some merely "radical chic" (according to Mercedes Garberi's catalogue published by Mazzotta, Milan, 1989). The opening exhibition (*Letteratura-Arte. Miti del Novecento* curated by Zeno Birolli and Gino Baratta) was interesting; a few were useful (*Nuove tendenze. Milano e l'altro Futurismo*), 1980; *Otto pittori Italian*, 1986). An occasional apt one-man show has been held (*Francesco Lo Savio*, 1979). Recent trends have also been examined (*Azimuth & Azimut*, 1984).

Good exhibitions put on by the Palazzo Reale include *Boccioni a Milano* (1982-83) and *Kandinsky a Parigi* (1985) as well as shows of a more documentary nature *Le Fantasie di Mafai* (1989). The Museum also helps to organise exhibitions abroad; Giorgio Morandi appeared in several Japanese exhibitions in 1989-90.

Directors. The Director before World War II was Giorgio Nicodemi. He was followed by Constantino Baroni (1945-56) who was responsible for expanding the Galleria Civica. Then came Paolo Annigoni (1956-65) and Gian Guido Belloni (1965-72). Mercedes Garberi, director from 1972-1992, bought numerous major works and reorganised the exhibition space.

Catalogues. G. Nicodemi, M. Bezzola, *La Galleria d'Arte Moderna. I dipinti*, Milan 1935-39. Idem, *Le sculture*, 1938. *Galleria d'Arte Moderna, Padiglione d'Arte Contemporanea, Raccolta Grassi*, by C. Pirovano and L. Caramel, Milan 1973. *Galleria d'Arte Moderna, Opere del Novecento* by L. Caramel and C. Pirovano, Milan 1974. *Galleria d'Arte Moderna Collezione Boschi*, by L. Caramel, C. Pirovano, and M. T. Fiorio, with an introduction by M. Garberi, Milan 1980. *Arte Contemporanea per un museo. 10 anni di acquisizioni delle Raccolte d'Arte di Milano*, the accompanying exhibition catalogue, with an introduction by M. Garberi, Milan 1989. *La collezione Jucker acquistate dal Comune di Milano*, by C. Porro and F. Caroli, Finarte, Milan 1992.

Fin de siècle. The museum currently boasts some forty rooms on the second floor of the Palazzo Reale next door to Milan Cathedral. They offer a choice of two different itineraries with one section devoted to works of accepted renown (1900-1960) and a "workshop" section which is re-installed constantly depending on space restrictions. Both itineraries ultimately take the visitor to the Jucker collection, acquired by the museum in 1982.

These premises are only temporary and designed to last only until such time as the municipal authorities decide to provide the museum with a permanent home. This must also be suitable for the sort of works that have been emerging recently (i.e., not solely within the realms of painting and sculpture). The museum also needs to improve its relationships with the Villa Reale in Via Palestro, which houses the Grassi and Vismara collections, and with the Marino Marini Museum.

The Museum is clearly growing too quickly for its own good: it has too many art works and too little space. The Palazzo Reale premises are unsuitable and municipal management may not be the ideal solution. Maria Teresa Fiorio has been director since 1992 and put on some splendid exhibitions such as: *Morandi e Milano* (1990-91, Palazzo Reale), *Da Modigliani a Fontana. Disegno italiano del XX secolo nelle raccolte civiche di Milano* (1991), *L'idea del classico. Temi Classici nell'arte italiana degli anni Venti* (1992). She has also ventured into border territory, for example with one exhibition devoted to Ignazio Gardella in 1992.

Milan - Pinacoteca di Brera (The Brera Gallery)
Collectors began donating paintings to Milan's best-loved museum back in the Forties. The two most important donations arrived almost simultaneously: the Riccardo Jucker and Emilio Jesi collections. However, the former was subsequently withdrawn and now only part of it is on show at CIMAC. The Jesi donation came in two sections. The first dates back to 1981 and covers Italian paintings; the second included major European works by artists such as Picasso and Braque.

The catalogue by Gian Alberto Dell'Acqua with a preface by L. Vitali (Milan, 1981) presents fifty seven paintings from Modigliani to the Futurists, from Metaphysical painters (Carrà and Morandi) to a small group of early *Novecento* paintings and sculptures by Medardo Rosso and Arturo Martini. This almost amounts to a short history of Italian art.

Modena - Galleria Civica *(Civic Gallery)*

History. The Gallery began in 1958 as a cultural salon responsible for organising an annual art show. In the Seventies, it organized one-man retrospective shows on Enrico Prampolini, Mauro Reggiani and others. In the Eighties, Fabrizio D'Amico organised an exhibition entitled *Disegno Italian tra le due guerre, Roma 1934* as well as a cycle of one-man shows devoted to artists, photographers and architects of the past and present, held in Palazzina dei Giardini.

Directors. Pier Giovanni Castagnoli (1982-87), Flaminio Gualdoni.

Fin de siècle. The Gallery has put on some dozen exhibition a year. Some have been one-man shows (*Lucio Fontana*, 1990, *Luigi Veronesi*, 1990, *Enzo Cucchi*, 1990), others retrospectives with emphasis on the Roman School (*Raphael*, 1991, *Alberto Ziveri*, 1992, *Ferruccio Ferrazzi*, 1993). Each exhibition is supported by an Educational workshop. Major acquisitions by the Gallery include more than one thousand photographs by Franco Fontana. Its most ambitious project, in progress since 1988, is the creation of a Contemporary Drawing Collection. In spring 1995, the Gallery hopes to open new premises, in Palazzo Santa Margherita, which will house permanent collections, archives and a workshop. This space will be easier to organise for exhibitions.

Naples - Museo di Capodimonte *(Capodimonte Museum)*

The Fine Arts Superintendent at Capodimonte is Nicola Spinosa, who is also responsible for the museum's modern art collections and exhibitions. Capodimonte Palace is now under restoration and both the Royal Apartments and the historical collections are expected to open in Autumn 1995. Several exhibitions have been held in Castel Sant'Elmo, including *Fuori dall'ombra* in 1992, a successful review of the figurative arts in Twentieth-century Naples. The museum has benefited from major legacies such as Andy Warhol's Vesuvius series (Lucio Amelio donation,1994).

The Museo Diego Aragona Pignatelli Cortes (director Angela Tecce) also holds exhibitions, most recently, *In plastica, Forme e colori dei materiali plastici* and *Giornate napoletane del design*. Over the next three years, the third floor of Capodimonte Palace will reopen to house the museum's Modern Art collection.

Palermo - Civica Galleria d'Arte Moderna "Empedocle Restivo" *(Empedocle Restivo Civic Gallery of Modern Art)*

History. Empedocle Restivo was responsible for organising the opening of this gallery himself. It was inaugurated on May 25, 1910 at a ceremony held in the splendid Teatro Politeama Garibaldi and attended by King Vittorio Emanuele III. It started out with works collected from exhibitions put on for the express purpose of providing art for the museum, or contributed by donors. Other works came from the stores of the National Gallery of Modern Art in Rome. A 1932 article in *Emporium* suggests that the character of the Gallery was formed at a very early stage. In recent times it has presented exhibitions of regional interest. But it has not ignored the work of the avant-garde.

Collections. The initial collection covered Sicilian artists of the Nineteenth and Twentieth century such as Mario Rutelli. We also find the occasional non-Italian, such as Franz Von Stuck. The gallery's coverage of the Twentieth century is primarily concerned with Sicilian painters: Francesco Trombadori, Fausto Pirandello, Renato Guttuso. But works are also included by Carrà, Sironi, Casorati, Campigli and Severini.

Exhibitions. Since 1960, the gallery has presented several splendid exhibitions, such as *Pietro Consagra* (1973), *Liberty a Palermo* (1973) and a 1972 exhibition of Sicilian artists. I also remember *Revort I*, an avante-garde event presented by "Gruppo 63".

Catalogues. O. Gurrieri, "La Galleria Civica d'Arte Moderna di Palermo", in *Emporium*, July 1932. R. Collura, *La Civica Galleria d'Arte Moderna "Empedocle Restivo" di Palermo*, 1974.

Fin de Siècle. Director Antonella Purpura plans more educational work as well as reviews of the artists represented in the Gallery's collection.

Parma - Centro studi e archivio della Comunicazione - CSAC (Communication Research Centre and Archive)

The Centre is the brainchild of Arturo Carlo Quintavalle and has been directed by Gloria Bianchino since 1989. It does a great deal of archive and collecting work and also puts on periodic exhibitions of its material. In the Seventies it put on major one-man exhibitions, in many cases making the name of the young artist concerned. Examples are *Giulio Paolini* (1976), *Toti Scialoja* (1971), and *Mario Schifano* (1974).

Two major shows of recent years have been devoted to Atanasio Soldati and the Vasari Archive. CSAC also cooperates with other institutions. It organized the *Auto Dipinta* exhibition for the Palazzo Te in Mantova as well as the *Muri di carta* photographic exhibition for the 1993 Venice Biennale. Recent acquisitions by CSAC include a thousand or more photographic prints by contemporary photographers like Mario Giacomelli, Luigi Ghirri, and Mimmo Jodice, as well as the "Atanasio Soldati" Fondo di Studio (research fund). Its most ambitious future plan is the cataloguing of its various artistic and photographic collections. It also hopes to develop an efficient system of consultation and communication.

Piacenza - Galleria d'Arte Moderna Giuseppe Ricci-Oddi (Giuseppe Ricci-Oddi Modern Art Gallery)

History. This Modern Art Gallery takes its name from the magnificent aristocrat who first endowed it: Giuseppe Ricci-Oddi. It is housed in a major modernist building designed by Ulisse Arata. This private foundation has recently received additional support from sponsors such as the Piacenza Amici dell'Arte (Piacenza Friends of Art) and the local Savings Bank.

Collections. The early Twentieth century is represented by the Divisionists (Morbelli, Pellizza da Volpedo) and the occasional major name (Mario Cavaglieri, Camillo Innocenti, a group of works by Amedeo Bocchi and Armando Spadini). One noteworthy item is Boccioni's marvellous *La madre*. From the *Novecento*, I remember Carlo Carrà, the three Carenas, Massimo Campigli, Filippo de Pisis and Felice Casorati. Non-Italians include Klimt (*Portrait of a Lady*) and Carl Larsson. More acquisitions were made after the War. Among sculptors represented I remember Medardo Rosso and Adolfo Wildt.

Catalogues. G. Sidoli, *Galleria d'Arte Moderna Ricci-Oddi*, Piacenza 1931. L. Ozzola, *Galleria d'Arte Moderna Giuseppe Ricci-Oddi a Piacenza*, Bergamo 1956.

Fin de siècle. Stefano Fugazza has been director since 1993. Since 1990 purchases have concentrated on works by local artists. Noteworthy exhibitions have been devoted to *Mario Cavaglieri a Piacenza* (1990), *Rotella* (1991), and *Siro Penagini* (1992), and another show outlined proposals for the expansion of the Gallery in 1990. Fugazza is currently working on exhibitions devoted to Cascella (*Michele Cascella a Piacenza nel 1927*) and the architect Giulio Ulisse Arata.

Pistoia - Museo Civico (Civic Museum)

Re-opened in 1982, the museum planned a series of exhibitions devoted to Pistoian artists ranging from Marino Marini to Mario Nigro and Gualtiero Nativi. Bruno Corà was appointed director in 1993. Since then he has organised exhibitions (*Jannis Kounellis*, 1993-94, *Luciano Fabro*, 1994), international symposia and an educational programme. There are now plans to turn the Palazzo Fabroni into a museum of contemporary visual arts. New acquisitions are planned for it.

Prato - Centro per l'Arte Contemporanea Luigi Pecci (Luigi Pecci Contemporary Art Centre)

History. The Centre's first acquisitions date back to 1988 and have been exhibited several times since 1990. The Centre is a private association one of whose shareholders is the Municipality of Prato. (Additional funds come from the Regional Government and the Ministry of Culture.) Its first director was Amnon Barzel, who was followed by Ida Panicelli (1992 - November 1994).

Collections. The Centre owns about seventy works of art which are unique in having been created for the Centro Pecci. They range from examples of "Arte Povera" (Mario Merz, Gilberto Zorio), to conceptual art (Sol LeWitt) and the "Transavangardia" (Enzo Cucchi). Other works are by Julian Schnabel, Vito Acconci and Mauro Staccioli, and there are installations by younger artists, too.

Exhibitions. As a "living museum" the Centre considers exhibitions to be of fundamental importance: indeed these are the source of its collections (due to an extremely thoughtful purchasing policy). Noteworthy examples include exhibitions on Julian Schnabel and Mario Merz (1990), Vito Acconci and Gilberto Zorio (1992), in addition to experimental cycles entitled *Carta bianca* and *Sosta vietata*. The Centre's interest in the past has been more spasmodic, though I remember exhibitions on Miró and Fellini this year. The museum also publishes art books and held an exhibition on this subject in 1994.

Fin de siécle. The Centre's most ambitious current project is to open new premises for its permanent collection. Meanwhile it continues with Education programs especially for young people who will be museum visitors in the future. In particular, I remember a specific project entitled "Playing with art in Prato", created by Bruno Munari.

Rome - Galleria Nazionale d'Arte Moderna (National Gallery of Modern Art)

History. The building, on the grounds of Villa Giulia, was designed by Cesare Bazzani for the 1911 Exhibition and has housed Rome's Modern Art collection since 1915. Before this date, the works were kept either in the Palazzo delle Esposizioni or at the Ministry of Education. The new Gallery launched an intensive campaign of purchases at the Venice Biennale and sought work by Italian and non-Italian artists from other institutions. It also received substantial donations: a large collection of Divisionist works donated by Vittore Grubicy in 1932; a major group of Medardo Rosso sculptures donated by his son in 1931; a major Filippo di Pisis collection in 1960; and a donation from the family of Armando Spadino in 1951. Palma Bucarelli was made director before the War and re-opened the Gallery in 1944. She then launched an enthusiastic acquisitions policy despite huge rows and political hurdles. By 1951, the collections had been properly reorganised with Nineteenth-century work concentrated to the left of the building and Twentieth-century work on the right. The Gallery began to acquire significant gifts which provided an accurate picture of the contemporary art scene. Current donations include works by Alberto Burri, Lucio Fontana and Giuseppe Capogrossi. More have followed recently. The Gallery also purchases art on the open market or from the artists themselves.

Following comprehensive refurbishment, the efficient new-look Gallery re-opened in 1987 under Eraldo Gaudioso. The installation of the Twentieth-century rooms was carried out by Bruno Mantura and the architect Constantino Dardi. Important donations of more recent years have included paintings by Giacomo Balla (1980-84), Renato Guttuso (1987) and Giorgio de Chiri-

Rome, the catalogue by Arduino Colasanti, 1923.

Rome. National Gallery of Modern Art, Room XXIV as it appeared in a 1938 installation (from the Gallery archives)

Rome, Mussolini Gallery: one room as it appeared in a 1939 installation with Giacomo Catta's monochrome "Il Dubbio" on the right.

co (1989). Paintings are queing up to be hung. There have also been additions to the Giacomo Manzù donation, which is housed separately in the sculptor's old studio in Ardea.

Collections. The Italian National Gallery owns over 1,500 paintings and sculptures covering the period 1900-1945. Since 1987, some four hundred of special historical significance and artistic quality have been on permanent display. One of the first rooms contains a masterpiece by Gustav Klimt (*The Three Ages*) next to a Van Dongen acquired at the Secession, a de Chirico in the style of Böcklin next to a modest Cézanne. This weak survey of Futurism rubs shoulders with an excellent review of Metaphysical Art (Carrà, *L'ovale delle apparizioni*).

We then move on to three groups that form the core of the National Gallery collection. The Twentieth century is represented by a large number of masterpieces from the Twenties and Thirties: Carrà, Severini, a fine room devoted to Filippo de Pisis, Sironi and Campigli. After years in exile, the Roman School has been brought back together with new additions: next to Amerigo Bartoli's allegorical painting *Amici al Caffè* (bought at the 1920 Venice Biennale) we find masterpieces of magic realism and the Via Cavour School. Substantial groups of tonal and realist paintings can also be seen, together with sculptures. Sculpture forms the museum's third core subject with works by Arturo Martini and Marino Marini (plus the Manzù annex in Ardea). Another room is devoted to portraits with great effect (installed by Bruno Mantura). The group of rooms ends with a few examples of Thirties Abstract Art (abruptly punctuated by a Kandinsky) and a group of *Corrente* works. The Gallery also owns an important collection of war-time and post-war paintings by Renato Guttuso. The star attraction is a crucifixion scene donated in 1941.

The airy halls of this part of the gallery were designed by Cesare Bazzani and refurbished by Constantino Dardi. Here the art works benefit from an exemplary play of space and light. The period covered in this section of the gallery (1915-1945) is reviewed in a brief catalogue.

The Rome Museum is matched only by Milan's CIMAC in its coverage of the post-war period with entire rooms devoted to the leading artists of the period. The section covering the last half century of art movements has yet to be coordinated and much of it is never on display. A central, outstanding group of works centres on the battle between abstract and realist artists during Italy's reconstruction at the end of World War II. The Gallery also owns works by Giuseppe Capogrossi, Alberto Burri, Ettore Colla and Emilio Vedova. Shrewd acquisitions of high quality works from the Sixties have been made over the past thirty years, such as the works by Pino Pascali. The museum also owns an immense collection of drawings and prints. These include thousands of items from the Twentieth century, which are displayed in rotation.

The museum has yet to find the right setting for an exhaustive collection of works donated by Giacomo Balla and Giorgio de Chirico.

Exhibitions. The National Gallery has produced outstanding exhibitions and educational activity, especially under the directorship of Palma Bucarelli. Exhibitions of British, French, Belgian and American art were put on immediately after the war. In the Fifties, well-timed exhibitions were devoted to *Alberto Savinio* (1952), *Picasso* (1953), *Scipione* (1954), *Mondrian* (1956-57), *Jackson Pollock* (1958), *Kandinskij* (1958), *Modigliani* (1959), and *Malevic* (1959). The museum Art Club also put on some highly impressive international shows of work by young artists who received encouragement in the form of Ministry of Education prizes. International exhibitions held in the Sixties did a great deal to promote the work of young artists. *De Stijl e Bauhaus* (1961), *Mark Rothko* (1962), *Dada* (1966), and *Arshile Gorky* (1967). In addition, retrospectives were devoted to recently deceased artists like *Pino Pascali* (1968), *Ettore Colla* (1970) and *Piero Manzoni* (1971). In 1971-72 *Giacomo Balla* retrospective was organized followed by another on *Giorgio Morandi* in 1973. Palma Bucarelli's last major exhibition was on *Giuseppe Capogrossi* (1975). Palma Bucarelli's directorship lasted just thirty years. Although she was fiercely criticised during that time, now we can only mourn her.

Among the exhibitions organised by the subsequent director, Italo Faldi, I remember *Alberto Burri* (1976), *Fausto Pirandello* (1976-77), *Afro* (1978), and *Camuccini* (1978). High spots of the Eighties included *Arte astratta italiana* (Italian Abstract Art) (1980), *Roma 1911* (1980), *Giorgio de Chirico* retrospective (1982), *Giulio Paolini* (1981-82), *Fausto Melotti* (1983), *Armando Spadini* (1983-84), *Piero Dorazio* (1983-84), *Fazzini* and *Siveri* (1984-85), and *Giulio Turcato* (1986). A dreadful *Van Gogh* exhibition held in the winter of 1987-88 was memorable for the huge crowds it drew. The next director was Dario Durbè, followed by Augusta Monferini.

Catalogues: P. Piroli, *Galleria Nazionale d'Arte Moderna*, Rome 1917. A. Colasanti, *La Galleria Nazionale d'Arte Moderna di Roma*, Milan-Rome 1923. P. Bucarelli, *La Galleria Nazionale d'Arte Moderna*, Rome 1951 (updated and expanded edition, 1973). *Galleria Nazionale d'Arte Moderna: Pittura e scultura del XX secolo*, by G. de Marchis, Rome. (Only Vol I: *Opere fino al 1910* has appeared.) *Collezioni del XX secolo: Il primo Novecento*, with an introduction by E. Gaudioso, edited by B. Mantura, C. Dardi, L. Velani, G. de Feo, and P. Rosazza, Florence 1987. Note: no catalogue on the Gallery collection is avaiable. Information on it is scattered and sporadic.

Fin de siècle. The Gallery has seemed rather lacklustre in recent years, as if oppressed by its own history. This is borne out by the exhibitions it now puts on, such as its less than adventurous presentations of the Balla and de Chirico donations. Or the often overblown one-man shows (*Toti Scialoja*, 1990, *Fabio Mauri*, 1994). Other exhibitions intended to be of historic significance have been of questionable academic value (*Filippo de Pisis*, 1993, *Mario Sironi*, 1993-94). The gallery has also given house-room to the occasional oddity such as a show devoted to kites (*Aquiloni d'Artista*, 1992). Overall the Gallery appears to be suffering from a certain lack of planning. It is now about to open a one-man exhibition of Carlo Carrà's work, and Paul Klee's juvenile works will be on show in the spring. Augusta Monferini Calvesi has been director since 1988. By contrast, the Gallery is particularly good at educational activity and was one of the first to enter this field.

The museum works are not displayed to full advantage. The Nineteenth-century collection is almost entirely closed; only a portion of the donations can be viewed. (Giacomo Balla suffers particularly.) The recently reorganised Twentieth-century section is mostly closed for lack of staff. On the positive side, this is the only museum in Rome that stays open until 7 pm.

Rome, National Gallery of Modern Art, Exhibition of Contemporary Italian art curated by Palma Bucarelli 1944-45. (Italian and English language edition of the catalogue produced for the re-opening of the national Gallery of Modern Art, cover by Orfeo Tamburi).

Rome - Galleria Comunale d'Arte Moderna e Contemporanea (Municipal Gallery of Modern and Contemporary Art)

History. This collection dates back to 1903, when the municipality received its first works of art as gifts. These were housed in the Palazzetto della Farnesina. Acquisitions and then new arrivals followed thick and fast: from the International Exposition in 1911, from the "Secessione", from "Amatori e Cultori" exhibitions and from the Rome Biennale. In 1925, the collection occupied six rooms of the Palazzo Caffarelli on the Campidoglio. It was then closed for a time and reopened as the Museo Mussolini in 1931. Antonio Muñoz was the architect responsible for the twelve rooms subsequently graced by a major collection acquired at the Quadriennale in 1931 and 1935 (seventy works of art, all important). The museum closed down in 1938 and its contents were stored in the Italian National Gallery of Modern Art. The Municipal Museum reopened in 1949 on the third and fourth floors of the Palazzo Braschi (director: Carlo d'Aloisio da Vasto) and then closed again. Carlo Pietroangeli decided to exhibited a group of selected works in the Palazzo delle Esposizioni for several years in the 1960's).

For almost half a century, this major collection has been closed to the public and is almost inaccessible to academics. Under the directorship of Gemma di Domenico Cortese, however, the museum has been very generous with loans to specialised exhibitions of the *Novecento* and on the Roman School.

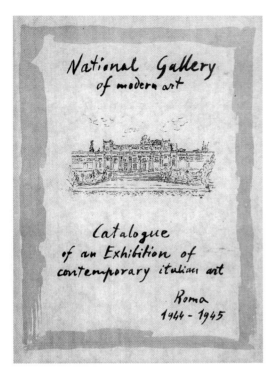

Collections. The museum concentrates, naturally enough, on the Roman School, or on works with a Roman link. Nevertheless it also owns masterpieces by Carlo Carrà, Mario Sironi, Giorgio Morandi, Felice Casorati, Gino Severini, Alberto Savinio and many others (all purchased at the Quadriennale and other exhibitions during the Thirties). Its coverage of Roman art starts with the best years of Divisionism: Enrico Lionne, Giacomo Balla, Camillo Innocenti and Sartorio. The musuem's extraordinary Roman School collection ranges from the magic realism of Francesco Trombadori and Antonio Donghi to the expressionism of Scipione and Mario Mafai (with some exceptional paintings and drawings). Several artists are represented by superb works: Fausto Pirandello, Ferruccio Ferrazzi, Roberto Melli, Giuseppe Capogrossi, Guglielmo Janni, Afro, Franco Gentilini, Alberto Ziveri and many others. Other works acquired out of documentary interest include views of the city painted by Donghi and Benvenuto Ferrazzi, as well as Tamburi's *Demolizioni.*

Catalogues. La Galleria Mussolini by A. Munoz, Rome 1931. *Il Museo di Roma e la Galleria Comunale d'Arte Moderna a Palazzo Braschi,* by C. Pietrangeli, Rome 1952. C. Pietrangeli, *Galleria Comunale d'Arte Moderna e Contemporanea. Mostra di una selezione di opere,* Rome 1963. Note: a catalogue of the collection is being produced by a team of academics whose files may be consulted on request.

Fin de siècle. Giovanna Bonasegale, the museum director since 1992, hopes to re-open the collections. At first they will be exhibited by rotation at the Gallery's premises in Via Francesco Crispi, but later they will be moved to a new permanent home in the former Peroni Brewery.

Rome - *Accademia nazionale di San Luca (The San Luca National Academy)*
The Academy owns a few collections of contemporary art as an offshoot of its impressive museum and archive (Director: Angela Cipriani). Early in this century, the Müller and Mancini prizes endowed the Academy with several major works. (I remember Giacomo Balla.) The collection also covers works by Roman artists such as Ferruccio Ferrazzi, Mino Maccari, Fausto Pirandello and Amedeo Bocchi. The Academy is now building up a collection of portraits and self-portraits (from Carlo Carrà and Amerigo Bartoli to the present day). The collection is neither open to the public nor systematically catalogued. The Academy has put on some exhibitions: *Trombadori, Janni, Francalancia* (1986), and *Fabrizio Clerici* (1984), for instance.

Rome - *Città del Vaticano - Collezione d'Arte Religiosa Moderna (Collection of Modern Religious Art)*
The collection opened in June 1973 after a brief gestation period and contains five hundred and forty works by two hundred and fifty artists. These are housed in a ring of fifty rooms around the Sistine Chapel and are connected to the Vatican Museums. The aim of the project was described in an address by Pope Paul VI: "We have every reason to hope that by setting this first exhibition of Modern Religious Art in harmony with rather than in opposition to the surrounding splendours of the Vatican collections, we will spark off a new artistic tradition and convince the artists of the world that the Catholic Church is still their admirer, patron and protector".

Though the definition of Religious art is questionable, the collection nevertheless includes paintings by major European artists (Van Gogh, Gauguin, Bacon) and sculptors (Marino Marini, Francesco Messina) along with an occasional masterpiece (Armando Spadini, Scipione). The eight hundred or so works in the collection are listed in an original catalogue (M. Ferrazza and P. Pignotti, *L'appartamento Borgia l'Arte contemporanea in Vaticano*, Rome 1974). The director, Mario Ferrazza, also informs me that a systematic catalogue is about to be published.

Rome - Collezione dell'Assitalia (Assitalia Collection)

The Assitalia insurance company collection was the brainchild of Giovanni Pieraccini and includes a good number of excellent paintings by artists of the calibre of Umberto Boccioni, Giorgio de Chirico, Alberto Savinio and Gino Severini. The small collection of Roman School paintings is outstanding: Antonio Donghi, Mario Mafai, Alberto Ziveri, Giuseppe Capogrossi and others. The collection catalogue was edited by M. Fagiolo (Electa, Milan 1987). Sadly, the quality of the collection has somewhat deteriorated in recent years because acquisitions have concentrated more on "bankable" names than quality.

Rome - Collezione della Banca di Roma (Bank of Rome Collection)

Some good-quality Twentieth-century (Giacomo Balla, Giorgio de Chirico) and Roman School works. (I remember a Donghi group from the Pennacchini collection.) The bank has also sponsored exhibitions including one devoted to Donghi in the City Hall in 1985.

Rome - Collezione della Banca Nazionale del Lavoro (Banca Nazionale del Lavoro Collection)

This includes the important "Roma 1948" collection. This group of fifty small Roman landscapes, collected by Cesare Zavattini, illustrates the artistic trends of that particular year.

Rome - Collezione della Camera dei Deputati (Chamber of Deputies Collection)

The Chamber of Deputies owns some three hundred works of art. As its recent catalogue points out, "Though far from comprehensive, this interesting collection contains a few masterpieces ably flanked by a good number of substantial works". One group of works was acquired from exhibitions in the Thirties and Forties. I remember Gino Severini, Giorgio de Chirico, and Morandi, as well as nearly all the Roman School painters.

  Other purchases have been more random: the Gallery houses a collection of drawings and an interesting series of busts of notable figures, some by major sculptors. This little-known collection is now described in an excellent catalogue: *Camera dei Deputati, Catalogo delle opere d'arte*, by V. Rivosecchi, A. Trombadori, and G. Selvaggi, Leonardo, Milan 1993.

Rome - Collezione del Quirinale (Quirinale Palace Collection)

The recent catalogue lists 1,868 works of art. The collection has been built up through sporadic acquisitions made over a long period (I remember a Balla commissioned by Queen Margherita in 1914) or through acquisitions made at national or unions exhibitions. (There are masterpieces by Mario Mafai, Alberto Savinio, Giuseppe Capogrossi, Mario Cavaglieri, Arturo Martini, and Armando Spadini.) Though patchy, this collection nevertheless contains a number of outstanding items. At long a catalogue has been issued in: *Il patrimonio artistico del Quirinale. La quadreria e le sculture* by M. Damigella, B. Mantura, and M. Quesada, Milan 1991.

Rome - Istituto Nazionale per la Grafica e Gabinetto delle Stampe alle Farnesina (National Institute of Graphic Arts and Farnesina Print Collection)

The little-known collections owned by these two institutions offer some pleasant surprises. I remember pre-Futurist works by Giacomo Balla, a group of drawings by Scipione and a collection of plates and etchings by Giorgio Morandi. An intelligent acquisitions campaign has been undertaken over recent years. Purchases have included the Francesco Sapori collection of 2,000 ex libris, an Enrico Drei research bequest (Fondo di Studio), a group of engravings

Turin. Opening of the Antonio Fontanesi exhibition at the Modern Art Gallery in 1932. The director Vittorio Viale is seen with Prince Umberto.

by Arturo Martini and another of Achille Funi drawings. One remarkable printer of the modern era, Renzo Romero, has also donated his collection of post-war dies and prints. These were put on show in a recent exhibition.

Turin - Galleria Civica d'Arte Moderna e Contemporanea (Civic Gallery of Modern and Contemporary Art)

History. The Gallery dates back to 1863 and housed Italy's first collection of modern art following the unification of Italy. Today, more than a thousand works are on permanent display and the Gallery owns works by four hundred and forty different artists. The Museum has pursued a shrewd acquisitions policy and also worked hard to attract donations. Vittorio Viale first reorganised the collection in 1931 following its transfer to the Palazzo Madama. During World War II, Turin was badly bombed, and so the city decided to build a new home for its Modern Art collection once the war had ended. Plans were invited and a design by Carlo Bassi and Goffredo Boschetti (then an employee of the Luigi Mallè Museum) was selected in 1952. The art works were transferred to the offices of the *Società Promotrice* in Valentino Park while work proceeded at a furious pace. The new Gallery on Via Magenta opened on October 31, 1959. It also housed Civic Museum's Library and Photo Library. Major international exhibitions have always been a gallery policy. Luigi Mallè became director in 1965. In 1967 an Experimental Museum created by Eugenio Battisti opened in Turin after the idea had been turned down by Genoa. In 1978, the Museum received the Ettore de Fornaris donation. This breathed new life into its collection.

In 1981 it was decided to close down the building because it had become almost unusable. However, cataloguing and purchases went on under Rosanna Maggio Serra. Several exhibitions held during the museum's period of closure reminded the general public and academics what they were missing. This is perhaps one of the most active museums in Italy. I remember the *Museo Sperimentale* exhibition in 1985-86 and a selection of works from the De Fornaris Foundation Collections exhibited in 1986 and 1993. In the meantime, the Gallery building and its paintings and sculptures were being restored. The Museum re-opened in 1993 with all its collections systematically catalogued.

Collections. The early Twentieth century is mainly represented by the work of Piedmontese artists from Giacomo Grosso to Leonardo Bistolfe. The Futurists are represented by Umberto Boccioni and Giacomo Balla's extraordinary *Compenetrazioni Iridiscenti* (incidentally purchased at an exhibition I curated at the Galleria l'Obelisco, Rome in 1968). The Gallery recently bought a de Chirico still life. Astute acquisitions at national and city exhibitions have endowed the Gallery with works by all leading *Novecento* masters: Giorgio de Chirico and Alberto Savinio, Carlo Carrà and Fillippo de Pisis, and others. Artists from Piedmont and Turin are naturally also well represented (from Felice Casorati to the "Turin Six") and more are continually being collected. The gallery's own exhibitions prompted a series of shrewdly timed purchases. And the exhibitions themselves were also well-timed. (The Gallery's interest in the Abstract artists of the Thirties is a good example.) The Museum has also maintained good relations with Turin's commercial galleries and this has brought it several masterpieces as well as works by lesser lights who form the connective tissue of the Twentieth century. One fascinating small room houses paintings by European artists (Francis Picabia, Max Ernst) acquired as a result of exhibitions curated by Luigi Carluccio.

The *Informel* painters are extremely well represented by Lucio Fontana, Alberto Burri, Ettore Colla and Emilio Vedova. The Museum's collection of Sixties work is also extremely perceptive, and benefited from the takeover of Eugenio Battisti's museum in Genoa. The collection of *Arte Povera* (a new movement to emerge from Turin) is also exemplary.

Exhibitions: This sector probably promises most for the museum's future. The first exhibition was put on by Mario Valsecchi to celebrate the post-war re-opening on October 31, 1959. Apart from

Turin. Civic Gallery of Modern Art. Part of a 1969 exhibition of "New Dada and Pop Art from New York ".

Turin. Civic Gallery of Modern Art: a room on the second floor, 1970 (from the Civic Museums photographic archives, Turin).

two rooms devoted to Casorati and Spazzapan respectively, that exhibition brought together the best from the past in the form of a Gianni Mattioli collection and two stunning groups (Tosi and Giovanardi) from Milan. Though neither Vittorio Viale nor the subsequent director, Luigi Mallè, were modernists, the museum soon gained renown for its modern approach. In a symbiotic relationship, art galleries fed the museum and in return the museum stimulated collectors and the art market. They began with the tried and tested (Robert and Sonia Delaunay, 1960) but also risked a modern classic (Nicolas de Staël, 1960). In 1962, Crispolti and Galvano presented *Aspetti del Secondo FuturismoTorinese* (Aspects of the second Turinese futurism), and in the same year Tapié and Luigi Moretti presented *Strutture e stile* (Structures and style). Then came the one-man shows: *Hans Richter* and *Francis Bacon* (two faces of the avant garde) in 1962. In 1963, a great *Giacomo Balla* exhibition was organised by Enrico Crispolti and Maria Drudi Gambillo. This was followed by the heavyweights: *Franz Kline* in 1963, *Felice Casorati* and *Maria Helena Vieira da Silva* in 1964. In 1965, the exhibitions ranged from *Hans Hoffmann* to the photographer *Steichen*, the *"Turin Six"* and *Graham Sutherland*. 1966 was the year of *Hans Hartung, Robert Motherwell* and *Bram van Velde*. One very special event in 1967 was the presentation of the Experimental Museum of Contemporary Art organised for Genoa by Eugenio Battisti. In 1968, ten years after his death, a retrospective was devoted to *Osvaldo Licini*. 1969 saw *Louise Nevelson, New Dada and New York Pop Art* (curated by Luigi Mallè) and also an exhibition on the work of *Atanasio Soldati*. Abstract painters were represented in 1970 by *Lucio Fontana*. (The series continued in 1972 with *Fausto Melotti* and in 1973 with *Mauro Reggiani*.) Several memorable shows were also held in the early seventies: *Conceptual Art, Arte Povera, Land Art* and *Yves Klein* in 1970 and *Alberto Burri* in 1971. I myself was responsible for a major retrospective on *Francis Picabia* in 1974.

Directors. Enrico Thovez took over in 1913. He was succeeded in 1922 by a physician, Lorenzo Rovere. In 1930 Vittorio Viale was called in to reorganise the museum on its transfer to Palazzo Madama. Luigi Mallè replaced Viale in 1965, added a great many works to the collection and organised several major exhibitions. Aldo Passoni took over in 1973 only to die in the following year. His work was carried on by A.S. Fava, Silvana Pettenati, and Rosanna Maggio Serra.

Catalogues. *I dipinti della Galleria d'Arte Moderna* by L. Mallè, Turin 1968. *I musei Civici di Torino. Acquisti e doni 1966-1970* by L. Mallè, Turin 1970. *Il museo Sperimentale di Torino. Arte italiana degli anni Sessanta nelle collezioni della Galleria Civica d'Arte Moderna*, by M. Bandini and R. Maggio Serra, Castello di Rivoli, 1985-86. *Le collezioni della Galleria Civica d'Arte Moderna di Torino 1945-1965* by P. Fossati, R. Maggio Serra, Promotrice delle Belle Arti, 1987. *Fondazione Guido ed Ettore De Fornaris, Arte Moderna a Torino: 200 opere d'arte acquisite per la Galleria d'Arte Moderna* by R. Maggio Serra, 1986. *Fondazione Guido ed Ettore De Fornaris, Arte Moderna a Torino II. Opere d'arte e documenti acquisiti per la Galleria Civica d'Arte Moderna e Contemporanea di Torino, 1986-1992*, by R. Maggio Serra, Turin 1993. *Il Novecento. Catalogo delle opere esposte*, by R. Maggio Serra and R. Passoni, Turin 1993. Note: Since cataloguing was first entrusted to a young student of Lionello Venturi's (Mario Soldati), the Gallery has appeared to suffer from a want of method, yet correct cataloguing is essential if the museum's collections are to be properly displayed.

Fin de siècle. The museum is currently managed by an Artistic Committee (Ugo Perone, Rosanna Maggio Serra, Silvana Pettenati, Antes Bortolotti, Angelo Bucarelli, Rossana Bossaglia and Edoardo di Mauro). The art collection Director is Rosanna Maggio Serra. The museum reopened with a wide-ranging exhibition: *Torino 1902. Le arti decorative internazionali del nuovo secolo* (Turin 1902. International decorative arts of the new century) (1994). Future exhibitions are planned over the coming years: *Luigi Mainolfi, Omaggio ad Alighiero Boetti* (Homage to Alighiero Boetti), *I Nuovi Nuovi* (New newcomers) and *Una storia italiana. Gli ultimi vent'anni di arte italiana* (An Italian history: The last twenty years of Italian art). An historical exhibition is also being prepared:

Dall'Art Autre al gruppo Gutai: Michel Tapié nella Torino degli anni Cinquanta (From Art Autre to the Gutai group: Michel Tapié in Fifties Turin).

Turin - Rivoli - Castello di Rivoli Museo d'arte contemporanea (Rivoli Castle Museum of Contemporary Art)

History. Now ten years old, this museum was set up on a new basis. In the beginning, it was managed jointly by the Regional Government of Piedmont and a group of private shareholders. Later the task was handed on to the "Committee for Art in Piedmont" (composed of the Regional Government, the CRT bank, Fiat and the GFT Group). The idea of making Filippo Juvarra's eighteenth-century palace into a museum of contemporary art was as original as the concept of joint public-private sector management for a cultural asset. The museum became a stopping-off point on the international circuit under the chairmanship of Marco Rivetti of GFT and its first director Rudi Fuchs. In 1990 Fuchs was replaced by Ida Gianelli, who has carried on the policy of putting on exhibitions while continuing to acquire new works for the permanent collection.

Collections. The exhibition in December 1994 showed to good advantage all the acquisitions of the previous ten years, which have come from various sources. Today, Rivoli Castle owns about forty works which range from traditional paintings and sculptures (Fausto Melotti, Emilio Vedova, Lucio Fontana) to carefully selected examples of *Arte Povera* (Michelangelo Pistoletto, Gilberto Zorio, Mario Merz, Luciano Fabro) and large installations, some created specifically for the museum (Giulio Paolini, Sol LeWitt).

Exhibitions. Exhibitions have to be a priority for any new museum and Rudi Fuchs organised some truly memorable shows such as those devoted to Jannis Kounellis, Nicola de Maria and Mario Merz. Ida Gianelli has continued along the same lines, but has not neglected the need to settle accounts with the art history of the present century as it approaches its end. I remember her first project *Arte & Arte* (Art & Art) as well as memorable shows devoted to *Alberto Burri, Giuseppe Penone, Enzo Cucchi* and *Carla Accardi*. One particularly imposing project was *Una avventura internazionale. Torino e le arti 1950-1970* (An international adventure: Turin and the arts 1950-1970).

Fin de Siècle. Ida Gianelli continues her acquisition policy and arrange exchanges with other museums. Despite some controversy, this approach has succeeded in making Rivoli Castle an international name to be reckoned with. The museum also shows a keen interest in peripheral areas such as photography (*Mario Giacomelli* 1992) and publications (*Letteratura artistica*, 1991). Gianelli is now planning exhibitions on Marlene Dumas, Francis Bacon and Haim Steinbach. Rivoli Castle will continue to run of educational programmes with more courses on contemporary art and photography to be run by the curators.

Turin - Collezione della RAI (RAI Collection)

The RAI (Italian state broadcasting company) collection is based on acquisitions but also works commissioned for special programmes. It includes the occasional masterpiece (Felice Casorati, *Concerto*, 1924), one or two de Chirico oddities, some groups of works by recent artists (Luigi Spazzapan, Bepi Santomaso, and Piero Ruggeri). A short catalogue of the collection was produced by M. Bernardi (Milan 1962), while P. Vivarelli wrote the catalogue for a recent exhibition (Turin, 1994).

Trento and Rovereto Museo d'Arte Contemporanea [MART] (Museum of Contemporary Art)

History. Over the past few years, Fortunato Depero's former museum in Rovereto and the Palazzo delle Albere in Trento have come to form an important cultural nexus. It all began with the works of Depero himself, plus various bequests (Umberto Maggioli, Tullio Garbari). Since then, MART has acquired works by Alberto Savinio, Osvaldo Licini and Luigi Veronesi, and is still making regular purchases. The Museum takes a particular interest in purchasing archives and libraries (that of Carlo Belli, for example).

Exhibitions. Exhibitions are MART's dominant activity. I remember some devoted to the (rather obvious) major movements of the past: *Divisionismo italiano* (1990), *Romanticismo. Il nuovo sentimento della natura* (1993). One very selective exhibition curated by M. Fagiolo offered the opportunity to re-examine the opus of Fortunato Depero (1988-89). Other exhibitions have displayed acquisitions from the estates of artists and intellectuals: in 1993 these included a bequest from A.D. Pica and an archive from Mino Somenzi and Carlo Belli. Naturally Trento's own artists are a special concern; I remember an exhibition devoted to *Gigiotti Zanini* in 1992-93.

Directors. Gabriella Belli has been director since MART was established in 1987.

Catalogue. The collection has not been systematically catalogued, but a Nineteenth-century filing system exists. Some work was done on Fortunato Depero at the time of the exhibitions devoted to that artist.

Fin de siècle. Due to its location in one of Italy's "autonomous regions", the museum is outstandingly well funded. It offers an effective educational programme (the "Museum School" project) together with lectures and conferences. In spring 1995, the museum expects to inaugurate a revised exhibition sequence. Works in the permanent collection will be sequenced from Jugendstil to the Seventies. It will continue to arrange exhibitions of new purchases and is already planning to exhibit its Figini-Pollini and Tullio Crali collection next autumn.

Trieste - Galleria d'Arte Moderna Civico Museo Revoltella (Revoltella Museum and Modern Art Gallery)

History. The Gallery traces its origins back to the bequest of Baron Pasquale Revoltella in 1869. However, it really took off in the Thirties with purchases at major and minor exhibitions. In 1932, the museum building gained a second wind and a new floor. After an eventful life featuring years of closure, the Gallery finally re-opened in 1991.

Collections. Like many other museums, this starts with the neoclassical period. The collection includes a small group of European paintings (Franz Von Stuck, Zuloaga, Zorn) and works by early Twentieth-century artists (Mancini, Bistolfi). The museum owns many more works by later Twentieth-century artists such as Felice Casorati (*Il meriggio*), Carlo Carrà (*Donne al mare*), Felice Carena and Giorgio Morandi. The artists of the Veneto and Trieste are particularly well represented: Piero Marussig, Mario Cavaglieri, Arturo Nathan, Carlo Sbisà, Guido Cadorin and Vittorio Bolaffio. The collection ends with a choice group of works by post-war painters: Emilio Vedova, Renato Guttuso, Afro, Giuseppe Santomaso, Giuseppe Capogrossi and others.

Catalogues. *Il Civico Museo Revoltella Catalogo della Galleria d'Arte Moderna*, Trieste 1933, L. Sambo, *Civico Museo Revoltella - Galleria d'Arte Moderna*, Trieste 1953.

Fin de siècle. Since the museum reopened in 1991, it has put on several important exhibitions, mostly centred on its own Revoltella collections. I remember *L'ottocento ritrovato* (The Eighteenth century rediscovered) (1991), *Da Canova a Burri: il Museo in mostra* (From Canova to Burri: a museum on show) (1992), *Il paesaggio dalle collezioni Revoltella* (Landscape of the Revoltella collections) (1994). Maria Masau Dan, director since 1991, plans an exhibition of works by the Trieste artist Carlo Sbisà in 1995 and, even more important, the publication of a general museum catalogue.

Udine - Galleria d'Arte Moderna Marangoni (Marangoni Gallery of Modern Art)

History. The gallery was originally housed in a Sixteenth-century castle, which opened in 1906

Venice. City of Venice International Modern Art Gallery, the first catalogue, 1902.

as an annex to the museum of ancient art. That home had to be abandoned after the earthquake in 1976. Carlo Someda de Marco was museum director from 1932 to the Fifties. In 1983 the museum was transferred to the Palamostre Exhibition Centre, where it occupies two whole floors including lecture rooms and storage facilities.

Collections. Donations of works from exhibitions have endowed the gallery with a substantial collection, including works by Giorgio de Chirico, Fausto Pirandello, and Mirko (the model for the gate in front of the Fosse Ardeatine Memorial). In the Seventies, the Afro exhibition (1978) led to the acquisition of an outstanding group of works by the Basaldella group: Corrado Cagli, Mario Mafai and Orfeo Tamburi. A group of drawings by Raimondo d'Aronco, the great Art Nouveau architect, also constituted a significant acquisition. A donation by Mario Luisa and Sante Astaldi in 1983 brought the museum nearly two hundred new items (see M. Bentivoglio, *Catalogo della Collezione Astaldi*, Rome 1971): works by de Chirico, Savinio, Mafai, Pirandello, Severini, de Pisis, and Guttuso.

Catalogues. C. Someda de Marco, *Il Museo civico e la Galleria d'arte antica e moderna di Udine*, Udine 1956. *Acquisizioni 1975-1986.* Catalogue by A. Rizzi, Udine 1980. Cristina Donazzolo Cristante, Isabella Reale, Tiziana Ribezzi, *Acquisizioni e restauri, 1981-1991*, Udine 1991.

Fin de siècle. The present directors (Giuseppe Bergamini and Isabella Reale) have recently produced a new catalogue of the exhaustive Astaldi collection, to be published by Electa. The museum has shown a particular interest in the acquisition of complete archives, most recently those of Raimondo d'Aronco, Giuseppe Zanini, etc. It is also working to expand its collections, especially with works by artists of the past half-century.

Venice - Galleria d'Arte Moderna, Ca' Pesaro (Ca' Pesaro Modern Art Gallery)

History. The first catalogue, printed in 1902, adopted the same graphic design as the Biennale catalogues and listed nearly two hundred works. The collection began with Count Filippo Giovannelli's donation of works by Italian and foreign artists. "It is from that generous and imaginative gesture that Venice derives its international Gallery of Modern Art". In 1902, seventeen different nations were represented in the collection: an internationalist dream. Baldassare Longhena's imposing Ca' Pesaro was originally intended as a transitory resting place for the collection, but in the event no temporary billet has ever proved more permanent. The 1913 catalogue describes the museum as "Italy's leading collection of modern art and one of the most important in the world". From the start, the Gallery pursued a policy of systematic purchases at the Biennale. The 1938 catalogue, which describes the Gallery as "The City of Venice International Gallery of Modern Art", is by Rodolfo Pallucchini, who assured his readers that "Ca' Pesaro constitutes an ideal expansion of the Royal Galleries of the Accademia". In the same year Ca' Pesaro arranged an exchange of works with the Royal Gallery of Modern Art in Rome, from which it acquired new additions to its collection. The most recent catalogue (1991) is by G. Romanelli: a meticulous review of past achievements. This catalogue lists the collection and details the Gallery's conservation projects. It also describes the state of the building, which requires urgent restoration work, no simple task given the nature of the construction. The publication also mentions a plan to devote the second floor to the permanent collection and the third floor to service facilities.

Collections. Romanelli speaks eloquently of the fate of this museum: "its historically significant record of Venice's conflicting yet always vital relationship with modern art and contemporary culture is pursued within and through or even (as in the case of the Ca' Pesaro 'Secession') against the Bienniale itself". The collections cover almost all of the Venetian school from Neoclassicism to the early Twentieth century. The Twentieth-century collection starts with Sartorio's monumental frieze, which was transferred to Ca' Pesaro from the central hall of the 1907 Biennale. Venice's place at the heart of the mittle European tradition is reflected in major acqusitions from artists such as Ferdinand Knopff, Franz von Stuck, Max Klinger, Gustav Klimt (whose extraordinary *Judith* was purchased at the 1910 Biennale) and the Munich period of Wassily Kandinsky.

Ca' Pesaro reserves a special place for its earliest exhibits, works by artists such as Arturo Martini, Gino Rossi and Ugo Valeri. Particular attention is devoted to a collection of works by Medardo Rosso, a leading light in the turn-of-the-century art world. The Italian Novecento movement bought several major new works to Ca' Pesaro by artists such as Mario Sironi, Filippo de Pisis, Antonio Donghi and Giorgio Morandi. Just as the Biennale remains a window on the whole world of art, Ca' Pesaro never failed in its European vocation, acquiring works by Pierre Bonnard, Paul Klee and Max Ernst. Post-war art movements involving the use of marks, gestures and various materials are also represented by important works, many of them timely acquisitions from the Biennale.

Directors: Vittorio Pica was the founding father of this institution which continues to owe much to nineteenth-century internationalist tendencies. The committees set up every two years to buy art works from the Biennale exhibitions played a major role in the development of Ca' Pesaro. In 1938, Rodolfo Pallucchini was appointed director by the Municipal Department of Arts and Education. He was succeeded after the War by the art historian Guido Perocco, who did much to bring the gallery on. The present director is Giandomenico Romanelli.

Exhibitions. One of the earliest was *Primi espositori di Ca' Pesaro 1908-1919* (Early exhibitors at Ca' Pesaro 1908-1919), organised by G. Perocco in 1958. The Eighties saw another review of Ca' Pesaro's achievements over the years (1987) as well as a one-man show by *Guglielmo Ciardi* (1988), a review of Italian art in 1920-1950 entitled *Oltre il Novecento* (1989), a one-man show on *Adolfo Wildt* (1989) and a review of various avant-garde movements of the past, illustrated by works from the Gallery's own collections (1990).

Catalogues. Galleria Internazionale d'Arte Moderna della Città di Venezia, Venice 1902. *Catalogo della Galleria Internazionale d'Arte Moderna della Città di Venezia*, 1913. *La Galleria Internazionale d'Arte Moderna della Città di Venezia*, introduction by R. Pallucchini, Venice 1938. *Ca' Pesaro, La Galleria d'Arte Moderna*, by G. Romanelli, Milan 1991.

Verona - Galleria d'Arte Moderna e Contemporanea (Palazzo Forti) (Palazzo Forti Gallery of Modern and Contemporary Art)

History . The Gallery's small permanent collection has been accumulated through the Verona Prize: one winner I remember was a masterpiece by Mario Mafai. The policy of the present director, Giorgio Cortenova, seems to suggest a preference for block buster exhibitions.

Exhibitions. These appear to constitute the true voice of this municipal gallery. Among the most successful *De Chirico, gli anni Venti* (De Chirico, the Twenties) (1987), *Modigliani a Montparnasse* (Modigliani in Montparnasse) (1988), *Renato Birolli* (1989), *Savinio: gli anni di Parigi* (Savinio: the Parisian years) (1990) organised in cooperation with the galleria dello Scudo. On its own account, Palazzo Forti has organised a number of shows, among which I remember a one-man exhibition on *Claudio Cintoli* (1984); *Astratta. Secessioni astratte nell'Italia dal dopoguerra al 1990* (1988). *Da Cézanne all'arte astratta. Omaggio a Lionello Venturi* (1991) was a good exhibition which vacillated between art history and criticism.

Fin de siècle. Restoration work on the Palazzo Forti will restart in 1995. The aim is to do something about the 65% of the building that has yet to be put to good use. The Gallery will continue to put on exhibitions. In recent years these have been of a popularising nature. Among them I remember *Da Magritte a Magritte* (1991), *Paul Klee* (1992), *Wassily Kandinsky* (1993), *Toulouse-Lautrec* (1994).

the Collection

Carla *Accardi*

Carla Accardi was born in Trapani in 1924. She moved to Rome in 1946, when she began to work as an artist. In 1947, she signed the manifesto of the abstract art group "Forma 1", with whom she began to exhibit. Her work evolved from an initial geometrical and constructional approach toward a form of painting based on marks reminiscent of writing. At that time, her work took the form of tangles white marks on a black ground.

Carla Accardi is one of the most interesting personalities in the field of abstract art. She combines painting with hints of the unconscious to produce a sort of effusive, lyrical writing which nevertheless obeys specific rhythmic paths. The artist speaks of the drive behind her compositions in terms of two complementary concepts: a progressive geometrical approach and a random approach – though it must be appreciated that the events underlying her "randomness" may be partly pre-ordained. During the Sixties, she took to colour with a vengeance, and used it to imbue the surface of the canvas with emotion. She went on to enhance this emotional function to the point where a sort of perceptive and psychological interference is created in the eyes of the spectator through the additive properties of colour. The artist herself stated in this respect: "When one colour is placed next to another (the colours may be pure or mixed but always 'clean', in other words always equivalent to a beam of coloured light) a lighter glow is created along the margin of contact between the two adjacent colours. This property is termed 'additive' to denote the increase in light (…). " The effect of the resulting enhanced light-mark is almost blinding and reminiscent of Matisse's work, except that in this case non-traditional materials are used as the emotional trigger.

In the work owned by the Castello di Rivoli, fluorescent colour and sheets of plastic foil replace the more traditional medium of canvas and oil or tempera colours previously used by the artist. These decidedly non-organic and highly artificial elements are typical of a society in full industrial spate, as was the case during the Sixties, the period when the works were completed. Accardi set herself the task of placing emotion in the heart of artifice. Her choice of sicofoil, clear plastic sheets, was entirely appropriate to the task she set herself. The transparency of the medium reveals the structure of the painting, in other words the frame, and opens up the work to interaction with space. The painting's own light is juxtaposed with the light of its surroundings. The throng of short diagonal marks that writhe across the plastic in her works *Rosa-Nero* (Pink-Black) and *Giallo-Nero* (Yellow-Black) is rendered more complex by overlapping. Individual squiggles lose their integrity and take on the overall appearance of broader, woven bands. Accardi typically exercised great freedom in her choice of support material during this period and this tendency reached new and radical heights in the elements which make up the set entitled *Rotoli* (Rolls) and *Cono giallo* (Yellow cone). Here the "canvas" has become a transparent membrane, freed from the constrictions of a frame. The plastic sheet is bent back onto itself to produce its own shape. In this way, Accardi succeeds in producing a brand-new visual form, half way between painting and sculpture, which contrasts its own inherent fragility with an intense burst of colour. The artist followed these successes shortly afterwords with works such as *Triplice tenda* (Triple curtain) (1969-1971), where her coloured marks take the form of writing in space and carry the spectator into a sensory adventure not intended solely for the eyes. The work goes beyond a two-dimensional plane to erupt into space itself. Her painting thus becomes a space that the spectator may cross in physical terms or simply accept for its archetypal value.

Rosa-Nero, Giallo-Nero (Pink-Black, Yellow-Black), 1967
varnish on plastic foil,
165 x 165 cm, 165 x 165 cm
Gift of Mario Pieroni, Rome, 1991

Selected Bibliography

V. Bramanti, *Carla Accardi*, Ravenna: Loggetta Lombardesca, Essegi Editrice, 1983.*Carla Accardi*, Modena: Galleria Civica, Edizioni Cooptip, 1989. *Carla Accardi*. Gibellina: Museo Civico, 1990. *Carla Accard*, Rivoli: Castello di Rivoli, Charta, 1994.

Rotoli (Rolls), 1966-72; *Cono giallo (Yellow Cone)*, 1966
varnish on plastic foil, ten units
Gift of Mario Pieroni, Rome and Massimo Minini, Brescia, 1991

Giovanni
Anselmo

Giovanni Anselmo was born in Borgofranco (Turin) in 1934 and became an artist in 1965. In his work, he sets out to reveal the energy inherent in the material he uses for his works. This is revealed by effects brought about by the force of gravity or changes brought about by using combinations of rigid and malleable materials. His work has followed thematic cycles: in an early example entitled *Particolare* (Detail) (from 1972), slides bearing the word "particolare" were projected into space or against objects. In this case the artist's intent was to draw the spectator's attention to general concepts (infinite and invisible, as in another cycle of work he began in 1971). These may be seen as an abstract category which the artist wishes to allow us to experience, at least in terms of tension.

Verso oltremare (Toward ultramarine) forms part of a cycle of works, all with the same title, begun in 1984. The thematic premises were, however, laid down in several earlier works. In *Senza titolo* (Untitled) completed in 1969, as the artist describes it: "… a stone weighing some 75kg is hung as high as possible and fastened to the wall by a steel cable. The laws of physics dictate that when a stone is moved further from the centre of the earth it becomes imperceptibly lighter. It is therefore worth reflecting that when the stone is moved higher than a certain point in the universe, between the sun and the earth for example, it will lose its weight totally and actually embody the idea of flight." Anselmo thus uses the force of gravity to depict the overcoming of gravity and an image or sign to suggest an experience of infinity. The theme of ultramarine appeared for the first time in 1979, when it took the form of a straight ultramarine line drawn directly on the wall. Ultramarine, or beyond the ocean, is a real dimension, beyond our geographical world. Centuries ago, the mineral used to produce the type of blue pigment we call ultramarine was brought from over the ocean. At the same time the name conveys the idea of beyond, a dimension where our spatial and time coordinates fall apart to be replaced by others, which we may experience only through the act of pure thought.

In 1980, the stone was described as 'grey' and had thus 'lightened' in relation to the ultramarine. This revealed a change in its empirical properties. This is juxtaposed with another empirical element, which is brought to us solely by thought, but should not be seen as in any way metaphysical. The artist says that the sky begins on the terrestrial crust we inhabit. We ourselves are thus "details" in infinity. Much of Anselmo's work is based on these themes. Since 1982, he has applied ultramarine blue to the walls in the form of rectangles while his 'lightened grey stones' appeared to sway above, attached to the wall by steel cables tied with slip knots. In 1984 Anselmo began his *Verso oltremare* cycle of which the Castello di Rivoli owns an example. The granite no longer takes the form of blocks, but great triangular slabs with roughly hewn outlines. These works are reminiscent of the artist's first works, entitled *Direzione* (Direction) (1967-1968), which took the form of great triangular stones positioned on the ground and set with a compass. The top of the stone block always faces north, like the needle of a compass. Even in terms of its arrangement, the work therefore indicates an overcoming of spatial limits despite the fact that the weight of the material binds the stone to the ground. The great stone in *Verso oltremare* is located in an upright position, tilted toward the wall and held in balance by a steel cable. Here too, the arrangement alludes to a loss of weight and alludes to a transmutation of material properties once the stone is attracted 'over the ocean', i.e., towards the ultramarine colour on the wall. The top of the stone triangle does in fact point to a small painted rectangle of intense blue on the wall. This suggests the stone striving for infinity, but never reaching it. The two substances and the two different universes they symbolise are depicted as not yet commensurable because they belong to the here and now of the observer, to his own space and time, to his own finite condition. The installation suggests the force inherent in the material, a force occurring in a time we can form no part of. Yet the artist tells us we may appreciate this different dimension through images and poetic intuition.

Selected Bibliography

Giovanni Anselmo. Grenoble: Musée de Peinture et Sculpture, 1980. *Giovanni Anselmo*. Basel: Kunsthalle; Eindhoven: Stedelijk Van Abbemuseum, 1979. *Giovanni Anselmo*. Paris: Musée d'Art Moderne de la Ville de Paris, 1985. *Giovanni Anselmo*. Modena: Galleria Civica; Lyon: Musée d'Art Contemporain, Hopefulmonster, 1989.

Translator's note: the Italian term "oltremare" can convey two meanings: that of the colour "ultramarine" and also that of "beyond the ocean" in the sense of "overseas" or "over the horizon".

Verso oltremare
(Towards Ultramarine), 1984
Luserna granite, steel, acrylic painting,
321.8 x 131 x 2.8 cm
Castello di Rivoli Purchase, 1987

Marco Bagnoli was born in Empoli in 1949 and plays a major role in the artistic movements which began to arise at the end of the Seventies. Bagnoli's work takes the form of complex installations which seek to involve the environment through the introduction of various expressive media, which may take the form of drawings, paintings, prints or even sculpture. His works are based on possible relationships between the cognitive potential of the imagination, intuitive thought and emotion (traditionally the province of artistic expression) and the awareness which comes from rationality (traditionally an attribute of scientific thought).

The two works by Marco Bagnoli owned by the Castello di Rivoli stand as a single relationship between structure and meaning. The first work is a white-painted wooden sculpture produced by piling different sized rings upon one another. Their rotation determines the shape and volume of the sculpture at will. The sculpture is struck by a source of artificial light and throws the shadow of a double human profile against the facing wall, like a doorway beyond which all duality breaks down.

Thus the title of the work, *Colui che sta* (He who stands). The stance of the double figure indicates its lack of decision over which course to take, or indeed whether to undertake any action which involves movement. Yet paradoxically the figure is actually generated by another form of movement: the circular movement of its constituent rings. The figure is seen as a potentially dynamic factor which does not become dynamic because it is held between contrasting possibilities, as denoted by its dual prospect.

The second work is a broad-meshed copper structure, supported by a steel frame, which forms a grid studded with small yellow boxwood roots. The structure represents a map of the heavens, where the roots are stars and the grid indicates the spatial coordinates used to identify the constellations. The title of this second work is *Benché sia notte* (Although it is night), which alludes to the main function of the object, to allow someone setting out at night under poor conditions to guide himself by fixed points. This second curved and slightly tapering structure appears to bend around the first figure in a protective way, because it provides the means for *Colui che sta* to overcome its stasis and express its inherent dynamism. The locked dual outlook becomes a trajectory, a course, an experience of direction.

The two works are linked by the structural relationship between statue and niche: the rounded sculpture fits into the concave grid. This relationship and function hark back to classical art. This suggests that classic art is still the standard and thus lies at the root of every directional relationship which drives experience; first and foremost an artistic experience. However, this fact does not exclude its opposite: absence of foundation and disorientation. In *Colui che sta*, these are also represented as possible options for experience, creativity and awareness. The awareness produced by art, and the scientific awareness promoted by Bagnoli make the rule and an instance of the rule into two complementary factors which are moulded by the subject of awareness into an ever-changing series of new syntheses.

Selected Bibliography

Marco Bagnoli. Lyons: Musée Saint Pierre, Octobre des Arts, 1987. *Marco Bagnoli*, Quba. Rome: Edizioni Inonia, 1988. *Marco Bagnoli*. Grenoble: Centre National d'Art Contemporain Le Magasin, 1991. *Marco Bagnoli*. Rivoli: Castello di Rivoli, 1992. *Marco Bagnoli*. Spazio x Tempo. Florence, 1992. *Marco Bagnoli*. Spazio x Tempo. Florence: Edizioni Plostampa, 1994.

Colui che sta (He Who stands),
model, 1991-92
wood, gold tempera, silver, iron,
256 x 120 x 120 cm
Benché sia notte (Although it is Night), 1991-92
iron, copper, boxwood root,
440 x 316 x 55 cm
Gift of Publitalia '80, 1992

Lothar Baumgarten was born in Rheinsberg, Germany in 1944.

Yurupari – Stanza di Rheinsberg was initially shown in Düsseldorf 1969. The title refers to the artist's place of origin, Rheinsberg, a town in East Germany's Brandenburg. Relocated and adjusted to its new surroundings, the work was presented a second time in 1984 at the Castello di Rivoli – in its actual form.

The works alludes to the phenomenon of *Time* in a double-fold manner: to historical time, through the dialogue it searches with the architectural surroundings in which it stands; and to the transience of time, by the choice of its materials. Unbound cobalt pigment, as used for the colouring of the walls, gives expression to an inherent quality of the tropics: their transient impermanence.

Scattered over the walls are names of plants and animals found in the southern hemisphere of the New World. These names conjure up a composite scenery of tropical America; moreover, they evoke the verbal appropriation of these lands by the Europeans and their incorporation into an encyclopedic body of knowledge. Thus, they recall the hungry era of classification, in which the distinct desires for acquisition and for new experiences merged in the practice of naming out a world hintherto unknown. The names chosen for this space, their juxtaposition and interrelation, set in motion various layers of associations with a continent: as it might be perceived by the five senses; as it was captured in an irrevocable process os discovery; and as it might be imagined, from descriptions in books, read in a room at Rheinsberg.

Selected Bibliography

America Señores naturales. Venice: La Biennale di Venezia, 1984. *Tierra de los Perros mudos*. Amsterdam: Stedelijk Museum, 1985. *Accès aux quais, tableaux parisiens*. Paris: Musée d'Art moderne de la Ville de Paris, 1985. *Makunaíma*. New York: Marian Goodman Gallery, 1987. *Carbon*. Los Angeles: Museum of Contemporary Art, 1991. *America Invention*. New York: The Solomon R. Guggenheim Museum, 1993.

Yurupari, Stanza di Rheinsberg (Yurupari, Rheinsberg Room), 1969-84 (detail)
pigment, tempera and feathers on wall, dimensions given by the environment
Castello di Rivoli Purchase, 1986

Domenico *Bianchi*

Born in the countryside near Rome in 1955, Domenico Bianchi began to emerge at the beginning of the Eighties as one of the most interesting members of a group who were beginning to see pictorial language as a tradition in need of revitalisation. Together with the other artists with whom he undertook a sort of union (Bruno Ceccobelli, Gianni Dessì and Giuseppe Gallo) Bianchi bases his work on premises other than those adopted by the contemporary "Transavanguardia" group. For painters in the Transavanguardia group do not base their work on figuration but a form of expression mid-way between iconism and true abstraction. The work *Senza titolo* (Untitled), dating from 1988 owned by the Castello di Rivoli exemplifies the meaning that painting assumes for Bianchi. A tangle of clearly defined, overlapping lines describing a curved and sinuous path in the middle of the composition seems to describe a form which is not defined but "becoming", a route from unform to image - or perhaps the other way round. The more definite and well-defined the painted mark, the more ambiguous the resulting figure. It is not clear whether the resulting image is produced by a centripetal force which is causing the line to coil up into a tighter construction or whether the force is centrifugal and the line is unwinding. The figure stands out against a background painted in a uniform dark, flat, gloomy colour. Two upper and lower bands in warm yellow add an elementary spatial poetry of their own. The two bands appear to perform the function of a frame or act to vicariously emphasise the centrality of the surface and the figure it bears.

This structural relationship soon reveals itself to be more complex than is apparent at first sight. The surfaces are not continuous and whole, but made up of small fibre-glass panels, and the colour is not produced by the painting material but by wax, which has been used instead of paint. In intrinsic terms too, the work is an organism undergoing change. The materials of which the work is formed display the same ambiguity as the resulting marks and language. A return to the tradition of painting which was handed down to us by previous generations after the years of artistic experimentation may be symbolically described as a rediscovery of the centre as an ordering principle of artistry. Bianchi attempts this rediscovery without hesitation, but also brings a new critical awareness inherited from the avant-garde movement, which irrevocably questioned the idea of the centre and centrality. For this reason, the central position of the image or rather the place where the pictorial language is displayed is a constant feature of Bianchi's compositions. Indeed the artist constructs a true rhetoric around the theme of centrality. His surfaces always contain a nuclear mark which is conceived as a generator of form, a point from which his images radiate. Yet these images never achieve certainty: they remain open to meaning but do not allow themselves to convey full meaning. Just at the point art is again able to express all its potential meaning through the use of markings, colour and material, the practice of painting undergoes another change. The paint itself becomes mixed with the most disparate array of materials or replaced by other materials just as in the tradition of historical avant-garde movements and neo-avant-garde movements.

Selected Bibliography

Bianchi, Charlton, Förg, Kruger, Verhoef. Rivoli: Castello di Rivoli, 1989. *Bianchi.* Bologna: Galleria Comunale d'Arte Moderna Villa delle Rose, 1993. *Domenico Bianchi.* Amsterdam: Stedelijk Museum, 1994.

Senza titolo (Untitled), 1988
wax on fibreglass, 286 x 363 cm
Castello di Rivoli Purchase, 1990

Dara Birnbaum was born in New York in 1946 and has worked with video images since 1978. During the first stage of her work in this field, she took material from television. Her sources ranged from soap operas to Television advertising. Due to its status as the most widely diffused medium, television is the main vehicle of mass culture. Birnbaum uses the contents of this culture to reveal the ideological suggestions which often lie hidden in it. The artist breaks up the television sequence and repeats certain moments considered particularly crucial. The behaviour of characters, both fictitious and real, is analysed in terms of expressive codes. Thus Birnbaum dissects the character of Wonder Woman, the super-heroine with supernatural powers; the neurotic behaviour of girls competing in TV quizzes; or TV news reports from Tienammen Square in Peking. Since 1982, when she began to produce works such as *P M Magazine* (based on an evening news programme), Birnbaum's work has consistently taken the form of a multimedia, environmental installation.

The trilogy *Damnation of Faust* (1983 - 1987) marks a shift from Birnbaum's previous works because the video images used do not come exclusively from television programmes, but are selected and processed to illustrate a personal interpretation of a literary character. The sections of the triptych are entitled *Evocation* (1983), *Will-O'-the-Wisp* (1985) and *Charming Landscape* (1987). In all three sections, Birnbaum has used various expressive media: monitors projecting images accompanied by music and sound effects; panels bearing gigantic images taken from the same audiovisual source and chosen for their particular significance; and paintings on the walls of the space in which the screens are installed. The installations also reflect the colours and decorative architecture of their surroundings. In the case of *Will-O'-The-Wisp*, the work owned by the Castello di Rivoli, three monitors are arranged in the middle of a large panel, which also bears eight photographs arranged in an arc. A shape formed at the top of the panel reflects the shape described by the stucco decoration in the room of the castle where the work was originally exhibited. The photographs depict a single, slightly unfocused image of a woman's face shown with closed eyes together with the bough of a tree. The same image can be seen on the screen, accompanied by a female voice speaking softly of a lost love. These images alternate with scenes of children playing in a road and pictures of natural landscapes. The female figure corresponds to the character of Margaret, Faust's counterpart, who the artist sees as an archetypal example of the relationship between men and women as determined and given legitimacy by western culture. By using contemporary images, Birnbaum seeks to bring the literary myth up to date and locate the female figure in her submissive role by linking her to the historical and cultural process that produced her.

Selected Bibliography

D. Birnbaum, *Rough Edits: Popular Image Video Works 1977-1980*. Halifax: The Press of Nova Scotia College of Art and Design, 1987. *Dara Birnbaum*. Valencia: IVAM Centre del Carme, 1990. Birnbaum, D. *Every TV needs revolution*. Gand: IC Series Imschoot, 1992.

Will-O'-The-Wisp, 1985
painted wood, photographs, television sets
Gift of Zerynthia Association for
Contemporary Art, 1992

James Lee Byars

James Lee Byars was born in Detroit in 1932. An interest in philosophy and Oriental religions led him to Japan, which he visited on numerous occasions between 1957 and 1967. While there, he taught English to Buddhist monks and nuns. The artist has developed his own personal visual language by combining his understanding of learnt from Oriental cultures with the results of the most advanced scientific research. The artist's language is based on simple forms endowed with deep symbolic significance: geometrical circles, spheres, cylinders or pyramids. He also uses materials and colours important in a symbolic sense, such as marble and velvet or black and gold. Whether they take the form of three-dimensional objects, installations, actions or poems, Byars' works never carry a clear message. Their symbolism is varied, open to interpretation and indeterminate. The texts the artist writes to accompany his exhibitions always take the form of an aphorism or fragmentary extract. Sometimes these are made up of abbreviated words or words elaborated to the point that they become illegible. These enigmatic "statements" often end with a question mark. The artist also chooses to celebrate the opening of his exhibitions through another set of enigmatic actions: he meets his public in a golden gown and with a blindfold over his eyes. For him, the important thing is to pose the question. The work itself then invites the spectator to search his own cultural memories in order to find an answer, a meaning.

The two works owned by the Castello di Rivoli incorporate an emblem and a material used frequently by the artist: a sphere and gold. The sphere is displayed inside a wooden cabinet with glass walls similar to the sort of display case used in museums to exhibit small *objets d'art*, applied art, archaeological finds, or natural history subjects. The slightly antiquated appearance of the cabinet conjures up an impression of a similarly dilapidated museum atmosphere, designed to preserve a somewhat conventional idea of classicism. Inside, however, we find a perfect sphere of sandstone, not associated in any way with the materials described above. This highly ambiguous figure is somehow related to the past, yet also with the most remote future. It is endowed with all the polysemy of a symbol, for which a genealogy may be constructed, but yet can also be given new meaning. In our own culture, and in many cultures distant from our own such as that of the Japanese, the sphere is a cosmic symbol charged with meanings relating to spirituality, a state which transcends the terrestrial world. The fragment of nature represented by the sandstone has been smoothed and made perfect even though this would not occur in nature. It is exhibited inside a cabinet, which assumes the function of a display "device" in restoring visibility to a sacred object. The stone sphere also recalls the idea of a celestial body, and the work's title, *The spherical book*, prompts us to imagine that this fragment of the cosmos contains the secret of our existence, in the same way that a book about occult science does. As Thomas McEvilley perceptively noted, the figures of the sphere and its progenitor, the circle (also often used by Byars) often occur in Oriental philosophies (such as Tantrism, Taoism or Shintoism) to convey transcendent meanings, but have fallen into disuse within our own culture since Renaissance times. They are now adopted instead by unofficial, occult disciplines such as Cabalism or Alchemy. Our Western culture chooses to express its rationality through the straight line, which always leads in a specific direction, or the square, construction element par excellence, particularly of our modern age. A curved line, however, returns to its original point and embodies all possible movements in its potential for rotation. This is no building block but rather an evocation of the incessant living rhythm of nature: a nature with religious overtones. The Oriental philosophies to which Byars indirectly refers are religions of nature, which the artist contrasts with our own scientific, utilitarian beliefs. Gold is also a cosmic symbol. This material is used as a uniform background in Byzantine and Gothic paintings, where it is used to convey an idea of infinity and divinity. Gold has increasingly lost this meaning since the Renaissance. Nowadays, if anything, both element and symbol are used to denote the idea of earthly riches and also the negative connotations linked with such wealth. Byars often uses gold to convey an original spiritual meaning. The long golden wand that rises up through the entire height of the Castello di Rivoli staircase is heading towards heaven, as if wishing to draw our attention up towards the infinite in an attempt to transcend real space.

The Spherical Book, 1981-83
Berne sandstone, wood, glass, sculpture
diam. 27 cm, display case 175 x 146 x 46 cm
Castello di Rivoli Purchase, 1986

Selected Bibliography

James Lee Byars. Berne: Kunsthalle, 1978. *James Lee Byars. The Philosophical Palace*. Düsseldorf: Kunsthalle, 1986. *James Lee Byars. The Palace of Good Luck*. Rivoli: Castello di Rivoli, 1989. *James Lee Byars. The Perfect Thought*. Houston: University Art Museum - Contemporary Art Museum, 1991. *James Lee Byars, Sonne Mond und Sterne*. Stuttgart: Wurttembergischer Kunstverein, 1993.

The Wand, 1989
gilded aluminium, 1650 x 7.5 x 7.5 cm
Castello di Rivoli Purchase, 1991

Pier Paolo *Calzolari*

The first works of Pier Paolo Calzolari, who was born in Bologna in 1943, are closely related to the American school of neo-Dadaism. But since the end of the Sixties, the artist has directed his efforts towards work of a more complex nature by working on installations involving a wide range of materials or actions taking place in real time. He uses natural elements such as tobacco and banana leaves, wax, salt, margarine, moss and other more technological elements such as neon light in order to create highly imaginative works which are autobiographical in origin and provide an opportunity to reflect on the role of the artist. One of his most explored themes is the transformation of material by mechanical means. *Sedie* (Chairs) directly refers to an installation created by the artist in 1975 as part of a performance. Calzolari created a complex work consisting of actions and installations located within different rooms of a villa and outside the villa itself. In this work, figures alluding to infinity such as circles, spirals, upturned figure eights and triangles formed from objects or commonplace actions were exhibited as a unifying theme. One element in this series of *tableaux vivants* was a pair of seats with a bread stick balancing on their backs. The length of the bread stick was determined by the size of part of the artist's body. That particular component of the former ephemeral performance event has now been taken out of its original context and used to create a different work. *Sedie* used two ordinary objects to convey the idea of everyday life and the domestic environment, though Calzolari introduced a new formal relationship in order to transfigure the image: instead of being two real objects, taken directly from everyday life, the two chairs were made out of terracotta, in other words a material which forms part of the artistic tradition. The work thus takes its rightful place in the field of sculpture. The everyday world is still present, described by the simple truth of a bread stick. This organic element evokes everyday life because it carries its own anthropometric associations and thus stands as the substance and symbol of bodiliness. This created world is also forced to undergo processes of its own (the bread stick dries and deteriorates, it must be changed) which directly recall the process of baking earth, in other words the process responsible for converting organic material into a rigid structure (into a sculpture, in fact) and thus, by association, turning a natural element into an element of culture. After allowing us to experience this ongoing relationship with the organic world and examine the vitality of meaning evident in form, the artist asks us to compare this process with another process, of which we are shown only the effects. The chair seats and sculpture base are made of lead, also a natural element processed by human labour, which the artist has chosen for its malleability. The lead parts are connected to a refrigerator motor, which freezes the material until it takes on a uniform white colour. The work thus undergoes a transformation which suspends it in an indeterminate dimension: an organic material becomes form and everyday objects become signs, but both are now transformed by a mechanical process which does not belong to nature or the artistic tradition and cannot even be properly controlled by the artist because it depends on the climatic conditions in the environment where the work is located. The object is entirely transformed in an almost biological way, and transported to a universe outside the realms of utilitarian experience or even simple visual enjoyment. We could experience the transformation ourselves by touching the frosted parts, but we know that ice burns like fire and that we risk spoiling the integrity of the work. The precise formal structure is at odds with the variety of substances used and the partly randomly-determined extent of their visibility. Suspended in this way between different shades of meaning, the work becomes a strongly ambiguous image which seems to frame for us, in other words to present, the actual idea of a limit, of which the ice or frost constitutes an ironic emblem.

The work entitled *Senza titolo (Omaggio a Fontana)* (Untitled [Homage to Fontana]) also adopts the same principle of icing. In this case the rectangular metal surface out of which the work is made undergoes the transformation. The white frosting produced on the surface takes the place of white paint. Calzolari considers this the essence of white, an absolute idea, incapable of being classified (as just one more colour in the infinite array of white paint shades on a colour chart). All Calzolari's work reveals the same quest for the absolute. The artist tackles this theme in an attempt to "relativize" the absolute (the essence) by bringing it into confrontation or contact with the phenomenological world. In *Omaggio a Fontana*, the holes studding the surface of this work are a reference to a lesson learnt from this earlier artist, who was engaged in a similar quest.

Senza titolo (Omaggio a Fontana)
(Untitled - Homage to Fontana), 1989
freezing structure, copper, lead, motor,
127 x 92 x 3 cm
Given anonymously, 1994

Selected Bibliography

Pier Paolo Calzolari. Opere: 1968-1986.
Modena: Galleria Civica, 1986. *Pier Paolo
Calzolari.* New York: Barbara Gladstone
Gallery, 1988. *Day After Day. Pier Paolo
Calzolari.* Turin: Canale-Pedrini-Persano
Editori, 1994. *Pier Paolo Calzolari.* Paris:
Galerie nationale du Jeu de Paume, 1994.
Pier Paolo Calzolari. Rivoli: Castello di
Rivoli, Charta, 1994.

Sedie (Chairs), 1986
copper, lead, bread-stick, refrigerator motor,
100 x 346 x 95 cm
Gift of Giorgiana and Giorgio Persano,
1991

Enrico
Castellani

Born in Castelmassa (Rovigo) in 1930, Enrico Castellani produced his first work within the context of the poetic pictorialism of the *Informel* movement. He later opposed the interior streak which arose within this movement and in 1959 became one of the leaders of a group of artists who systematically opposed this stance. During the same year, he founded a review and art gallery entitled "Azimuth" together with Piero Manzoni. Both gallery and review were engaged in examining the rationalistic, analytical and constructive climate then arising in the international field. Castellani's interests lay in the direction not of recording unconscious urges and subjective will but rather of wishing to see painting as an independent, essential linguistic element within a general system of painting. This new-found autonomy is emphasised by the fact that all Castellani's works are described by the title *Superficie* (Surface), as well as a few further details including the colour with which the painting is coloured. The first works he carried out in this new direction were monochrome canvasses. The format he used did not conform to the traditional two-dimensional appearance of painted works. His surfaces were angular, either constructed out of intersecting or jutting planes. Sometimes the artist replaced his monochrome surfaces with scored canvasses which interfere with our optical perception of lines when used in free-form works. This aspect of his work represented a contribution to contemporary efforts in the field of kinetic and programmed art.

Castellani is specifically interested in the relationship between space and light, which are both seen as playing an active part in the process of endowing a work with meaning. The artist does not hesitate to alter the structure of the painting itself in order to bring space and light into play. The painting thus becomes a surface full of bumps and pits obtained by banging nails into strips of wood at the back of the canvas. The canvas covering is therefore broken up by a succession of bumps and depressions which may be constant, when lines of bumps and pits alternate to cover the whole surface. The rhythm may, however, be varied infinitely by imposing different asymmetrical patterns, always determined in accordance with rules of mathematical progression. The work in the Castello di Rivoli collection, entitled *Superficie IBI* (IBI surface), is ordered in accordance with a diagonal pattern. Because such rules exist, we may assume that the general features of this work will be present in every other work by Castellani, even when the artist's work fills the entire available space. In most cases, the integrity of the surface is affected without startling effects, in other words without breaking down the structure of the painting as such. The work activates empirical, environmental and temporal factors which govern perception. A time factor comes into play due to the visual rhythm triggered by the sequence of bumps and pits (the rate may remain steady, speed up or slow down). Also, our perception of the work itself is affected by the light in the environment where the painting is hung. The surface projects more or less pronounced shadows depending on how much light strikes the painting and in what direction. The shadows introduce another morphological factor, because they move and change as the observer moves and thus complement the actual morphology inherent in each work.

Selected Bibliography

Enrico Castellani. Parma: Università di Parma, 1976. Zevi, A. *Enrico Castellani*. Ravenna: Loggetta Lombardesca, Essegi Editrice, 1984. *Enrico Castellani*. Rome: Netta Vespignani - Plinio De Martiis, 1991.

Superficie IBI (IBI Surface), 1978
acrylic on canvas, 150 x 150 cm
Long-term loan of the artist

Maurizio *Cattelan*

Born in Padua in 1960, Maurizio Cattelan first worked within the field of design before devoting himself to the visual arts at the end of the Eighties. One of the most interesting members of the group of younger Italian artists, Cattelan's declared intention is to work with the lack of alignment between systems for the transmission of specialised knowledge in order to carve out space for reflection upon the problematic relationship between life and art. The works exhibited by the artist include such examples as a series of safes bearing signs of attempted break-ins (real), or portraits produced using police identikits, and refer directly to the social dynamics of his age. Significant in this regard are two sculptures from 1994, which the artist made out of the rubble left after the Milan Contemporary Art Pavilion was destroyed in a terrorist attack. The same line of thought applies to more complex operations, such as the occasion when he created a football team made up of non-European immigrants and then promoted this team by selling gadgets from an illegal stand at the Bologna Arts Fair. This type of activity enables Cattelan to display an interest in the popularity of football while also examining the racist prejudices emerging within Italy. The illegality of the stand is meant to remind us that this form of selling is the only way most Third World immigrants can support themselves.

Cattelan has also questioned the relationship between socio-economic structure and artistic production by making bizarre, almost intolerably provocative requests to artistic institutions. In reality, Cattelan's aim was simply to add ironic emphasis to the privileged role enjoyed by the artist when he succeeded in arranging for a gallery entrance to be bricked up so that the exhibition could be viewed only through the windows, or even when he insisted that employees should wear carnival costumes for the entire duration of the exhibition. He also underscored the close relationship between artists and the consumer system by selling his stand at the 1993 Venice Biennale to a perfume manufacturer, which installed an advertising board on it.

The work *Il Bel Paese* (The Fine Country), which Cattelan produced specifically for the "Soggetto-Soggetto" (Subject-Subject) exhibition held at the Castello di Rivoli and subsequently donated to the museum, is typical of the disturbing self-deprecating line the artist takes with artistic institutions. The work consists of a simple round mat which he intends should be treated just as any ordinary mat. In the course of the exhibition, the artist laid his work on the floor of the museum entrance so that visitors could tread on it. Similarly, everyone is free to walk over the mat whenever the work is exhibited within the museum rooms. Yet the mat is also something else: it acquires artistic connotations simply through being exhibited in a museum. Thus Cattelan suggests that the institute is directly responsible for the attribution of value. The image on the mat is the famous logo used on Bel Paese cheese packets. Italy itself is described as "Il Bel Paese" (The Fine Country) on the packet, which we can now only accept as an ironic statement although it was almost certainly not intended as such originally. Cattelan also seeks to undermine the undeniable seriousness surrounding works of art in two further ways. Firstly, he uses an advertising logo lacking any artistic qualities and made humdrum because it is so common. Secondly, he cheekily uses his art as a vantage point for poking fun at the artistry Italian nation.

Selected Bibliography

Biologia delle passioni. Ravenna: Essegi Editrice, 1989. Daolio, R. *Il re crede di essere nudo*. Ravenna: Essegi Editrice, 1990.

Il Bel Paese (The Fine Country), 1994
wool carpet, diam. 300 cm
Gift of Pulsar Group Insurance Brokers,
Milan-Turin, 1994

Alan *Charlton*

Grey is the only colour used by painter Alan Charlton and this is invariably applied as a monochrome layer. In the works of Charlton (born in Sheffield, Great Britain in 1948), the uniform application of this most neutral of colours represents a radical nullification of all expressive characteristics. Thus he reduces the entire system of painting to this option, the entire linguistic repertoire to this single possibility. His painting is executed in different shades of grey and defers to a few highly specific self-imposed rules which he uses as devices to overcome the unquantifiable problem of adapting to the changing phenomenology of the spaces within which he works. Each space has its own particular light, and the artist selects the shade of grey on the basis of that light. The shade also changes from work to work if the works are produced in a different size and remains the same if the formats change. The formats themselves are often determined by the exhibition space, and prepared after visiting the site. For Charlton, monochrome painting (as for many other artists, beginning with Ad Reinhardt) is important as a category, as an absolute. Through metonymic association, monochrome grey can be seen as embracing all possible types of painting if considered from a categorical, purely ontological viewpoint. Unlike Reinhardt but like Fontana, Charlton juxtaposes this absolute with something that contradicts it: the space. The status of the work is altered because we are forced to consider the surrounding space.

Although seven years divide the two works by Alan Charlton owned by the Castello di Rivoli, both display the same pictorial features. The sole difference between these two monochrome grey canvases lies in the shape of the medium. In the square painting entitled *Single Panel Painting*, we do not see merely a square canvas painted grey but more specifically "a picture", the code traditionally most favoured for bearing the particular system of markings known as "painting." The entire system is asserted and the form of expression bluntly stated in this assertion of category. The declaratory intent is also underscored by the tautology inherent in the title. This particular manifestation of the category described is nevertheless partly affected, in its specific form of expression, by an experienced event, the light conditions at the site where this specific painting was painted. This relationship may be seen even more clearly in the work *Multiple Line Painting*. In this case, one of the main features of a monochrome work has been transmuted: wholeness. Yet this transmutation is still achieved within the terms of the self-imposed code. The monochrome is not broken down, its integral structure has simply been delineated in virtual terms. The subdivision into long rectangular segments causes the work to lose its structure, albeit in accordance with a consistent visual rhythm. This rhythm acts upon the space, in the sense that it sets up a dynamic relationship with the light at the exhibition site and the movements of the spectator to create shadows. In fact, the structure of the work looks different when observed from different angles. In this way, the absolute is not denied, but made to form part of a dialectic. The absolute is measured in terms of phenomena in the sense that a spectator's ability to perceive the work visually depends partly on the phenomena and events of the real world.

Single Panel Painting, 1977
acrylic on canvas, 100 x 100 cm
Castello di Rivoli Purchase, 1986

Selected Bibliography

Alan Charlton. Drawings of Paintings. Eindhoven: Stedelijk Van Abbemuseum, 1975. *Alan Charlton. Selected Paintings 1969-1981.* Eindhoven: Stedelijk Van Abbemuseum, 1982. *Alan Charlton. One Man Exhibitions: Invitation Cards and Installation Photographs.* Charleroi: Palais des Beaux-Arts; Paris: Musée d'Art Moderne de la Ville de Paris, 1989. *Alan Charlton.* Schaffausen: Halle für neue Kunst, 1991. *Alan Charlton.* Krefeld: Museum Hans Esters, 1992.

Multiple Line Painting, 1984
acrylic on canvas, 216 x 319 cm
Castello di Rivoli Purchase, 1986

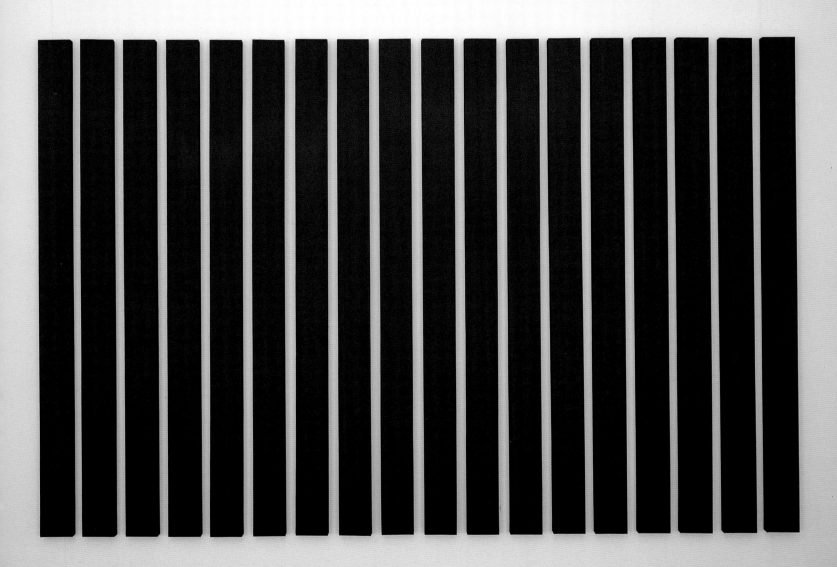

Enzo Cucchi

Born in Morro d'Alba (Ancona) in 1949, Enzo Cucchi became a self-taught painter before abandoning this activity to become a poet halfway through the Seventies. Then he moved to Rome and recovered his interest in the visual arts when he worked in close contact with Sandro Chia and Francesco Clemente. Together with these painters, and also Nicola De Maria and Mimmo Paladino, he formed part of a group dubbed the "Transavanguardia" by the critic Achille Bonito Oliva. At the beginning of the Eighties, he began to win international acclaim as one of the most representative artists of that cultural climate, so typical of the decade, whose distinctive characteristic was a return to neo-expressionist figuration. From 1984, Cucchi produced several works under th title of *Vitebsk/Harar*, terms which describe two places, evidently chosen for their emblematic nature. In 1883, Arthur Rimbaud finally abandoned his life as a poet and decided to live in voluntary exile. He chose the Ethiopian city of Harar, were he worked as a trader in skin and ivory. From 1919, Kasimir Malevič taught at Vitebsk at a school founded by Marc Chagall. Back in 1921, the Russian artist began to experience pressure from police authorities who attempted to halt the spread of his artistic theories. The works of Cucchi therefore apparently reflect upon two different experiences of poetic crisis. In the case of Rimbaud, this experience was determined by an existential choice, while the experience was brought about induced by the powers that be in the case of Malevič. In an 1984 work painted in memory of the two artists, Cucchi combines the image of a desert landscape with a piano in the foreground with a series of skulls enclosed in an oblong shape lying above the horizon. The skull image, in particular, always makes an appearance in other compositions with the same title. These paintings of Cucchi's reveal much about his passionate nature: the substantive nature of his colours, the vibrancy of his markings and the complexity of his page layouts, which often take the form of actual installations in space. This is the case with the *Vitebsk/Harar* compositions presented in 1984 at the Mary Boone Gallery in New York, where the work, painted in oils on canvas or on wooden beams with violently expressive brush-strokes, is accompanied by mounds of a wide array of materials piled up on the floor. The same expressive violence is found in his drawings of the same title, particularly the ink drawings on paper. Here the skull image is used in its traditional connotation as a symbol of death and is joined by other disquieting figures, such as a jackal playing a violin in the desert. Like another very similar work dating from 1985 entitled *Arthur Rimbaud a Harar* (Arthur Rimbaud in Harar), the work owned by the Castello di Rivoli differs from these briefly described works and from most of Cucchi's other works in general due to its sombre tone. The artist has chosen to work on a large uniformly black iron surface touched with brush-strokes of black paint which is visible due to its different colour. Only two images emerge on this extensive surface: a skull at the bottom and the moon at top left. The images are defined in reductive terms. Almost all pictorial traces have been lost from this work, as if the surface has absorbed all their vitality. The surface itself is restricted to sending out deadened signals in the form of inventions which exploit the shape of the material. The moon is defined by cutting away a small circle from the iron, while the skull is produced by embossing and scoring the surface. This area has rusted and thus isolates the image chromatically. The iron surface is seen as a non-artistic, found object which bears the sign of use and wear (the rust or dents which cover the entire surface) and apparently locate this particular work by Cucchi within the tradition of experimenting with the poetic qualities of material as exemplified by artists from Burri to the "Arte Povera" movement. The two figures of the skull and the moon act as sole indicators of space, yet are sufficient to suggest a deserted and desolate night landscape. When associated with the title, which describes the artist's failure to achieve his mission, this space becomes a psychological dimension, a mental space which refers to absence, death and mourning.

Although imagery maintains a strong metaphorical validity within the work of Cucchi, it is nevertheless generated by a practice close to free association and cannot relate to a single, certain meaning. The artist produces images which belong to a collective memory, often those of the peasant community to which the artist himself belongs, or challange popular culture, which the artist sets out to reinterpret in terms of its ambiguity. According to the parameters of this culture, the drama of existence revolves around acceptance of the laws of life and death. Thus the symbol of the skull in Cucchi's paintings is not linked to particularly tragic connotations but more to a peaceful reflection on the vanity of things. The artist himself writes: "The cemetery forms part of my landscape: it is one of the things I know best. I have always lived in remote places where the cemetery was the most important thing of all. Skulls may frequently be found in the countryside. This is an image, not a subject. It is a very strong spiritual and moral link with everything around me. It is a natural thing. Women in Naples go to talk with a skull between one purchase and the next. It is the same thing, there is nothing dramatic about it. Cezanne painted apples. My skulls are my apples."

Senza titolo (Untitled), 1988
iron and resin wood, 295 x 485 cm
Long-term loan of a private collector

Selected Bibliography

Enzo Cucchi. Amsterdam: Stedelijk Museum, 1984. *Enzo Cucchi*. New York: The Solomon R. Guggenheim Museum, 1986. *Enzo Cucchi. Testa*. Munich: Stadtische Galerie im Lenbachhaus; Edinburgh: The Fruit-Market Gallery; Nice: Musées de la Ville de Nice, 1978. *Enzo Cucchi*. Prato: Museo d'Arte Contemporanea, 1989. Perucchi-Petri, U. *Enzo Cucchi. Drawings 1975-1989. "La Disegna"*. New York: Rizzoli International, 1990. Roma. Modena: Galleria Civica; Trento: Galleria Civica d'Arte Contemporanea, 1990. *Enzo Cucchi. Disegno*. Nîmes: Carré d'Art, Musée d'Art Contemporain, 1991. *Enzo Cucchi*. Rivoli: Castello di Rivoli, Charta, 1993.

Vitebsk/Harar, 1984
paint on steel, 400 x 500 cm
Castello di Rivoli Purchase, 1986

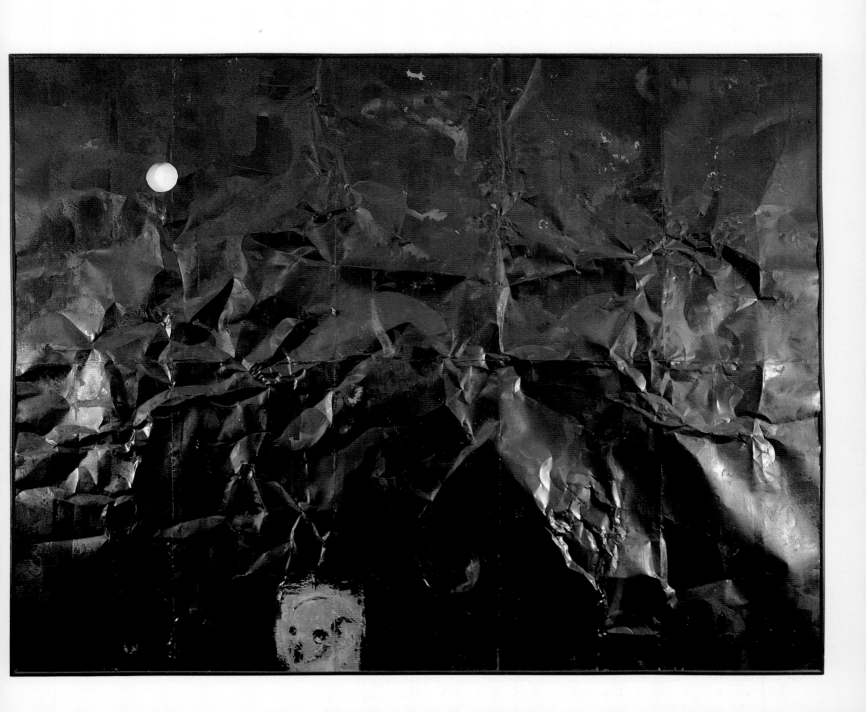

Wim Delvoye

An exponent of the younger artistic generation, Wim Delvoye was born in Werwik, Belgium in 1965 and is remarkable for the ironic intent with which his installations tackle cultural issues of a certain depth. The artist appropriates images widely disseminated throughout the mass media and considered "artistic" in the common sense of the word, such as the distinctive figures of Delft pottery, the abstract patterns of Oriental carpets or, more generally, the emblems we often find on various items of domestic decoration. He then forces these emblems to undergo a sort of decontextualisation by associating them with objects other than those for which they were originally destined. The Delft decorations are applied to metal saws, the Oriental patterns to abstract paintings, the mimetic patterns of military canvasses to plant pots. The effect of these incongruous juxtapositions is humorous and helps to defuse potential psychological conflict. The result is a played down yet effective criticism of lifestyles within which we are all individually involved.

The installation Wim Delvoye has produced specially for the Castello di Rivoli consists of a wooden sculpture in the form of an inlaid cement mixer and a hundred or so shovels whose blades are painted to depict the coats of arms of European cities. At one level of reading, according to the explicit intention of the artist, the work sets out to be a monument to work in the general sense, where the tools used here are very typical of a building site and represent a metonymic figure. But a second level of reading associated with the first is obviously at work here, too. This is determined by the treatment the objects have undergone, a treatment which deliberately manipulates the discrepancy between the "meaning" explicit in the objects themselves and their formal development. The cement mixer is made out of wood and elaborately inlaid like a wardrobe in imitation antique style. The object is 'fake' because although it is an item, a cement mixer, at the same time it conjures up the idea of another, a wardrobe. It is therefore deliberately related to a kitsch object. This monument working immediately reveals its ironic side and irony is a constant feature of all Wim Delvoye's output.

By juxtaposing the cement mixer and the shovels, we perceive a third level of reading which, now more implicitly, conveys the 'theme' of the installation itself. All the shovels have been transformed into heraldic coats of arms and each one bears the insignia of a town. The heraldic emblem recalls the idea of an ancient town or city state, in other words the concept of a distinctive closed community, proud of its individual nature. Yet the incongruous association of the coats of arms and the shovels questions this concept. The artist is trying to tell us that contemporary society requires us to overcome all individuality in order to accept that our society is becoming a multi-racial world. The need for different cultures to live together has become the greatest requirement of our age. The idea of this living together is inherent in the association of shovels and cement mixer: significantly enough, all these tools of common toil are here engaged in that most constructive of activities, building. Irony and parody are used here as undermining devices because the artist really sees the blending of cultures and the acceptance of difference as positive attributes and not as something forced. These positive values work against the negative values of ethnic prejudice and racism which still rear their ugly heads on our continent.

Selected Bibliography

Wim Delvoye. Rivoli: Castello di Rivoli, Fabbri, 1991.

Installazione Castello di Rivoli (Castello di Rivoli Installation), 1990-91
wood, shovels, paint on iron, dimensions determined by the environment
Gift of Rosita and Ottavio Missoni, 1992

Jan Dibbets

Born in Weert, Holland in 1941, Jan Dibbets is a leading figure in European conceptual art. His work makes use of photography as a tool for examining space and our use of space. The artist sees photography as a means of conditioning our visual perception and space as a shifting phenomenon, impossible to define with clarity. Since the end of the Sixties, Dibbets has been ordering photographic sequences into visual patterns to record changes in the chromatic intensity of natural light as it filters through the windows of certain architectural environments. During the Seventies, his photographic sequences were arranged in curves or other spatial and temporal patterns designed to confound the spectator's normal psychological expectations.

The work *Spoleto Floor* is a photographic sequence showing a detail from the floor in the Spoleto Cathedral and resembles other works such as *Spoleto Duomo* and *Spoleto Duomo 270°* (both dating from 1980). Here the artist has installed the camera upon a tripod pointing at the floor and gradually turned the lens throughout a semi-circle in order to take photographs at regular intervals. This objective documentation of environment and architectural detail is made possible due to the objectivity of the technical equipment. The camera's most outstanding potential resource is exploited in this case, in other words its ability to document external realities with a completely clear eye. In order to achieve this result, Dibbets uses the camera in as neutral a manner as possible. He uses no light sources other than natural light, for example, in order to achieve shadows and light effects which are also natural and linked to the moment when the photograph was taken. The circular sequence reveals the effect an observer could achieve if he or she looked at that same portion of the floor in the Spoleto Cathedral Floor while turning round on the spot. This affirmation to realism is overlaid by the artist's own work, evident in the way the images are assembled. These are not placed side by side, but overlap one another to ensure that each deliberately square photograph does not contain details visible in the others. The visual structure therefore assumes a semi-circular form and we obtain an optical allusion of continuity. Yet the artist is less concerned with reflecting a visual experience than he is with creating a concept of space which does not tally perfectly with true space. The first three image fragments, on the bottom right hand side of the composition do not reflect the floor as a continuous whole but repeat three semi-circular portions. The ordering principle of the composition is not determined by the real space investigated by the mechanical eye, but by an element intrinsic to the portrayed image. In fact, a sequence of stone slabs and inlaid sections located at the lower edge of the sequence are ordered into an overlapping semi-circle and ultimately form three concentric rings which alternate with three areas ordered in a straight line. This interplay of visual elements, lines and geometrical forms orders the composition and impinges upon the actual conditions in real space. Yet the visual result is not determined by the actual coordinates of real space. For example, the parts overlap to leave certain details which do not fit perfectly together because these inaccuracies do not actually affect our visual perception of the pattern on the floor. In his photograph, Dibbets takes spatial experience as a starting point but does not stop here. Space is cut up, removed from its continuity and introduced into a different continuity created wholly by the artist from assembled images. It is not immediately obvious that certain parts do not fit together properly. This indicates that the artist sees his first task as highlighting the mechanisms of visual perception by examining them outside their connection with more general sensorial perception.

The semi-circular shape of the photographic sequence is emphasised by the addition of pastel lines which indicate the simultaneous presence of many vanishing points. The aim of these lines is to overturn the constructive rules of traditional perspective and hint at the idea of spatial ambiguity. Dibbet's use of rotating viewpoints within architectural spaces always induces a sense of vertigo, which is accentuated by the disorientating effect of rotation. The open ring shape suggests a will to join up the circle, a figure where beginning and end coincide, and even go on to form a spiral. These curving images of space are diametrically opposed to the traditional image of space imposed by classical canons of perspective, and can be virtually projected into infinity.

Selected Bibliography

Jan Dibbets. Audio-visuelle Dokumentationen. Krefeld: Museum Haus Lange, 1969. *Jan Dibbets*. Amsterdam: Stedelijk Museum, 1972. *Jan Dibbets. Photographic Works 1967-1980.* Eindhoven: Stedelijk Van Abbemuseum; Paris: Musée d'Art Moderne de la Ville de Paris; Berne: Kunsthalle, 1980. *Jan Dibbets*. Minneapolis: Walker Art Center, 1987. Fuchs, R. and Moure, G. J*an Dibbets. Interior Light. Works on Architecture 1969-1990.* Barcelona: Ediciones Poligrafa, 1991.

Spoleto Floor, 1981
photographs, acrylic, crayon, paper on wood, 130 x 175 cm
Castello di Rivoli Purchase, 1986

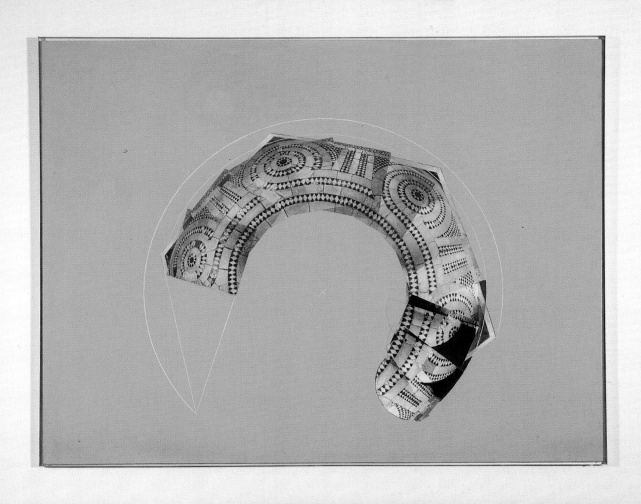

Luciano
Fabro

Luciano Fabro was born in Turin in 1936, and has been working as an artist since 1963. Since the beginning of his career, he has displayed a specific interest in space, which he sees as a communicative dimension or environment woven out of the relationships between external reality and interior life. His first works were made out of glass and exploited the relationship between transparency and mirror-like reflection. Other works made out of iron piping investigated the environment by altering the way in which it is perceived. His interest in space then prompted him to involve the spectator physically in a sensory adventure (*In cubo, Allestimento teatrale*, 1966-67) (In Square, Theatrical Event). He then pursued another tack and produced works he termed 'tautologies', in other words pure statements, not conditioned by experience. One example of such work was *Concetto Spaziale* (Spatial Concept) dating from 1967, where a portion of floor is covered by newspapers. Later, his work centred around the idea of removing the collective symbolic function from widely recognizable images. For example, he made images of Italy out of a range of materials and located them in completely unexpected positions. On another front, he prompted a debate on the linguistic specificity of sculpture by adopting materials from the standard canon, such as marble, and then going on to use other incongruous, innovative materials such as glass and coloured silk or canvas on bronze (*Piedi*) (Feet, 1968-1972), *Attaccapanni*, (Clothes Pegs, 1976-1977). In more recent works, he develops his environmental theme through installations which are entitled *Habitat* or defined in accordance with his critical re-reading of the codes of classical perspective.

The date in the title of his work *Paolo Uccello (1450-1989)* suggests that here the artist is extrapolating his ideas of perspective through time. The work was displayed for the first time in 1985 in the open air on the occasion of a group show in Geneva City Park, where it was simply entitled *Paolo Ucello* without any further description. The work was given its current title, with the date tag 145O-1989, when it was exhibited on the occasion of the artist's one-man show at the Castello di Rivoli in 1989. The work therefore changes name and meaning according to the context in which it is exhibited to the public. In fact the work is constructed in a similar fashion to another work by the artist, entitled *Opus Euclide*, produced in 1984. It differs only in adopting a more solid structure suitable for exhibition in the open air. The work consists of two square metal frames, standard elements of metal scaffolding, placed in front of one another to form a virtual cube. This is then suspended in the air in the same way as other similar works made during the same period. An upright metal rod applied to each of the two frames is fastened in the middle of the two squares, while another rod is connected to the first square by means of metal hoops. The two rods float in space, one horizontal and one angled forward. The hoop can slide to alter the position of the two floating lines so that they are free of firm connections. The virtual cube naturally outlines a perspective box with the frame and metal rods as its coordinates. These coordinates are given only partially and suggest units of a fixed a priori structure designed in accordance with the spatial laws of Euclidean geometry. The unfixed nature of some of the coordinates implies the impermanent nature of what they define. The historical reference to Paolo Uccello and the date 1450 indicate the possibility of violating the laws of perspective. The frescoes relating the story of Noah painted by Paolo Uccello in the green cloister of Santa Maria Novella in Florence date back to 1450. The unusual perspective in these paintings (several points of view aligned along the same central axis, or lines which do not converge to a single point and so on) result in fantastic, irrational visions. In Fabro's work, Euclid, the rule, sits shoulder to shoulder with Paolo Uccello, the violation of the rule. Because the work is located outside in the world, rational thought, of which perspective is an emblem, is forced to measure itself against the unimaginable truth of the real as perceived by the moving eye of the observer.

Selected Bibliography

Fabro, L. *Attaccapanni*. Turin: Einaudi, 1978. Fabro, L. *Regole d'Arte*. Milan: Casa degli Artisti, 1980. *Luciano Fabro. Sehnsucht*. Essen: Museum Folkwang; Rotterdam: Museum Boymans van Beuningen, 1981. De Sanna, J. *Fabro*. Ravenna: Essegi Editrice, 1983. *Luciano Fabro*. Rivoli: Castello di Rivoli, 1989. *Luciano Fabro*. Barcelona: Fundació Joan Miró, 1990. *Luciano Fabro*. Luzern: Kunstmuseum, 1991. *Luciano Fabro*. San Francisco: San Francisco Museum of Modern Art, 1992. *Luciano Fabro*. Pistoia: Palazzo Fabroni, Charta, 1994.

Paolo Uccello 1450-1989, 1989
iron, two units, 400 x 400 cm each
Long-term loan of the artist

Lucio *Fontana*

The son of a sculptor who emigrated to Argentina, Lucio Fontana was born in Rosario de Santa Fé in 1899. He moved back to Italy in 1905, and began his artistic activities in the Twenties, after studying under Adolfo Wildt at the Brera Academy. He did not ally himself with any of the official artistic movements of the time, being content to practice a type of non-academic figuration which took the form of vigorously modelled clay and ceramics painted in non-naturalistic colours. After 1931, and his work *Tavolette Graffite* (Scratched Boards), he produced images that were primitive if not completely abstract. In 1935, he went over to the abstract movement completely and created a series of sculptures out of two-dimensional plaster surfaces divided into irregular geometrical surfaces grooved with scratches. He then returned to figurative art with a long series of works in ceramic. The innovative appeal of these works lies in the skillful way Fontana was able to construct an image out of fragmented planes. He spent World War II in Argentina and then returned finally in 1947. This was the date when he began his greatest work, known as spatialism, which the artist promoted by gathering together a group of like-minded artists and drawing up manifestoes. Spatialist works are sculptures, paintings or cards crossed by holes, tears or cuts. These are "analogue" signs (a term coined by Crispolti in 1982) of real space: the phenomenological, tangible entity which shows through the holes. At the same time, they also allude to a spatiality that can only be defined as an "otherness", a dimension that cannot be defined except by thought. Fontana himself declared that "nothingness" was revealed through his holes.

Fontana's forays into spatial art were not restricted to the fields of painting and sculpture, but attempted to transcend such linguistic categories. His aim was to produce a new form of art with wider sensory appeal. The artist added holes and tears to canvas, clay, metal or paper in an effort to overcome the confines of surface and allude to a fourth dimension, a space beyond the surface.

Fontana saw this dimension in terms of measureless stellar spaces. With this idea of infinity as a backdrop, a subject could be perceived as pure spirit, a transcendent material in relation to the modern concept of spirituality which amounts simply to 'nothingness' (Fontana's nothingness is not a nothingness of destruction but a nothingness of creation). Fontana wished to do more than simply create an analogue language. He wished to bring all of space into the present moment, so that it could be directly experienced in sensory and mental terms. His *Ambienti Spaziali* (Spatial Environments), as he entitled the series of works he produced after 1949, are direct consequece of these thoughts.

On 5 February 1949, Fontana created his first *Ambiente Spaziale a luce nera* (Spatial Environments with black light) also called "Ambiente Nero" (Black Environment) at the Galleria del Naviglio in Milan. The gallery is lit by Wood lamps. The "black light" brings out the phosphorescent colours which cover certain abstract forms obscured by black drapes which hang from the ceiling. This same principle is approached in a different manner in the exhibition area at the Castello di Rivoli. Here the Wood light picks out a dual, sinuous linear series of circles painted in phosphorescent colours. The same approach is adopted in other environmental works prepared between 1964 and 1966. The artist's stated intention is that the spectator should come face to face with himself in the environment. This form of perception is not merely visual because it involves a collusion of all the senses to produce a more total, psychological and physical experience of perception. Fontana's environmental work represents the first of the projects outlined in the manifestoes of the Spatialist Movement (founded by the artist in Milan, 1947). "A work of art is eternal, but not immortal", stated the first Manifesto of Spatialism. For it to be immortal, art must break free of perishable material and make itself pure gesture, pure idea, through the aid of expressive tools borrowed from the world of technology. The second Manifesto (1948) states : "We want paintings to emerge from their frames and sculptures to leave their glass domes. It is as though a one-minute-long aerial display lasted a millennium, for eternity". The images Fontana outlines in his *Ambienti Spaziali* are just that, in other words aerial images, without bodies, which transcend their own physical nature. They are also abstract images, in other words disassociated from specific meaning to become universal. The artist deliberately uses such images to open up the imagination of the spectator. Fontana's works are therefore "open". They are not objects to be observed but sensations to be experienced. In his manifesto 'A Proposal for a Rule Governing Spatial Movements' (1950) he states: "A Spatial Artist no longer imposes a figurative theme on the spectator, but enables the spectator to create a theme himself through his own imagination and received emotions".

The artist created his spatial environment for the exhibition "Lo spazio dell'immagine" (Space of the Image), organised at Palazzo Trinci in Foligno in 1967. After Fontana's death at Comabbio (Varese) in 1968, the environment was re-constructed by Gino Marotta so that it could be exhibited at other exhibitions. The example owned by Castello di Rivoli is the only one not destroyed after the Rimini exhibition of 1982.

Selected Bibliography

Ballo, G. *Fontana: idea per un ritratto.* Turin: Ilte, 1970. Fossati, P. *Lucio Fontana. Concetti spaziali.* Turin: Einaudi, 1970. *Lucio Fontana.* Milan: Palazzo Reale, 1972. Crispolti, E. (edited by). *Lucio Fontana. Catalogo Generale.* Milan: Electa, 1986. *Lucio Fontana. La cultura dell'occhio.* Rivoli: Castello di Rivoli, 1986. *Lucio Fontana.* Paris: Musée national d'art moderne Centre Georges Pompidou, 1987. *Fontana e lo Spazialismo.* Lugano: Villa Malpensata, 1987. De Sanna, J. *Lucio Fontana. Materia Spazio Concetto.* Milan: Mursia, 1993.

Ambiente spaziale (Space Environment),
1967-81
fluorescent colours on wood, canvas,
Wood light, 300 x 500 x 300 cm
Teresita Rasini Fontana Donation, 1991

Günter Förg was born in Fuessen, Germany in 1952. Much of his work, which began in 1981, may be seen in terms of the modern tradition of monochrome painting and the quest for the absolute associated with paintings in a single colour. The point of Förg's work is the relationship between this absolute and the relativity of space. The artist uses a variety of expressive media, including painting (often applied directly to walls), and large photographs. Later he diversified into bas reliefs and sculptures – all in an attempt to open up his work to space on all fronts. This attempt involves the physical conquest of space and the simultaneous introduction of a virtual relationship between interior and exterior. Förg's installations vary according to the nature of the real space they occupy on each occasion, and the shifting relationship between the expressive media he uses. Mirrors are also used to alter perception. His photographs, which contain large reproductions of architecture in the European rationalist tradition, fulfill the function of alluding to external space. In other words, they describe what lies beyond the specific artistic environment yet inevitably defines that environment. The space Förg speaks of is not an abstraction but a living environment which art is invited to organise in a rational manner. The Förg work owned by the Castello de Rivoli consists of a panel of lead sheets fitted onto a wooden frame, whose surface is divided into three overlapping horizontal bands. The central band is covered with yellow and green paint; the other two remain untouched and exhibit the natural properties of the material used. Despite its simple layout, this sort of work denotes Förg's interest in a renewal of pictorial language through experiment. The intention is for the work to be seen as a relationship between itself and real space. Its experimental nature is evident in the choice of medium. The artist has abandoned canvas in favour of non-artistic materials such as fabric, aluminium, wood and glass.

The various materials are chosen on the basis of their intrinsic qualities of colour and thus the expressive possibilities permitted by their natural properties, particularly the way they react to environmental light. On this subject, the artist has stated: "Limit situations always stimulate me. For me, a square of material is a painting because it involves the resolution of certain problems of light". The painting owned by the Castello di Rivoli belongs to a cycle of similar works painted on lead and produced from 1986. All are untitled and identified by the simple name "Bleibilder". The problem of light in these works is apparently tackled by introducing a dialectic between backing and painting. The opacity of the lead absorbs the lights or reflects it very weakly. Yet light is allowed to flood into the composition by introducing bright colours in the painted section. The pictorial thread which runs through the "Bleibilder" cycle varies constantly due to an ever-changing relationship with the backing material. Sometimes the painting covers the entire backing. More frequently it leaves portions of varying size. Sometimes the material becomes visible below the layer of colour and damps its tones, preventing it from being seen to the full. On other occasions the colour emerges as victor and cancels out the dull lead colour to express itself in all its emotional richness. The painting examined here contains a particularly vivid yellow area of paint. A green patch shows through faintly in the centre. The paint bears evident gestural signs and these indications of previous artistic activity mark a further contrast with the two bands of lead. The lead does not simply represent not-light or watered down colour; it also stands as a symbol of pure objectivity when compared with the subjective nature of the painting. The metal belongs to another time frame, far removed from the phenomenological time frame of the subject. In other words, while the painting denotes relativity and a relationship with the here-and-now of time and space, the material denotes the absolute. One perceptive comment on these compositions (Corà, 1989) suggested that the various partitions between painting and untouched material act as fragments of a rhetoric, which may be used as a basis for interpreting what we see as part of a potentially infinite whole.

Selected Bibliography

Günther Förg. The Hague: Gemeente Museum, 1988. *Günther Förg, The Complete Editions 1974-1988*. Rotterdam: Museum Boymans van Beuningen, 1989. *Günther Förg*. Kassel: Museum Fridericianum, 1990. *Günther Förg*. Paris: Musée d'Art Moderne de la Ville de Paris, 1991. *Günther Förg. Druckgraphische Serien*. Bonn: Kunstmuseum, 1994.

Untitled (Bleibild), 1989
acrylic on lead and wood, 240 x 160 cm
Castello di Rivoli Purchase, 1990

Gilbert & George

Gilbert was born in Italy in 1943, while George was born in Devon, England, in 1942. The two artists met at St Martin's School of Art, London in 1967 and have lived and worked together ever since. They consider themselves a single artist divided into two people. Since the early Seventies, Gilbert and George have produced forms of art which tend to identify artistic work with everyday life. Their first works consisted of photographic books, engravings or cards sent to friends and acquaintances which contained writing and other information about their lives – and also about performances entitled *Living* or *Singing Sculptures*. In these works, the two artists stand on a table with their faces and hands covered with bronze or gold dust and sing old English songs to the accompaniment of robotic movements. They also use the term "sculptures" to describe big charcoal drawings (1970-1974) which portray the artists at various moments of their day, particularly while they are walking in public parks or relaxing in a pub. Their interests obviously centre on a desire to live and to be seen living. This desire represents not merely a new role for the artist but a new concept of individuality and thus of society. Their first photographic works date back to the beginning of the Seventies. These were initially envisaged as a set of visual fragments, first of all grouped freely on a wall and later, from about 1974 on, always arranged into squares or rectangles. The two artists consistently feature themselves as protagonists of these works. They can be seen as witnesses of an ambiguous account, which in these works always considers themes of existence and the human condition. The works were originally black and white, but in 1974 the artists began to colour certain sections red through the use of filters. For Gilbert & George, red is a symbol of blood and fire. Red is seen as a destructive force which is nevertheless responsible for regenerating life. They gradually added to their general symbolic use of colour in subsequent works, although the meaning of such symbols is never unequivocally stated in their works and remains open to the interpretation of the observer. Colour made a full appearance in the early Eighties, and at the same time their works became large or very large in size, though still broken up into rectangles. The rich use of colour and increasingly complex spatial relationships between images, which have reached the point of redundancy in more recent works, make one think of stained-glass windows in Gothic cathedrals with all their light and grandeur.

This religious reference is undoubtedly appropriate for Gilbert & George, who set out to involve their public in themes of a universal nature, such as life, death, love, hate sex and religion. The two artists now also show themselves with many other figures. These are invariably young men or adolescents, whom the two artists see as evocations of Christ, the young Man-God who sacrificed himself for humanity. The work *Doubles* of 1989 belongs to a cycle entitled "Cosmological Pictures" produced during the same year and exhibited between 1991 and 1993 in many European museums. All Gilbert & George's work may be defined as "cosmological" to a certain extent due to the themes to which it alludes, but in this cycle of twenty five works the two artists accentuate the pictorial use of their trademark photographs. Colour is applied to black and white photographs as though by turn of the century pictorial photographers. The image is built up by juxtaposing, combining and overlapping photographs within an extremely free spatial relationship. The end result bears no relationship to ordinary true-to-life photography. In this case, the full length portrait of the two artists is split twice in two directions: a split image of one stands behind an image of the other, in the sort of symmetrical relationship which often governs Gilbert & George's compositions. The meaning of their works is difficult to grasp unless specifically addressed to widely understood themes. In this case the "Doubles" referred to in the title (printed at the foot of the picture, as in all their works) are quite evident within the image we see. This arouses the sense of disquiet associated in our culture with the idea of a double or *doppelganger* identical to oneself. This theme is common in literature and the psychology of the unconscious. Gilbert & George, each flanked by the double of the other, express this fear in their shouting faces and the eerily bright colours of their faces and garments. Yet the tree blooming in the yellow background softens this sensation by conveying an idea of regeneration and regained peace.

Selected Bibliography

Gilbert & George 1968 to 1980. Eindhoven: Stedelijk Van Abbemuseum, 1980. *Gilbert & George*. New York: The Solomon R. Guggenheim Museum, 1985. Rutcliff, C. *Gilbert & George. The Complete Pictures 1971-1985*. London: Thames and Hudson, 1985. *Gilbert & George. The Charcoal on Paper Sculpture 1970-1974*. Bordeaux: Capc Musée d'Art Contemporain, 1986. Jahn, W. *The Art of Gilbert & George or An Aesthetic of Existence*. London: Thames and Hudson, 1989. *Gilbert & George. The Cosmological Pictures*. Rome: Palazzo delle Esposizioni, 1991. *Gilbert & George*. Lugano: Museo d'Arte Moderna, Electa, 1994.

Doubles, 1989
colour photographs, 338 x 355 cm
Castello di Rivoli Purchase, 1994

Per Kirkeby was born in Copenhagen in 1938. Before becoming an artist, he worked as a geologist; a profession that allowed him to experience nature in a manner both emotive and scientific. A geologist, says the artist, lives in direct contact with the earth and makes expeditions to mountainous areas (Kirkeby has even visited polar landscapes) to study the history of our planet in the rock strata. But then a geologist "returns home" and writes "a diary full of maps and diagrams, theories traced with a sharp pencil, written in a tent after a day spent wandering over the peaks of a great wasteland". This dual empathic and rational approach to nature is revealed in Kirkeby's paintings (although this is only one of his artistic achievements, because he is also a sculptor, poet, film maker and photographer). Kirkeby began to paint in 1964 and since that time his paintings have displayed great feeling and indicated a great range of gesture. Yet he never lacks a sense of the structure which binds his compositions together. The landscape in *Skumring* is built up out of swathes of colour which blend into one another. Yet each maintains its own identity and clearly states its function. The mass of dark layers on the left-hand side of the painting gives form to a strongly structured image, gloomy and solid as a mountain.

This mass is balanced on the right-hand side by a slender yet authoritative line which describes a similar shape. Down on the right, green splashes turn into white lines stretching out towards the line of the horizon. At the top right, a tangled mass of fluid, overlapping brush-strokes induces an atmospheric feeling of spatial depth. The resulting gentle blush in the background is reminiscent of the glowing colour of the sky at dawn. None of this is stated categorically in the painting; all is left to the intuition of the observer. Kirkeby's figures inhabit an ambiguous intermediate space. In his work, it is impossible to say whether formlessness is gathering the residues of stable form into itself or the formlessness is itself generating form. We cannot tell whether the image is celebrating a beginning or an end. The artist has said, "Geology is the doctrine of forces behind form, both destructive and constructive. And this means pure suppositions". Just as the geologist investigates a mountain with notes and diagrams, an observer may only decipher works of this kind through suppositions, in other words by endowing signs with an identificatory function. The structure of the work is nevertheless strongly expressed: Kirkeby's landscape is primeval, original, a place of strength. Yet the artist does not depict chaos or disordered urges. His expressive energy is shown at the point where it becomes language. Not form then, but formation: the artist is showing us the actual act of giving life to form.

Selected Bibliography

Per Kirkeby. Cologne: Museum Ludwig, 1985. *Per Kirkeby. Recent Painting & Sculpture*. London: Whitechapel Art Gallery, 1985. *Per Kirkeby. Skulpture und Druckgrafik*. Monchengladbach: Stadtisches Museum Abteiberg, 1986. *Per Kirkeby. Pinturas, esculturas, grabados y escritos*. Valencia: IVAM Centre del Carme, 1989. *Per Kirkeby 1964-1990*. Stockholm: Moderna Museet, 1990. Kirkeby, P. *Bravura*. Siracusa: Tema Celeste, 1991. *Per Kirkeby. Skulpturen*. Göppingen: Stadtische Galerie, 1992.

Skumring, 1983-84
oil on canvas, 250 x 200 cm
Castello di Rivoli Purchase, 1988

Born in Norfolk, Virginia in 1957, Annette Lemieux decided not to pursue her career as a painter at the beginning of the Eighties. Instead she directed her efforts into the reuse of existing images and objects, which she chooses and fits into new contexts and combinations in order to create unpredictable meanings. The artist favours images taken from illustrated magazines, publications and films produced during the Forties and Fifties, a period she considers particularly significant because it marks the origin of the American lifestyle and culture she focuses on (in a critical sense) in her work. For the same reasons her installations describe her own childhood memories or contain fragments of social history from her country, or the entire world. Her work suggests that interior life and external reality are not two opposing worlds but a single dimension. For the artist, this dimension is put to work in the name of her own specific social responsibility.

The work *Hobo Jungle* was completed by Annette Lemieux specially for her one-woman show held at the Castello di Rivoli in December 1992. The exhibition revolved around the theme of war and the breakdown this brings about in the lives of human beings. She took as her particular reference point the horrors of World War II, the Holocaust, and the Gulf War (the conflict between the United States, their European allies and Iraq) which aroused so much international public debate. All the works exhibited were made up out of documentary photographs or other existing images. These were chosen by the artist for their emblematic value and then enlarged and manipulated in various ways.

Hobo Jungle combines the general theme of war with the specific theme of the exhibition site. The photograph the American artist took as her starting point shows a room on the third floor of the Castello di Rivoli (the actual floor where Lemieux's exhibition was held) which was half destroyed by bombardment during World War II. The black and white photograph shows three soldiers armed with buckets looking for something among the remains of the roof, which lie strewn over the pavement. Certain elements have been added by Lemeiux to this dramatic reproduction of a real event to make the scene more ambiguous. The artist has applied different-sized cut-out circles of coloured fabric to the surface of the enlarged photograph. These are decorated with stars and other decorations and seem to be falling into the room through the hole in the roof. This simple addition interferes with the obvious original meaning of the image. Now it seems that the three soldiers are trying to collect the coloured spheres in their buckets and the atmosphere of the scene becomes strangely magical, or Fellinian as Trevor Fairbrother rightly noted in his introduction to Lemieux's exhibition. To complete the installation, the artist placed two cushions from an ancient armchair on the ground in front of the photograph. These are worn with use, torn and faded as though recovered from a bombardment. Their presence reinforces the ambiguous meaning presented by the title. The term *Hobo Jungle*, in other words a jungle inhabited by tramps, has little to do with war but a lot to do with the cruel reality experienced by the tramps and homeless who live in great cities and are engaged even now in a daily struggle for survival. The armchair cushions go beyond the historical reference to war contained in the photograph and refer to the way homeless people are forced to live, using all sorts of refuse from opulent society. The cushions are no longer signs of death but have now, like the coloured forms which rain down through the hole in the roof become signs of life and more specifically a will to live. Yet they serve to remind us again of the tragedy which still surrounds the lives of many today.

Selected Bibliography

Annette Lemieux. Kyoto: Art Random, Shoin, 1990. *Annette Lemieux*. Amsterdam: Stichting De Appel, 1991. *Annette Lemieux*. Rivoli: Castello di Rivoli, Charta, 1992. Meyer-Hermann, E. *Annette Lemieux*. Krefeld: Hans Esters, 1994. *Annette Lemieux: Time To Go*. Modena: Emilio Mazzoli, 1994.

Hobo Jungle, 1992
photograph, cloth, glue,
water-ink, resin on canvas,
canvas 214 x 316 x 4 cm;
pillows 20 x 74 x 59 cm; 20 x 48 x 51 cm
Gift of SIPEA s.r.l. Pubblicità, 1993

Sol
LeWitt

Sol LeWitt was born in Hartford, Connecticut, in 1928. In 1962, his artistic efforts began to be devoted to sculpture. His works were then made of wood and white canvas based on the form of a square. Since 1964, he has been making modular structures where the cube is used as the basic element for a virtually infinite series of combinations. Because the fundamental figure is defined by bars which contain an empty volume, we are made aware of the structural rules used to construct the figure. The artist's combinations are determined by arbitrary logic, but the rules, once stated, are rigorously respected. In 1967, LeWitt wrote his *Paragraphs on Conceptual Art:* a seminal text for this movement, in which the artist plays a leading role. Exponents of this movement see the idea as the all important action when producing art. The execution of the work itself is an act of peripheral importance and delegated to others, while the design stage is promoted to centre stage (drawings, diagrams, verbal notes). LeWitt began to create his *Wall Drawings* to fill the available environment during the late Sixties. In these works, simple elements (horizontal, vertical, diagonal and curved lines) are drawn on the wall and built up into complex works through a series of combinations and permutations. In more recent years, the artist has used ink and colour in the exhibition environment, whereas his sculptures have evolved into great white, irregular geometrical solids and cocrete block structures later.

The installation at the Castello de Rivoli consists of a heptagonal sculpture and a graphic "wall drawing" painted on the walls of room 4 of the museum. The work was designed specially for this room and recalls a similar work carried out by the artist for the exhibition "Arte e Arte" held at the museum in 1991. As in the previous work, the walls of the room are decorated with great rectangular shapes, produced by applying monochrome coats of different colours. The shapes are surrounded by a band of black paint and bear thick clusters of pencil marks scribbled on the surface.

The number of panels, seven in all, was conditioned by the available number of rectangular wall surfaces, taking into account the fact that doors are located on three of the walls, and two windows are situated on the fourth wall. Each wall drawing is mirrored in its "double", in other words, in each of the faces of the geometrical solid placed in the centre of the room. As always in the case of Sol LeWitt's work, the installation works through a juxtaposition of the basic linguistic elements of painting. The choice of colours is based on the three primary colours, red, yellow and blue (black is present in the chrome of the frames, white in the untouched wall sections). The other colours are produced by applying the main colours on top of one another, firstly the three possible pairs (red-yellow, red-blue and yellow-blue), and lastly all the colours. Graphite marks are added to build up grids and tangles on the surfaces. These add another basic element of artistic creation to the work – pencil line-drawing – and, above all, they render the process of perception dynamic. The spectator is invited to walk around the sculpture, observe, and take note of the different colours and the combinations generated. Yet LeWitt's installations do not stop at this act of observation by the spectator. The visitor is stimulated to become aware of the perceptive process he or she is experiencing. In this particular case, our perception of colour is put to the test by the interfering graphic signs on the painted surfaces and, above all, by environmental light. In some cases, the reflection of the light on the pencil signs prevents the underlying colour from being properly perceived. In other cases, the colour absorbs the light to emerge in all its brightness (this occurs with the walls and yellow sides). The autonomous properties of colour, the nature of light (frontal, radiant), the location of the painting in relation to the two windows, and the constantly changing position of the spectator are all factors which actively affect perception of the work. The size of the environment amplifies the effects of these factors, which reach the point where they cause incomplete perception or even visual distortion. The elements of the pictorial language – colour, surface and marking – are no longer purely stated, but caused to enter into an active relationship with one another and with the light and the physical movements of the observer. The object of the artist's work is now to capture this set of relationships in all their significant value.

Selected Bibliography

Sol LeWitt. Circle & Grids. Berne: Kunsthalle, 1972. *Sol LeWitt.* New York: The Museum of Modern Art, 1978. LeWitt, S. *Autobiography.* New York: Multiples Inc.; Boston: Torf, 1980. LeWitt, S. *Geometric Figures & Colors.* New York: Abrams, 1980. *Sol LeWitt Wall Drawings 1968-1984.* Amsterdam: Stedelijk Museum; Eindhoven: Van Abbemuseum; Hartford: Wadsworth Atheneum, 1984. *Sol LeWitt Prints.* Minneapolis: Walker Art Center, 1988. *Sol LeWitt Books.* Minneapolis: Minnesota Center for Book Arts, 1988. *Cube. A Cube Lighted from the Top, Four Sides, Four Corners and All Their Combinations.* New York: John Weber; Rome: Mario Pieroni; Cologne: Walther König, 1990. *Sol LeWitt Wall Drawings 1984-1992.* Berne: Kunsthalle; Andover: Addison Gallery of American Art, 1992. *Sol LeWitt Drawings 1958-1992.* The Hague: Gemeente Museum, 1992. *Sol LeWitt Structures 1962-1993.* Oxford: Museum of Modern Art, 1993.

Panels and Tower with Colours and Scribbles (All three colours and all their combinations), 1992
colour wash, graphite on wall and on wood
dimensions determined by the environment
Donation, 1993

Richard Long

Richard Long was born in Bristol in 1945 and is one of the most important and significant artists to have produced work within the last three decades. Since the end of the Sixties, Long has identified his brand of art through the medium of the elementary action of walking in the landscape. He then uses maps, text-works or photographs to record the walk itself, or changes he may have made along the way in the form of sculptures. These changes may involve the creation of simple geometric forms, considered fundamental in many visual cultures. For example, in 1967 Long crossed a field in such a way that his passing left a straight track in the grass. His decision to work with rural, un-industrialized landscapes such as the countryside of South-West England, the mountains of India and the Himalayas, African deserts and high planes in Bolivia operates partly as a criticism levelled at the separation between nature and culture on which our civilisation is based.

Some of Long's best-known works are now seen as representative of an entire period of artistic movements. They include the great stone circles of which his work *Romulus Circle* (1994) is a recent example. The circle (and also the spiral which he uses in other cases) represents a geometric shape produced by means of an act which can be seen as intellectual yet is rooted in the organic world and not distanced from this world. These characteristics are illustrated more clearly when the works are created in natural environments where the artist uses the materials of the chosen stopping places along his walks. Here rational design is literally juxtaposed with an organic background. The artist documents such formal acts by taking photographs. Yet the relationship Long creates between nature and culture is no less striking when the work is exhibited in places designed for the display of art. In these cases, the stones used are usually obtained from the area where the exhibition site is based. Long has produced another important set of works by forming circles out of hand-printed mud, or throwing streams of muddy water directly onto walls or the ground. The work *Waterline* is reminiscent of this set of works but differs significantly from them in using acrylic paint instead of "natural" mud for the purpose of practicality and permanence. Richard Long produced an uninterrupted pictorial mark on a black strip twenty-two metres in length by letting white acrylic colour fall onto the strip from above. The relationship between rational design and the organic is complementary.

Splashes of mud on walls do not suggest chaos or lack of form, but remind us that the origins of language and form lie in an organic drive. When an artist creates a formal event which is not entirely under his control, his gesture is impulsive and immediate. Yet language still results from that event. In *Waterline*, we see language at work at the time of its conception, when it is closely linked to impulse. At this point, this language is expressed not as form but as the potential for becoming form. The white paint on the black surface (black and white are two colours favoured by the artist) are an evident reference to the dripping technique Jackson Pollock and other abstract expressionist painters used to apply paint to the canvas. Direct and simple physicality is important for long, however, he shows no signs of the intense drama displayed by the great American painter. Here we see no excitement or emotional passion but simply a primary biological rhythm: that of a body moving along a long section of black cloth material and leaving a trail of white paint behind to mark a pure vital presence captured in the act of becoming significant. This presence is simply emphasised by the unusually large dimensions of the "canvas" and the fact that it is positioned on the ground, where the event took place. This positioning allows the spectator to experience the time, space, rhythm and energy, in other words the conditions which gave life to the formal act of pouring a water line.

Romulus Circle, 1994
Rome tufa, diam. 540 cm
Gift of Friends of Castello di Rivoli
and SIPEA s.r.l. Pubblicità, 1994

Selected Bibliography

Richard Long. Eindhoven: Stedelijk Van Abbemuseum, 1979. *Richard Long*. New York: The Solomon R. Guggenheim Museum, 1986. *Richard Long. Walking in Circles*. London: Hayward Gallery, 1991. *Richard Long. River to River*. Paris: Musée d'Art Moderne de la Ville de Paris, 1993. *Richard Long*. Roma: Palazzo delle Esposizioni, Electa, 1994.

Waterline, 1989
acrylic on vinyl, 200 x 2000 cm
Gift of Lisa and Tucci Russo, 1991

Luigi
Mainolfi

Luigi Mainolfi was born in Rotondi (Avellino) in 1948. At the end of the Seventies, he made a name for himself in Italy as one of the artists whose work was devoted to exploring new forms of pictorial and sculpting figuration linked in various ways to the cultural tradition of Italy.

Mainolfi also developed his own consistent personal language. He used this from the outset to produce sculptures made out of natural materials such as clay, plaster, wood, pumice and bronze castings. Mainolfi uses sculpture to evoke the popular culture from which he himself originates, combining such evocations with a cultural memory of his life as an artist.

The work *Colonna di Rivoli* dates from 1987-1988. This long, slender terracotta column grows out of the floor of the room where it is located and stretches up to the ceiling. It forms part of a thematic cycle which includes other similar works adapted to fit the height of the environment where the work is located. This feature therefore forms a continual strand running through his work, and also refers back to Brancusi's *Colonna infinita*. The artist has stamped an unbroken series of small figures alongside one another on the stem of the column. These represent small houses in a vertical city, a theme also developed by Mainolfi in other works.

The image of this town is fairy-tale and archaic at the same time, as always in the visual repertoire of this artist. Mainolfi has been engaged in building up his own imaginative world for some time, and these two traits have become virtually his hallmark. All his activities are aimed at bringing the act of sculpting back to its origins in the earth. The earth (or literally the clay in this particular case) is an element which may be manipulated and shaped with much greater immediacy than other more solid materials. Clay is a poor material, used to make household utensils in primitive communities, and retains links with popular forms of expression. The artist seeks to tie himself to these roots by producing figures reminiscent of places and moments which typify the traditions of his native earth, Campania. This reference is naturally transfigured in Mainolfi's personal poetic form of artistic expression. Here it involves the creation of Totemic ancestral images, based on the fantastic inventions of a zoomorphic or phytomorphic universe (this column looks like a tree trunk, for example) where different forms of nature are blended together with Arcadian feeling. These references to the archaic do not reflect real anthropological research but are a poetic development designed to create something like the archetypal figures of our collective unconscious. The *Colonna di Rivoli* forms part of this parallel, organic universe. The small emblems of a wholly made-up civilisation it bears are also rooted in contemporary culture because, lest we forget, the column also contributes to the foundation of contemporary art.

Selected Bibliography

Luigi Mainolfi. Il gioco delle palle. Turin: Edizioni Tucci Russo, 1985. *Luigi Mainolfi. La pelle del mondo è ruvida*. Aosta: Tour Fromage, Fabbri, 1987. *Luigi Mainolfi. Sculture*. Milan: Mazzotta, 1987. Beatrice, L. and Gualdoni, F. (edited by), *Mainolfi*. Ravenna: Essegi Editrice, 1993. *Luigi Mainolfi*. Bologna: Galleria Civica d'Arte Moderna, 1994.

Colonna di Rivoli (Rivoli Column), 1987-88
terracotta, h. 630 cm, diam. 15 cm
Gift of Antonio Tucci Russo and
Luigi Mainolfi, 1994

An engineering graduate and music lover, Fausto Melotti was born in Rovereto (Trento) in 1901 and died in Milan in 1986. In the Thirties, he exhibited at the Galleria del Milione in Milan. This site was then the centre of Italian abstract art, which set itself up in opposition to the figurative manner imposed by the imperious artistic "call to order." Melotti's work consists of plaster sculptures (instead of more traditional, canonic marble and bronze work), which are almost two-dimensional as opposed to standard well-rounded works or constructed in low relief around a harmonic series of peaks and troughs. The artist's intention was to create an art which appeals to the intellect rather than the senses. Despite this, he never devoted himself to rigorously geometric art, and still included figurative elements in his ceramic or clay constructions. These materials were his favoured materials during the Forties and Fifties. Starting in the Sixties, he also worked with metals (brass, steel and copper) to make aerial, wire-like three-dimensional constructions in which he emphasised the lightness of the work by adding coloured or painted fabrics. Melotti worked on two levels in all his creations, which achieved monumental size at the end of his life: on the one hand he created allusive, highly fantastic, almost fairy-tale forms while on the other hand the pure visual rhythms he produced are totally abstract and self-evident in construction. His work *Confronto* (Comparison) is a typical example of the type of sculptural language adopted by Fausto Melotti from the Sixties onward, and represents his decision to work with metals.

The decision to use metal does not alter the basic premises of Melotti's sculpture, which was expressed with the same lucidity as his earlier work. His non-figurative work is based on the creation of a pure series of peaks and troughs, where peaks prevail over the troughs and the "body" of the sculpted work. The rhythm the sculpture produces in space is born of a free, non-a priori use of geometry, here seen as a repertoire of signs which do not represent reality, but transfigure it (to use a term dear to the artist) into symbols. Geometry, always evidently rooted in the organic in Melotti's work, reflects abstract equivalents of real phenomena and converts them into pure forms and pure relationships between forms. Melotti treats his sculpture as a visual score: the equivalent of a musical phrase constructed according to the rules of counterpoint. His metal sculptures are most suitable for this treatment because the material of which they are made is so specific. This is apparent in the case of *Confronto*. Almost completely bodiless, the sculpture is made up of lines, wires and vibrating elements juxtaposed in a dynamic relationship. The comparison mentioned in the work's title is suggested by the different directions assumed by the three steel lines which make up the work. Two arrow-shaped lines point downwards, while a third line leads upward. Its flight is halted by a disk positioned on the top, and opposed by the horizontal position of three intersecting segments. These different movements are brought into harmony by the fact that all the linear segments share a common characteristic, a curved shape, and no straight lines are present (except for the two segments which support the middle line and anchor it to the base). The closed figure of the disk reflects the various degrees of curvature exhibited by the lines. The work is harmonious because each visual element needs the other elements in order to succeed. No part of the sculpture is superfluous, because each part portrays the same dynamic tension.

Selected Bibliography

Melotti. Turin: Galleria Civica d'Arte Moderna, 1972. *Melotti*. Milan: Palazzo Reale, Electa, 1979. *Melotti*. Florence: Forte di Belvedere, Electa, 1981. *Melotti*. Rome: Galleria Nazionale d'Arte Moderna, 1983. *Melotti*. Venice: Gallerie dell'Accademia, 1985. *Melotti. Opere 1954-1986*. Sartirana: Castello di Sartirana, 1986. *Fausto Melotti, l'acrobata invisibile*, Milan: Padiglione d'Arte Contemporanea, Mazzotta, 1987. *Fausto Melotti*. Venice: Palazzo Fortuny, Electa, 1990. Celant, G. (edited by), *Fausto Melotti. Catalogue raisonné*. Milan: Electa, 1994.

Confronto (Confrontation), 1972
steel, 290 x 200 x 63 cm
Gift of Cristina and Marta Melotti, 1991

Mario *Merz*

Born in Milan in 1925, Mario Merz became a self-taught painter after abandoning his studies. He started out in 1953 as an expressionist painter, but later turned to *Informel*. He exhibited at the first "Arte Povera" shows from 1967 onward sand became one of the leading lights of this movement. His work is based on experiments with non-artistic, often natural materials, and common objects struck by beams of neon light, which he uses to create installations that often involve the environment. The artist treats these beams of light in the same way as the arrows he originally used. In his work, they serve as images of the penetrative energy within all material. Since 1968, his work has centred around the igloo structure, which he sees as a primary and archetypal construction. He makes igloos out of a range of materials, including earth stones, glass fragments and wooden strips. In 1970 he began the nume-

rical progression works entitled Fibonacci. This was the pseudonym of Leonardo da Pisa, the mathematician who wrote "Liber Abaci" in 1202. This arithmetic progression summarised the growth processes of the organic world, such as the way rabbits breed, the arrangement of veins on a leaf or the number of spirals in a snail shell. This progression begins with one, and each successive number is calculated by adding the two previous numbers together. Merz adopts this progression as an emblem of the proliferative energy inherent in nature. He displays it by arranging neon numbers on his works or in a wide array of environments, such as, for example, the outside walls of the "Manica Lunga" at the Castello di Rivoli. In 1976, he began to produce spiral figures, another forceful emblem, often out of iron pipes combined with plates of glass or other material. At the end of the Seventies, he returned to a form of figuration related to the work he produced during his earliest days as a painter. He drew big images of primitive, archaic-looking animals on unbacked canvases which were then used as part of his installations. In formal terms, an igloo goes beyond the two-dimensional idea of a painting, which is normally fixed on a gallery wall and stands for the conquest of an absolute structure ("Thus the idea of an igloo as an idea of absolute space in itself: it is not modelled, it is a hemisphere resting on the ground".) but is not an a priori structure. Its origins are, on the contrary, organic: Merz sets out to explore a form of spatialism which is in contrast to Euclidean rationalisation, a form of geometry which transcends phenomenological data. In the world of phenomena, space is curved and a right angle is an a priori abstraction. An igloo is such a phenomenon. It is curved in a way our eye prevents us from perceiving, and assumes strong anthro-pological significance in Merz's work. The geometry thus becomes a scheme which enfolds in its shape all the "being in the world" inherent in its subject. The igloo primarily conveys the idea of home, which is also closely linked to a non-conflictual vision of the relationship between man and nature: a relationship which represents a radical departure from our usual way of relating to reality. Primitive man, the nomad, the eskimo tribe: Merz constructs a short-circuit between the space and time which make up our contemporary way of "being in the world". An igloo is a construction: the artist makes a frame out of steel piping and covers the structure with materials which belong to nature or suggest a primitive use: earth, stone slabs and glass fragments (sack-cloth in the case of *Tenda di Gheddafi* (Gheddafi's Tent). In this way, the igloo lives in communion with the material out of which it is made, and the home is given form by the materials present in the environment where the work is located. The igloo is seen as linked organically to the earth, part of the earth risen up, like a table – another form which often occurs in Merz's work. This form of construction goes against all the premisses of architecture. No stable connections connect one part of the igloo to another. Everything is simply supported or fastened with metal clips, as if the whole construction were defined but not finalised. The work is provisional, like the home of a nomad, or a tent in the desert, just as the title of the work in Castello di Rivoli suggests. Merz uses the figure of the igloo as an explicit tirade against the alienation experienced in towns and cities. An igloo is constructed in accordance with rules which also govern growth in nature. The canvas of *Tenda di Gheddafi* depicts painted emblems of these rules, represented by upturned cones. Cones with stalks were first used by Merz back in 1967 (a wooden cone with a plexiglass stalk fitted into a paralleliped of the same material) and are associated with the image of a spear or arrow. An upturned cone is thus a dynamic figure which describes a circular movement of penetration. (In more recent years, this symbol may be found associated with the image of a tree, for example in the painting *Foresta di conifere* [Coniferous Forest] from 1982). This same movement also gives us the spiral, another great symbolic theme constantly addressed by Merz. The artist states on this subject: "A true spiral is described when one spins around on one's own axis, just as dervishes do". The spiral moves from the middle outwards and serves as an emblem for the asymmetry (way out of oneself) which governs nature. A spiral is generated by a cone which in turn takes its form from the rotation of a triangle. Merz dwells on these dynamic figures because he considers them archetypes capable of synthesizing all images of nature. In other words, the actual idea of a living being is captured in all its primal form.

Fibonacci, 1976-90
neon lights, dimension determined
by the environment
Donation, 1990

Selected Bibliography

Mario Merz. Milan: Mazzotta, 1983. *Merz, M. Voglio fare subito un libro*. Aarau; Frankfurt am Main; Salzburg: Verlag Saverländer, 1985. *Mario Merz*. Zurich: Kunsthaus, 1985. *Merz, M. Voglio fare subito un libro*. Florence: Hopefulmonster, 1987. *Mario Merz*. New York: The Solomon R. Guggenheim Museum, 1989. *Mario Merz at Moca*. Los Angeles: The Museum of Contemporary Art, 1989. *Mario Merz. Terra elevata o la storia del disegno*. Rivoli: Castello di Rivoli, 1990. *Mario Merz*. Prato: Centro per l'Arte Contemporanea Luigi Pecci, Hopefulmonster, 1990. *Mario Merz*. Barcelona: Fundació Antoni Tàpies, 1993. *Mario Merz*. Amsterdam: Stedelijk Museum, 1994.

Igloo (Tenda di Gheddafi)
(Igloo - Gheddafi's Tent), 1988
iron tubes, acrylic on jute canvas,
240 x 500 x 500 cm
Castello di Rivoli Purchase, 1987

At the end of the Sixties, Marisa Merz adopted a non-traditional approach to the traditional and supposedly feminine activity of knitting. The artist used copper wire to produce square or triangular shapes, which she used to construct fragile structures installed in open spaces such as a beach, or groups of figures arranged on the wall. She also adopted natural materials or materials capable of changing state, such as wax or salt, to produce installations which alluded to the intimate space of everyday life. She also added furnishing elements with the aim of transfiguring the environment into a metaphorical space for artistic creation. From the beginning of the Eighties, the artist devoted much time to portraits, sometimes obviously self-portraits. These are executed both as pencil or ink drawings and as clay heads dried without firing and painted. The work owned by the Castello di Rivoli also conveys a sense of transfiguration and openness. The work is reminiscent of tradition, in this case the artistic tradition of portrait painting, but the codes have been changed.

A former exponent of "Arte Povera", Marisa Merz uses non-artistic principles in her work to give art a brand new identity. The colour and graphic design of her self-portrait are mainly blue and fully recognisable in their intent. The marks are cursive and greatly foreshortened. The colour does not respect natural canons and the figure looks hieratic and vaguely archaic because it retains only a few recognisable features. The brush-strokes and colour denote an emotional awakening which makes the image eery and prompts a sense of disquiet. This eeriness is accentuated by the layout of the work, in other words by the contribution of elements which "present" the portrait but nevertheless form an integral part of the work. The sheet bearing the image is framed and rests upon a structure similar to a console in order to suggest a domestic, intimate environment. The console actually forms part of a metal rack and the "frame" is a simple wooden container placed in front of the drawing. A sheet of glass is then rested over the frame. This sketchily evoked environment is transfigured into another dimension: even the conventional manner of presenting the work has been adopted only to be altered. None of the parts are fastened to any of the other parts, for example. Everything is simply propped together in an apparently improvised way. Furthermore, the objects used do not belong to art, but to life, and do not display characteristics which could be defined as aesthetic. Yet a new aesthetic sense is revealed in the combination of these elements: an apparent wish to reveal the artistic soul in the most common materials.

Selected Bibliography

Marisa Merz. Paris: Musée national d'art moderne Centre Georges Pompidou, 1994.

Senza titolo (Untitled), 1985
mixed media on cardboard, glass, wood and
iron, 284 x 150 x 50 cm
Castello di Rivoli Purchase, 1991

Liliana Moro was born in Milan in 1961 and became one of the founders of Spazio on Via Lazzaro Palazzi in Milan, an exhibition site self-managed by a group of artists. She is also one of the editors of the review "Tiracorrendo." Her first one-woman exhibition was held in 1990. Liliana Moro deals with the problematic relationship between subjective identity and the conditioning to which this identity is subjected by a wide range of behaviourial control devices that form part of our ideology and everyday life. Thus the artist confronts the stereotypes which govern the merchandising of sexuality, for example by taking her work to a Parisian peep-show or exhibiting pornographic inflatable dolls as in the case of "Documenta IX" in Kassel in 1992. She also deals with stereotypes which idealise the world of childhood, which is recalled by the artist through the use of cardboard dolls and other toys. Similar coercive structures are recognisable in language, when the artist reads the extremely detailed acting instructions written by Samuel Beckett for "Happy Days" in an audio-installation. These structures are contrasted with an emotional language which establishes loss as a strategy for resisting homogeneity.

The work *Aristocratica* (Aristocratic) dating from 1993 is a photographic development of a previous video work and consists of three short sequences centering on the idea of a self-portrait. The photograph repeats the image shown on the video, in other words the immobile face of the artist viewed in three-quarter profile without turning her eyes to the observer. The artist wears a sort of cap and a carnival-like pig's snout as if wishing to hide part of her features by adopting a self-denigrating disguise. The work therefore proposes a presence which immediately tends to absent itself, making identification impossible. This portrait does not explain itself by trying to establish a relationship with the observer. This is emphasised by the title, which in itself conjures up an idea of aloofness and detachment.

Selected Bibliography

Migrateurs. Paris: Musée d'Art Moderne de la Ville de Paris, 1993. *Torno subito*. Milan: Studio Casoli, 1994.

Aristocratica (Aristocratic), 1994
colour photograph, 155 x 200 cm
Given anonymously, 1994

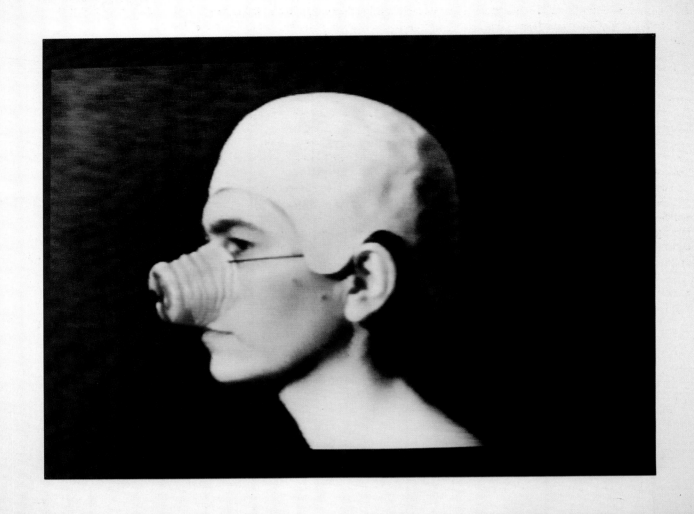

Matt Mullican was born in Santa Monica, California in 1951 and has always adopted various expressive means in his work. The range of forms he adopts includes performance, environmental installation, open-air sculpture and computer graphics. Since the mid-Seventies, he has worked within the field of performance art, which he carries out under hypnosis in order to experience states of regression or personality changes. Mind-body dualism is ever-present in the work of Mullican. He has built up an entire system of dualist thought he defines as "cosmology." Mullican's work consists of strongly synthetic images, which are taken directly from the everyday urban signs we find on the street, in public offices and in airports. The artist considers these an integral part of life for us all. He sees such signs first and foremost as an unconscious expression of a specific socio-cultural community. These symbols may be adopted just as they are, modified, or invented. The artist then associates them arbitrarily with meanings he selects himself. He applies meanings to all manner of media, ranging from a printed poster to a banner, granite slab, tapestry or drawing on paper. The symbols are classified into thematic groups and reappear throughout the artist's work in accordance with an underlying pattern of "cosmology". The symbols change also in colour according to their function. The first and lowest level concerns the physical world and is marked by the colour green. This is followed by the world of human beings and their social organisations, defined by the colour blue. A third yellow level describes artistic creation. Black and white, on the other hand, represent the abstraction of language. The final level, red, infers purely spiritual values. This final state was achieved in a total of twelve figures in 1984 and represents the peak of Mullican's output: an entire system of signs which denote the elevation of the material state of existence to a more sublime state. This can also be identified as an elevation from a relative object to a universal concept. Spirituality is expressed by the symbols of heaven, hell, death and life, pre-natal existence and subjectivity, fate, the world and its elements, and God. Spirituality is not envisaged as separate and incumbent on human beings, but rather as an expression of our interior energy.

The work *Senza Titolo* (Untitled) is an example of Mullican's idea of cosmology. An image on a blue background alludes to the organisation of community life by recalling the idea of an architectural structure. This and other symbols used by Mullican crop up again and again in his work, either alone or in groups, and reproduced on various types of material. Such juxtapositions give life to unexpected combinations of meaning, particularly when used in the large and complex installations the artist has produced recently. This nylon work takes on the appearance of a banner, an element often adopted by the artist because it recalls the archaic yet constantly revitalised social function (flags, streamers, etc.) of communicating particular messages to the community. Mullican often exhibits his banners in the open air in order to involve a wider public than normally benefits from seeing works of art.

Selected Bibliography

Mullican. Bath: Artside Gallery, 1988.
Matt Mullican. The MIT Project.
Cambridge: MIT List Visual Art Center, 1990. *Mullican: Die Struktur des Historischen*. Hannover: Sprengel Museum, 1991. *Matt Mullican, Works 1972-1992*.
Cologne: Walther König, 1993.

Senza titolo (edificio)
(Untitled - Building), 1991
nylon,
333 x 333 cm
Gift of Rivetti Collection, 1992

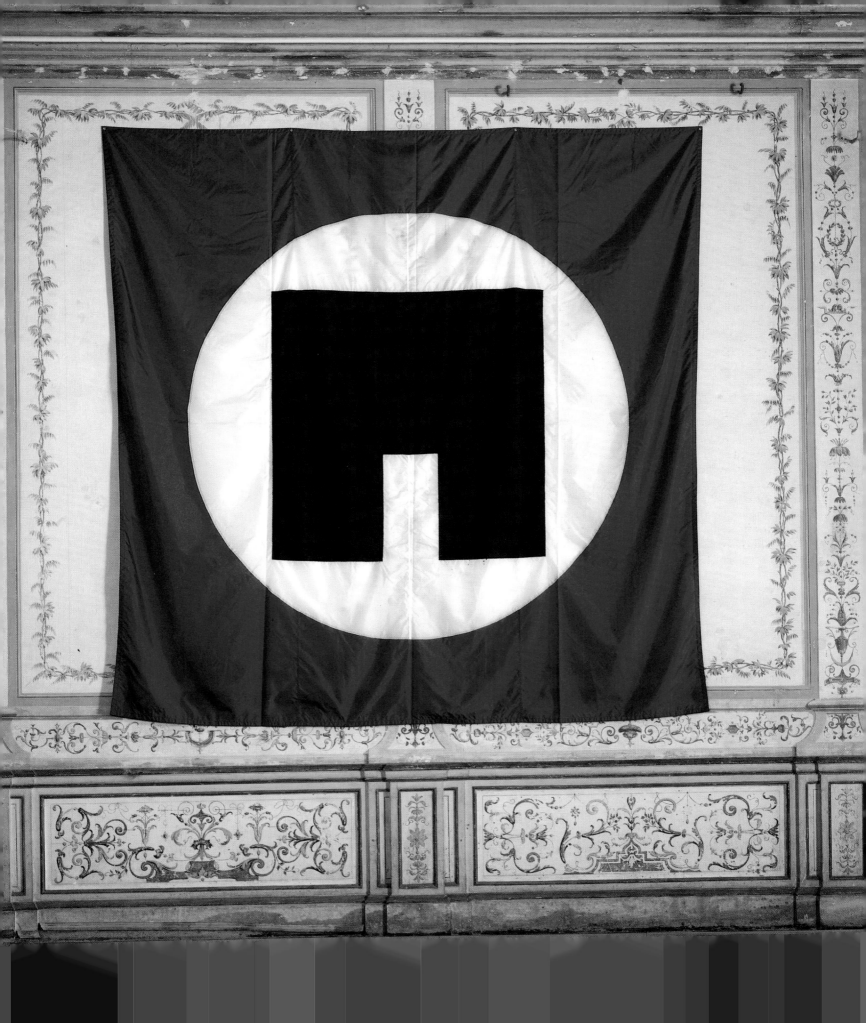

Maria *Nordman*

Born in Goerlitz, Silesia, Germany and living in Los Angeles and in the cities of her work, Maria Nordman's work began in 1967 on the streets of Los Angeles, *in places where people live and work* (De Sculptura. *Works in the City*, 1986). Leaving the confines of a pre-defined location during the first decade of work, and continuing with many realizations in cities into the present, *the work begins where there are no labels, or predisposed conditions, in rooms, parks, and streets of cities* (Nordman, 1967). The artist sees such spaces as dimensions to be experienced by the visitors in relation to each other, and works exclusively with natural light.

The material and resources are unlimited in this work; for example they can be made with the sun, water, or bronze, plaster, wood. The material chosen relates to the city where the work is located and the people with and for whom the work is made, rather than simply using material in an arbitrary manner. In the context of this work the coordinates refer to interpersonal conditions that could arise between the visitors considered as joint-constructors of the work itself. This work is further set apart from any predisposed labels or prefixed terms, such as electric lighting produced by repetitive sources. Maria Nordman also works in open structures which allude to everyday experience; these include seats and tables the public may or may not decide to use, or which refer to the idea of living area in the context of sculpture. This is exemplified by the fact that the works are means of working in different cultures tangentially.

Incontro tra la Dora e il Po (*Encounter of the Dora and the Po*) (1985) consists of two different works. One is set up inside a room selected by the artist within the Castello di Rivoli, and the other is located on a terrace adjacent to the outside building. The work is in part an homage to the architect Filippo Juvarra, using the Castello's corner stones to change our understanding of the term. These stones are joined at right angles to form a rectangle, which seems to reflect the castle corners. This theme is borrowed by Nordman and used as a basic constructive element of architecture (at least of western architecture). It is treated almost as an archetype.

Inside room 9 on the first floor of the castle the artist has built a constructional archetype, a great wooden room, with each outer wall painted in a different colour (red, black, blue and green). Access is through the four corners: Nordman has used double doors to make the construction habitable in an unorthodox way, which contradicts the basic rules of traditional architecture. As the artist states, *this room is precisely situated in relation to incoming sunlight from the adjacent rooms, from the terrace door and window of the room surrounding it.*

The corner or meeting point between two walls does not delimit here a closed room but forms a mobile element which can be opened. The artist uses this type of opening partly as a reference to the image of the winged figures of the eigtheen-century painting which decorates the ceiling of the room together with other figures. Once inside the room, the only light available to guide the visitor comes from the outside through four double doors. With the doors closed the light enters from the four directions in constantly changing intensities. The lack of other light sources accentuates the sensation of detachment from perceptive stimul operating on the outside and creates a changing dimension. As Nordman says, the quality of the room depends on whether another person enters the room while one person is inside. Each person will change the room in an individual way. The nature of the relationship between interior and exterior is paradoxical: the construction encloses an area but is in turn situated within a room, whereas its counterpart on the terrace is out in the open air but still within the building. These are not walls but possibly seats, made out of some stones used for the castle exterior and built on the corners of a virtual rectangle. Its exterior dimensions are identical to those of the construction inside the museum room. Nordman has made another archetype of living space for the outdoors, a seat. This concept takes the form of four identical corner elements which produce the idea of dialogue and thus of meeting, as is stated in the title of the work. The uncut marble also evokes the image of landscape, rivers and nature from which these elements are taken. The theme of a meeting is also reinforced by the figure of a cross, in other words lines intersecting at a point. These diagonals joint the opposing corners of an ideal rectangle, and are reflected in turn by the light seen through the doors jambs in the construction.

Selected Bibliography

Maria Nordman. Working Notes. Otterlo: Rijksmuseum Kröller-Müller, 1980. *Nordman, M. De Sculptura. Works in the City*. Munich: Schirmer-Mosel, 1986. *Nordman, M. De Civitate*. Lyons: Musée Saint Pierre Art Contemporain, 1987. *Nordman, M. Cité/ Sculpture*. Nice: Villa Arson Centre National d'Art Contemporain, 1989. Nordman, *M. De Musica. New Conjunct City Proposals*. Münster: Westfalischer Landesmuseum; Luzern: Kunstmuseum; New York: Public Art Fund Inc.; New York: DIA Center for the Arts; Hamburg: Kulturbehoerde; Rennes, FRAC Bretagne, 1991.

Incontro tra la Dora e il Po
(*Encounter of the Dora and the Po*), 1985
varnish on wood, marble; wood 261 x 251 x
400 cm; marble 48 x 251 x 400 cm
Castello di Rivoli Purchase, 1994

Claes Oldenburg was born in Stockholm in 1929. He grew up in Chicago and later became a naturalized American citizen. He has lived in New York since 1956. His initial interest was in the all-consuming communicative form of the "Neo Dada". In 1959, he turned to the contemporary urban environment and its subjects, which he reproduced in cardboard, papier maché and painted plaster. His style was deliberately coarse and intended as an ironic comment on the lifestyle of the masses and works of art in a traditional sense. He used a similar approach, midway between parody and sociological documentation, to construct environmental installations such as *The Street* (1960) or *The Store* (1962). At the beginning of the Sixties, he became one of the leading lights of the American Pop Art movement as a result of these and later works. The latter reproduced everyday objects on a grand scale and made use of incongruous materials to disquieting effect. Examples of such works were his famous soft sculptures, such as ice lollies made out of fake fur.

He also made items of furniture such as washbasins, baths, tools and typewriters out of polyurethane and vinyl. These works were so soft that they flopped down from the walls and became almost unrecognisable. From the mid Sixties, he produced monumental sculptures designed for public spaces (*Lipstick*) (1969). The size of these works was designed to emphasise the most banal features of contemporary life and American one in particular. Items depicted included clothes pegs and baseball bats.

Coosje van Bruggen is a contemporary art historian and former curator of the Stedelijk Museum of Amsterdam. She is also the author of monographs on such artists as Bruce Nauman (1988) and John Baldessari (1990). Since the Seventies, Oldenburg and van Bruggen have designed and constructed many works on a monumental scale. The monumental nature of these works emphasises a wish to involve the public. These artists are thus prompted to emerge from the shell of art galleries and museums to engage the public in a more direct manner. They employ a variety of approaches, which emerge during the course of all their activities. The work on show at the Castello di Rivoli is distinctive because it incorporates two projects. The piece was made for the Triennale in Milan in 1988, for the contribution to Art in Public Places of Miami, Florida. The model on the table is a model of a fountain by Oldenburg and van Bruggen, located in the city of Miami *entitled Dropped Bowl Scattered Slices and Peels*, inaugurated in March 1990. This installation effectively displays the artists' playfully critical intent, which is directed at the mores of everyday life and conventions which govern the presentation of works of art in museum spaces. A broken bowl with orange peels is a model of the fountain built in the City of Miami (1990), while the broken plate with scrambled eggs is a design for a work to be placed in a dining-room. Fractures and fragments floating in space: nothing less than an appraisal of the theme of catastrophe is employed to describe incredibly banal events. The amplification of such events to monumental scale makes them less recognisable and converts them into alarming images. A similar sense of alarm is raised by the act of combining these two pieces in the form of new installation. Fusion of the two works provides the setting for a sort of primeval upheaval: the fragmented bowl is positioned on a table within a room, while the wooden frame is left exposed and lifted. The frame's perilous position gives the installation a dynamic sense of spatial disorientation. The spectator finds himself at odds with the usual coordinates according to which works of art are installed in museum rooms.

Selected Bibliography

Claes Oldenburg. New York: The Museum of Modern Art, 1969. *Oldenburg, C. The Haunted House*. Krefeld: Hans Esters, 1987. Celant, G. *A Bottle of Notes. Claes Oldenburg, Coosje van Bruggen*, Sunderland: Northern Centre for Contemporary Art; Leeds: The Henry Moore Centre for Study of Sculpture, Leeds City Art Galleries; London: The Serpentine Gallery; Swansea: The Glynn Vivian Art Gallery; Valencia: IVAM Centre Julio Gonzales, 1988. Oldenburg, C. and Van Bruggen, C. *Nur Ein Auderer Raum*. Frankfurt am Main: Museum für Moderne Kunst, 1991. *Claes Oldenburg. Multiples in Retrospect 1964-1980*. New York: Rizzoli International, 1991. *Claes Oldenburg*. New York: Pace Gallery, 1992. Oldenburg, C. and van Bruggen, C. *Large Scale Projects*. New York: Monacelli Press, 1994.

Project for Walls of a Dining Room in Form of a Broken Plate with Scrambled Eggs, with Fabrication Model of the Dropped Bowl Fountain, 1987
aluminium, steel, wood, resin and polystyrene, 300 x 466.5 x 555 cm
Long-term loan of the artists

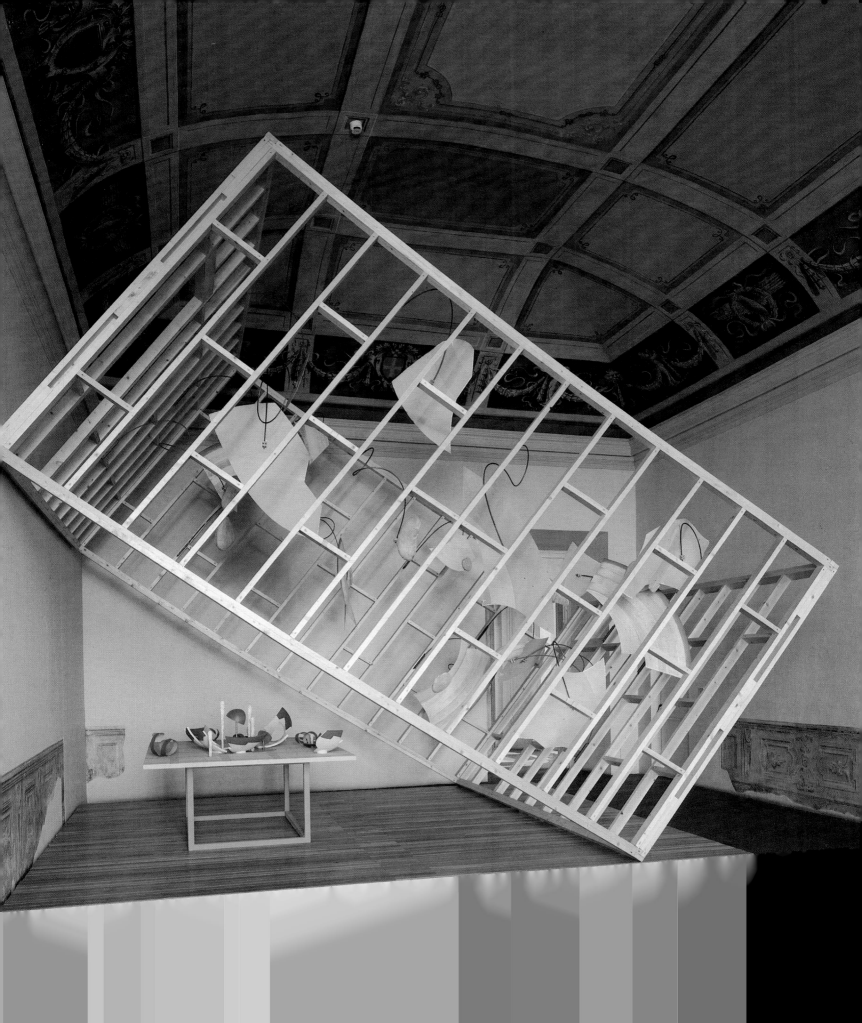

Giulio Paolini was born in Genoa in 1940, and has worked as an artist since 1960. In that year, he produced works such as *Disegno geometrico* (Geometric design), a canvas with inked squares on its surface. This was an analysis of the tools and environment of the artist, and such analysis emerges as a common theme throughout all Paolini's work. It is manifested through his exhibition of the material bases of painting (the canvas and frame, the paint-pot, the palette) as much as through his investigation of exhibition space and the artist as a manipulator of language. The investigation also stretches back into the past, to examine the functions of art throughout the course of its history: *Giovane che guarda Lorenzo Lotto* (*Young man looking at Lorenzo Lotto*) (1967) triggered a series of references which the artist incorporated in his work both through photographic reproductions and by making casts of classic statues. By the end of the Seventies, this investigation took the form of complex installations, almost theatrical in nature, where canvasses, drawings, casts, reproductions and everyday objects were used to prompt reflection on classic art as a fullness of meaning that we may no longer enjoy today except in fragments. Classicism thus becomes a great metaphor for today, something able to suggest the purpose and role of a work of art and its creator. The reference indicates an awareness that this role is fulfilled within a cultural environment whose specificity (linguistic and ideological) and content require examination. The installation in the Castello di Rivoli forms part of a cycle of works with the same title. These are all made up of similar materials, but the number of elements exhibited changes. Begun in 1981, the work began with a figure entitled *Labirinto* (Labyrinth), scratched on a pillar in the house known as "Casa del Poeta" (Poet's house) or "Casa di Lucrezio" (Lucretio's house) in Pompei. This mythical place depicted in effigy on a rural house and then buried by a catastrophic eruption prompted Paolini to produce several other "sites" (installations) which evoke the two "original" sites. He always evokes "originality" in the same way: as an impossibility. The evocation involves the presentation of two images, a labyrinth and a poet. These announce their essential precariousness (they are plaster casts) and their significant shortcomings. The image of the labyrinth found in Pompei was engraved on a plaster slab. This is shown in pieces to indicate that the significance of the myth so widespread among the citizens of Pompei, is lost to us today. The face of the poet is simply a form of iconography. It is a copy of an angel's head by Alessandro Algardi, a Bolognese sculptor who lived between 1595 and 1654. In both cases, the installation takes the form of a whole white cast supported on equally white bases. In the other two cases, we are left only fragments. These are enfolded in the red drapes which accompany each element and which in one case have fallen off the base. Algardi, a pupil of Ludovico Carracci and follower of Bernini, was also a restorer of classical statues, and references to Greek and Roman classicism are evident in his work. One element of the installation is an image from a Greek myth adopted by the Romans while the other element reveals a classical idea of art from the same source, but rethought for Baroque surroundings. Paolini's installation thus suggests an origin alluded to by many references, like variations around a theme whose true significance is impossible to know. The artist has said that we cannot know what antiquity was; we can only read the finds in our possession with the aid of clues which are in the end only assumptions. The "theme" of these "variations" is apparently a vacuum: the materials, such as plaster and cloth, are not chosen by chance because both casts and fabric contain a vacuum according to Paolini. The head of one of Algardi's angels is duplicated because the artist wishes to emphasise its status as a copy, which can be repeated an infinite number of times. The artist wishes to stress that the original work was lost and the current cast is based on the work of a Seventeenth-century artist who was not referring to a real object either, but to ideal, abstract, theoretical canons. The spoilt piece, in other words the set of fragments which do not constitute a whole, alludes to the necessarily incomplete enigma that the classical world constitutes for our culture just as it did for the culture in existence three centuries ago. Thus the labyrinth becomes a metaphor for artistic work. As Paolini himself stated with reference to his *Casa di Lucrezio*: "Once one has found one's way out of a labyrinth, one is free of the need to imagine innumerable other labyrinths which all lead to the starting point". And again: "The fragments of the labyrinth and enigmatic folds of the tunics, then, bear witness to nothing more than the undeniable visibility of innumerable dawns which lead to just as many dusks". All Paolini's work is in a certain sense labyrinthine because it defines the artistic environment as a closed place, which sets out in different directions but always returns to the same starting point. In other words, the same question is posed and re-posed: what is art and what do we learn when we experience art? Reflections on the past in Paolini's work also touch on different stages in the history of art. The traditional historical perception of art as a universal truth is, however, questioned by the artist. In the installation *Il cielo e dintorni* (The sky and surroundings) (1988), the critical attitude of the artist is almost ironic. On eighteen white silk flags Paolini reproduced details from works of art from the distant and near past (from Piero and Raphael to Gericault, Rousseau and Fontana). These images act as a metaphor not of the fundament but of the opposite, because they suggest the act of rising up to heaven, a loss of physical state, dematerialisation, flight and disappearance.

Casa di Lucrezio (Lucrezio's House), 1981-84
wood, plaster, cloth, four units
167 x 30 x 30 cm; 125 x 130 x 30 cm;
167 x 30 x 30 cm; 130 x 30 x 30 cm
Castello di Rivoli Purchase, 1986

Selected Bibliography

Celant, G. *Giulio Paolini*. New York: Sonnabend Press, 1972. Paolini, G. *Idem*. Turin: Einaudi, 1975. Paolini, G. *Figures - Intentiones; Images - Index*. Villeurbanne: Le Nouveau Musée, 1983. Bandini, M., Corà, B., Vertone, S. *Giulio Paolini. Tutto qui*. Ravenna: Loggetta Lombardesca, Essegi Editrice, 1985. Paolini, G. *Lo studio, il museo, il luogo, la visione*. Stuttgart: Staatsgalerie, 1986. Paolini, G. *Suspense. Breve storia del vuoto in tredici stanze*. Florence: Hopefulmonster, 1988. *Giulio Paolini*. Rome: Galleria Nazionale d'Arte Moderna; De Luca / Mondadori, 1989. Poli, F. *Giulio Paolini*. Turin: Lindau, 1990.

Cielo e dintorni (Sky and Surroundings), 1988
silkscreen on silk, eighteen units,
100 x 140 cm each
Castello di Rivoli Purchase, 1994

A. R. Penck

Born in Dresden in 1939, A. R. Penck moved to the German Federal Republic in 1980. Like the work of other German artists such as Georg Baselitz, Anselm Kiefer or Per Kirkeby, Penck's paintings and sculptures have been labelled Neo-Expressionist due to an essential gestuality which leads him to produce figures of strong, sometimes violent, expressive emphasis. All these artists achieved international notoriety during the Eighties, but had become active long before. They wished to generate a new set of images, linked to the Expressionist tradition yet rooted in the German culture and formed out of organic or vaguely archaic shapes. Penck chose the archaic option, and his work is distinctive because it has a specific pictorial language to which he has always remained faithful. As can be seen in his work *Kunsthar Auf-Leinwand* (Artist's Hair on Canvas) Penck's markings are deliberately primitive. Course brush-strokes depict anthropomorphic figures with highly schematic structures which at first sight look like the paintings of a child. For many artists, from Klee to Dubuffet, childhood is a mythical place from which art can take inspiration. It is often offset against the "adult" world, in other words the world of traditional rationality. The universe of primitive culture has been regarded as the world of childhood, in art.

Penck's figures suggest the world of our origins due to their somewhat totemic nature, and the archaic language such a picture evokes. As in archaic and popular visual cultures, the composition is built up with no regard for the rules of classical perspective. No relationship links figures and background, and no attention has been paid to the dimensional scale. We are left with only surface values, conditioned in different ways by the play of brush-strokes. These give rise to a different rhythm according to whether they build up an image or are considered simply an abstract pattern (though still constructed with a specific sense of visual order). Everything is expressed on the surface in the same way as writing. Penck's figures look like a pictogram and are reminiscent of a lost age when word and image were fused together, as in the case of hieroglyphics, before our own culture separated verbal signs from icons, the "text" from its "illustrations". This reminder brings no sense of pleasure or nostalgia, simply a will to bring those languages back to life in a form which involves imagination, or awareness, more than intellect. The choice of bright colours and artificial paints such as acrylic, to produce flowing figures, indicates a wish to distance the work from any aesthetic archaism. Penck's images recall a totem worshipped by primitive man, but also the graffitti written on a city wall: the tribe and the megalopolis, a religious relationship with nature and disenchantment with this technological age. The dramatic feeling which pervades Penck's compositions suggests that he superimposes the two dimensions (historical and psychological) to reveal an essential difference between them: a "state of nature", even if suspended in myth, involves a harmonious relationship with the environment that our contemporary age has lost.

Selected Bibliography

A. R. Penck. Concept Conceptruimnte. Rotterdam: Museum Boymans-van Beuningen, 1979. *A. R. Penck. Mike Hammer - Konsequenzen.* Monchengladbach: Stadtisches Museum Abteiberg, 1995. *A. R. Penck. Grafik Ost/West*, Braunschweig, Kunstverein, 1985. *Tekeningen: A. R. Penck.* The Hague: Gemeente Museum, 1988. *A. R. Penck.* Berlin: Nationalgalerie; Zurich: Kunsthaus, 1988. A. R. Penck, *Skulpturen und Zeichnungen 1971-1987.* Hannover: Kestner-Gesellschaft, 1988.

Kunsthar auf Leinwand
(Artist's Hair on Canvas), 1983
acrylic on canvas, 400 x 250 cm
Long-term loan of Eliana Guglielmi, Turin

Giuseppe Penone was born in Garessio (Cuneo) in 1947. His first works date back to 1968 and aim at achieving direct contact with the natural world. The artist is particularly interested in trees and uses them to produce works which reveal and modify the process of growth. The artist looks to nature as a generator of pre-cultural forms which are then processed and given meaning by culture. A tree became the best possible element for conveying this line of thought. To produce the decorticated *Alberi* (Trees) cycle, in which he has been engaged since 1969, he carves away wooden beams until he produces an image of the tree the beam used to be. The body and its relationships with the external environment also form part of nature. Thus Penone since 1970 has used slides bearing pencil marks to enlarge skin prints to gigantic proportions on the walls of exhibition environments. Natural, uncontrollable processes were used to produce other works, such as *Patate* (Potatoes), and *Zucche* (Pumpkins), (1977 and 1978-1979). In *Soffi* (Breaths) he used direct bodily contact to leave marks on materials (terracotta, leaves) and generate form. During the Eighties, he produced anthropomorphic work in bronze outlined by contact with sections of his own body. Shrubs were planted in the sections so that the work could not be finished until the plants had grown. In other words, body parts such as gigantic nails made out of glass are displayed in physical contact with leaves or stones to underscore their function as a link between the cultural and the natural (the artist sees a scratch as a sculpture). In similar recent works, natural finds (snakeskins) are used to bear witness to a formal, constructive rule.

The *Alberi* are probably the most typical and well-known work by Guiseppe Penone. The artist has often worked on this theme during his career. Since 1969, he has used trees in their capacity as a tool, a natural element converted by human work. The artist therefore takes a beam and identifies one of the rings visible on its base, which indicates years of growth. He then carves away the wood to recover the image of the tree at a given age. The trunk is revealed and the remains of branches protrude from the material. Thus the artist restores the tool to a state of nature through a manual operation, similar to that practised by a carpenter. This form of restoration can only be partial: if the act were complete, the tree would regain its natural form but the act of the artist would not be comprehensible. The image of a tree thus emerges only halfway along the horizontal axis. The contribution of the artist is more obvious and complex in the vertical *Alberi* which Penone began to produce in the Eighties: the work owned by the Castella di Rivoli is an example. The tree itself is cut and exhibited in two sections, and the upper and lower ends of the beam are left untouched to form the base of the two sculpted elements. While the growth period of a tree often exceeds our lifespan, our own existence, in these works the two timespans are in a certain sense unified through direct comparison between the different processes. The rules of biological growth governing the natural elements are thus compared with the rules governing the process of work: the long timespan of nature is compared with the accelerated timespan of creation. Penone sees the act of becoming letting the work speak for itself, by displaying the natural independent features of the tree and the features created by human work blend in an intermediate dimension which imbues the concept of a work of art, and sculpture in particular, with new meaning. In *Alberi* (each work is identified by this title, plus the height in metres) a classical neo-Platonist tradition is brought face to face with a Modernist, ready-made culture. The act of delving into a shaft of wood to find a pre-existing image makes explicit reference to the Platonic: the unchanging, eternal ideas expressed by neo-Platonic artistic theories of the Renaissance. These works express the essence of things, their generality, something which only thought may experience. The supremacy of thought which upgrades the artistic act (or "raises" it in the words of Michaelangelo) is the same supremacy found in Marcel Duchamp's ready-made work. An idea may be expressed by any object or sign, and the artistic act may be reduced simply to an act of designation. In his *Alberi* Penone puts this simple act of designation in context by comparing the specific nature of his own work in real time (the work often bears traces in the marks left by carving tools in the wood) with the generality embodied by nature and revealed by art in its essence. Penone addresses his criticism at the anthropocentric assumptions which dominate the relationship between man and nature. He expresses this criticism by adopting working methods designed to restore value to so-called craft activities, because he feels that in the past, craft and artistic activities were joined by an organic bond which the modern age has broken. An examination of such time-honoured occupations (Penone's output embraces themes of carpentry, pottery and farming) allows us to read in nature a set of processes which order themselves into a consistent system, and this adds life to the dry and logical system on which rational thought is based.

Selected Bibliography

Penone, G. *Rovesciare gli occhi*. Turin: Einaudi, 1977. *Giuseppe Penone*. Amsterdam: Stedelijk Museum, 1980. *Giuseppe Penone*. Paris: Musée d'Art Moderne de la Ville de Paris, 1984. Celant, G. *Giuseppe Penone*. Milan: Electa, 1989. *Penone*. Bologna: Galleria Civica d'Arte Moderna - Villa delle Rose, Nuova Alfa Editoriale, 1989. *Giuseppe Penone*. Rivoli: Castello di Rivoli, Fabbri, 1991. *Penone. L'espace de la main*. Strasbourg: Musée de la ville de Strasbourg, 1991. *Giuseppe Penone. La structure du temps*. Annecy: Musée Château, DAO - La petite Ecole, 1994. Robic, J. F. *Conversation avec Giuseppe Penone*. Strasbourg: Centre de recherches en Arts Plastiques, Université des Sciences Humains, 1994. *Giuseppe Penone*. Fossano: Centro Culturale Teresa Orsola Bussa de Rossi, 1994. *Giuseppe Penone. L'image du toucher*, Amiens: Fonds Régionals d'Art Contemporain de Picardie, 1994.

*Albero di undici metri
(Eleven-metres Tree)*, 1989
wood, two units, 516 x 45 x 45 cm each
Castello di Rivoli Purchase, 1994

Michelangelo *Pistoletto*

Born in Biella in 1933, Michelangelo Pistoletto mainly concentrated on self-portraiture when he started out as an artist at the end of the Fifties. In these early full-length, life-size paintings, his body stands out against uniform backgrounds. By 1961, in a series entitled *Il Presente* (The Present), the backgrounds had become black and reflective. After 1962, the human figure (now a photograph) was cut out and applied to mirrored steel sheets. His images portray everyday characters, while his backgrounds simply reflect real spaces and events beheld by the mirrored surface. The spectator becomes part of the picture by being mirrored in it and our field of view is doubled so that in front of us we see what is in fact behind us. By breaking up and multiplying the surroundings, the mirrored surface disorients the spectator, while the work itself is seen within the context of an ever-changing background. As a natural progression from his mirrored pictures, Pistoletto produced a set of works in 1965-1967 entitled *Oggetti in meno* (Fewer Objects) which reveal the fleeting, never-to-be-repeated nature of each individual creative moment. In these works, he swept away the notion of personal stylistic unity to introduce the idea of art being expressed in an evolving language. Starting in 1967, the artist's interest was directed toward installations composed of found objects. In 1968, he set up Gruppo Zoo, which was devoted to the idea of combining different expressive forms to produce performance art. He went back to the theme of mirrors in the seventies, with his cycle *Divisione e moltiplicazione dello specchio* (Division and Multiplication of the Mirror) based on disappearing images and dissected surfaces. At the same time, he continued to work with found-object installations.

In the Eighties, his art was devoted to sculpture, conceived as reconstructed fragments of collective and individual memories. His most recent works are organised into cycles, such as *Le Stanze* (Rooms) (1975-1976), *Arte dello Squallore. Quarta generazione* (Art of Squallor. Fourth generation) (1985), *Anno Bianco* (withe year) (1989), *Tartaruga felice* (Happy turtle) (1992), *Progetto Arte* (Project Art) (1994). His work *Persone nere* (Black figures) (1984) is one outcome of Pistoletto's intense foray into sculpture at the beginning of the Eighties. The sculpture is able to embody all that the artist understands by the term "soul" because of its historical context,

L'architettura dello specchio (Mirror Architecture), 1990
golden wood and mirror, three units,
380 x 200 cm each
Gift of Gruppo Dalle Carbonare, 1991

in other words the cultural richness of the community and values handed down from generation to generation that are subject to continual reappraisal. Assuming a work of art can and must be complemented by and complementary to the community in order to make up a whole, Pistoletto contrasts the "fullness" of his sculptures with the "emptiness" of his artistic ventures during the Seventies. He radically questions his earlier work for neglecting to examine this function, which touches upon the collective memory. The artist envisaged his sculpture as an exercise in remembering, and chose to depict this act of digging into the memory as a literal extraction of image fragments from a potentially infinite pool of visual stimuli. The image evoked by the fragment harks back to classical sculpture for reasons of function rather than style: the work of Pistoletto recalls an age (the artist cites both the Easter Island sculptures and Michelangelo's sculptures as examples) when the community was able to recognise itself in a work, particularly a monument, perceived as holding special meaning (for example, religious or ideological). Yet we do not look back on this age, which covers an extremely long span of time, with nostalgia. These meanings are no longer relevant to the art of our own time. Nowadays, a relationship with the community involves an awareness of history rather than ideology. This is the reason why Pistoletto's sculptures are figures; often in a style reminiscent of the classical period. In these works, the image is envisaged as a concealed object and also as a nascent state. We are presented with a rough version, a form barely emerging from a shapeless mass of substance; tending toward a meaning but not yet possessing full meaning. The *Persone nere* exhibited at Castello di Rivoli seem to be struggling with difficulty from their raw material. They are defined by economical cuts in expanded polyurethane. The memory triggered by the artist belongs as much to his own individual world as to the collective cultural history . The material used in this case (expanded polyurethane coated in black) does not belong to the classical tradition but allies itself to a new tradition of experimenting with materials not normally used by artists. Elsewhere the artist makes marble copies of his polyurethane originals. These works are treated in the same manner: a high proportion in the uncut state or highly recognisable image fragments heaped together to produce a sculpture comprising a collection or mass of meaningless bodies with no respect for rules of harmony. Size and height are the only criteria followed in his constructions. The resulting work therefore appears to tower over one and is best viewed from below. This is very evident in *Persone nere*, where roughly hewn faces peer toward the spectator and the entire sculpture bends

Continued on page 144

Selected Bibliography

Pistoletto. Florence: Forte di Belvedere, Electa, 1984. *Pistoletto*. Madrid: Palacio de Cristal, 1985. Corà, B. *Michelangelo Pistoletto. Lo spazio della riflessione*. Ravenna: Loggetta Lombardesca, Essegi Editrice, 1986. *Pistoletto. Division and Multiplication of the Mirror*. Long Island City, New York: The Institute of Contemporary Art P.S. 1 Museum, 1988. Pistoletto, M. *Un artista in meno*. Florence: Hopefulmonster, 1988. *Michelangelo Pistoletto. Oggetti in meno 1965-1966*. Basle: Kunsthalle, 1989. *Michelangelo Pistoletto*. Rome: Galleria Nazionale d'Arte Moderna, De Luca / Mondadori, 1990. Celant,G. *Pistoletto*. Milan: Fabbri Editori, 1992. *Pistoletto e la fotografia*. Oporto: Fundaçao de Serralves; Rotterdam: Witte de With Centrum voor Hedendaagse Kunst, 1993.

Persone nere (Black Figures), 1984
acrylic on polystyrene, 408 x 200 x 107 cm
Castello di Rivoli Purchase, 1986

Remo
Salvadori

Remo Salvadori was born in Cerreto Guidi (Florence) in 1947. At the beginning of the Seventies his work involved arranging photographs and everyday objects in space to reinterpret philosophical concepts, archetypal figures or figures linked to mythology such as the two-faced God Janus. The artist's main point of reference is always space, which he interprets as a source of creative psychic energy. His works therefore thematically recreate his thought and transform it into the spiritual resonances which always typify environments and objects in Salvadori's work. His work constantly features geometrical forms interpreted as symbols of existential status and cosmic entity (the square is a stable element and belongs to earth; the circle evokes an idea of the cosmos and transcendence), or recurrent though-provoking images with a range of possible meanings. The work *Modello* (Model) dating back to 1979 is an example, a ceramic object partly resulting from a period of self-observation while passing through four places, four galleries: gravity 0. The containing forms are elevated to a symbolic plane: they become linked to a universal categorical meaning and by extrapolation come to signify the crucible, the womb and the universe itself. In *Anfora e Modello* (Amphor and Model) (1979-1985), the vessel of the earth is united with the vessel of the sky, the model. An archetype, a reference to the iconography of Saint Christopher. The various works entitled *Triade* (Triad) (1982-1989) display an attempt to transcend rationalist thought founded on dualist dichotomies. The work *Nel momento* (In the moment) (1986-1991) displays "…works in lead leaf where the artist has cut and folded the material to produce full and empty spaces, figures and accumulations, whose result is always a different configuration" (lead, a subject tending towards light). "Square garden/listen,look/the visible all around./The position of the body,/the light,/the moment./Intervals in a musical scale./tactile values./A positive movement,/luminous./Radiance colours./Image colours,/gold". Thus Remo Salvadori's work arises out of a will to influence the perception of a work of art by placing it in relationship to the "interior sonority" of the space within which it is created. The work *Lampada* (Lamp) (1988-89) is presented as nine elements, each consisting of a sheet of paper placed in a diagonal position. In this way, the rectangle is perceived, and conceived by the artist, as a sort of diamond. Each sheet bears at its centre a watercolour with a central yellow area surrounded by a blue area. The area of colour is in turn surrounded by a ring of bronze. Each element of the whole contains its own specific nature, set in a dialectic relationship with the other elements. The arrangement of these sheets, with their bottom left hand corner facing downward, imparts a circular motion to the entire installation. The figure of the circle is reflected by the bronze ring, which seems to be the pivot about which each element rotates. The physical nature of the ring as a relief element gives this part of the work the prominence of a sculpture. The colour denotes immateriality and light, and the work is based on the relationship between sculpture (which compresses the luminous flow of colour and thus accentuates its irradiation) and a kindling of light. A relationship is also stated between bronze as an element of fire (metal is melted to give it form) and water-colour painting. Water-colour painting is a marriage between colour and water. The almost immaterial substance of which it is made conveys the idea of light, of colour/light as vibration and sublimation of material. The nine elements which make up the work also relate to the nine different places where each one was produced, and each displays a different degree of brightness because each piece was produced at a different time, and in a different place. The chosen colours, blue and yellow, complement one another. The yellow displays centrifugal force, and finds its opposite principle in the centripetal force of the blue, which is an element of balance. This choice of colours recalls the theories of the anthroposopher Rudolph Steiner, who re-examined and expanded upon Goethe's colour theory. According to Steiner, blue, yellow and red are so-called "radiance colours" and differ from white, black, green and pink (which are "peach bloom" in his terminology). These latter colours are termed "image colours", and also include gold as a manifestation of the spiritual on earth. Something radiates within yellow, blue and red: the glow in these colours represents "the outer edge of essentiality" (Steiner 1921). All Salvadori's work is based on the idea of overcoming principles of opposition. He takes this idea from his view of anthroposophy as an interior discipline, which can be expressed in art in order to achieve a spiritual perception of reality.

Selected Bibliography

Remo Salvadori: Divided Attention, Toronto: Art Gallery of Ontario, 1987. Celant, G. *Remo Salvadori*. Milan: Electa, 1991.

Lampada (Lamp), 1988-89
watercolour on French paper and bronze,
nine units, 50 x 70 cm each
Gift of Reconta Ernst & Young, 1989

Born in Prague in 1944, Katharine Sieverding has always expressed herself through photography, and self-portraiture in particular. Since the end of the Sixties, Sieverding has produced sequences of her own face repeated to fill the entire available surface, shot very close up, made-up and illuminated by carefully arranged lighting. In this way, the image of the artist assumes unreal or fantastical features. Her aim is not to reveal an identity but to provide a setting for psychological states of emotional unease, in which the artist's subjectivity is lost in a play of masquerade. Sieverding has produced her work on a large scale since the mid-Seventies. She often produces single, greatly enlarged images where her unnatural use of colour emphasises the fictitious nature of the character revealed in the self portrait. The sentences which appear together with the images convey a comment on the socio-cultural situation to which the images allude. At the end of the Seventies, the artist produced many works directly inspired by the advertising hoardings particularly typical of the United States, with their impeccably coloured images and invariably optimistic "messages". The work owned by the Castello di Rivoli forms part of this cycle. A portrait of the artist shown from the waist upward acts as an icon which inspires a sense of well-being and *joie de vivre* through carefully observed, essential features: an attractive woman, a summer dress, a sporty hat, made-up face, painted nails, and the specific healthiness of the glass of milk the artist holds in her hand. Yet two elements interact to diminish the reassuring tone of this self-representation: the wording *The Great White Way Goes Black* crosses the surface horizontally, passing over the portrait and the dark background which prevents spatial coordinates from being deciphered. The wording suggests an imminent and strange transformation. It may allude to the black of the background, which seems to invade the space and devour the light. It may be that soon the background will cancel out the image itself. All Sieverding's self-portraits are designed in such a way as to arouse similar questions. The artist's approach is disquieting. Extreme close-ups of her face are sometimes shot in sequence to produce innumerable images. Other works take the form of vastly enlarged faces occupying enormous areas. Her insistence on repetition does not help to reinforce an identity, but causes the identity to be lost because the image undergoes processing. Such treatments include the use of coloured filters, superimposition of geometrical patterns, or more simply, the shooting of multiple sequences at different distances, lit by light of varying strength. The bodily features change constantly and the portrait apparently becomes a presence which varies between the totemic and spectral. In the photograph illustrated, the ambiguity lies in a subcutaneous tension, a hint that this reassuring icon has another, darker face. The transformation to which the work alludes suggests the unease with which we view our own psychophysical identity in relation to existential stereotypes propagated by the mass media.

In *The Great White Way Goes Black*, the wording also refers to a real event Sieverding experienced and has used as inspiration: a sudden and impressive black-out which occurred on 13 July 1977 in New York. This event raised socio-political issues, such as attacks on shops by underprivileged people who were then arrested for theft, or the way the electric company made New Yorkers pay for the cost of repairs. This event was "The Great White Way Goes Black", the unpredictable catastrophe which lies in wait within the heart of technological civilisations and which exposes the negative aspects concealed by the optimismistic way our society presents itself.

Selected Bibliography

Katharina Sieverding. Grosfotos I-X / 75-77. Essen: Museum Folkwang; Eindhoven: Stedelijk Van Abbemuseum, 1977.
Katharina Sieverding. Monchengladbach: Stadtisches Museum Abteiberg, 1984.
Katharina Sieverding. Bilder aus den Zyklen XXVII - XI, 1987-1978, Karlsruhe: Badischer Kunstverein, 1987. *Sieverding.* Bonn: Bonner Kunstverein; Sindelfingen: Kunst+Projekte; Erlangen: Stadtische Galerie; Salzburg: Salzburger Kunstverein; Wiesbaden: Nassauscher Kunstverein, 1989.

The Great White Way Goes Black, 1977
colour photograph on canvas,
280 x 462 cm
Gift of Scott S.p.A., 1988

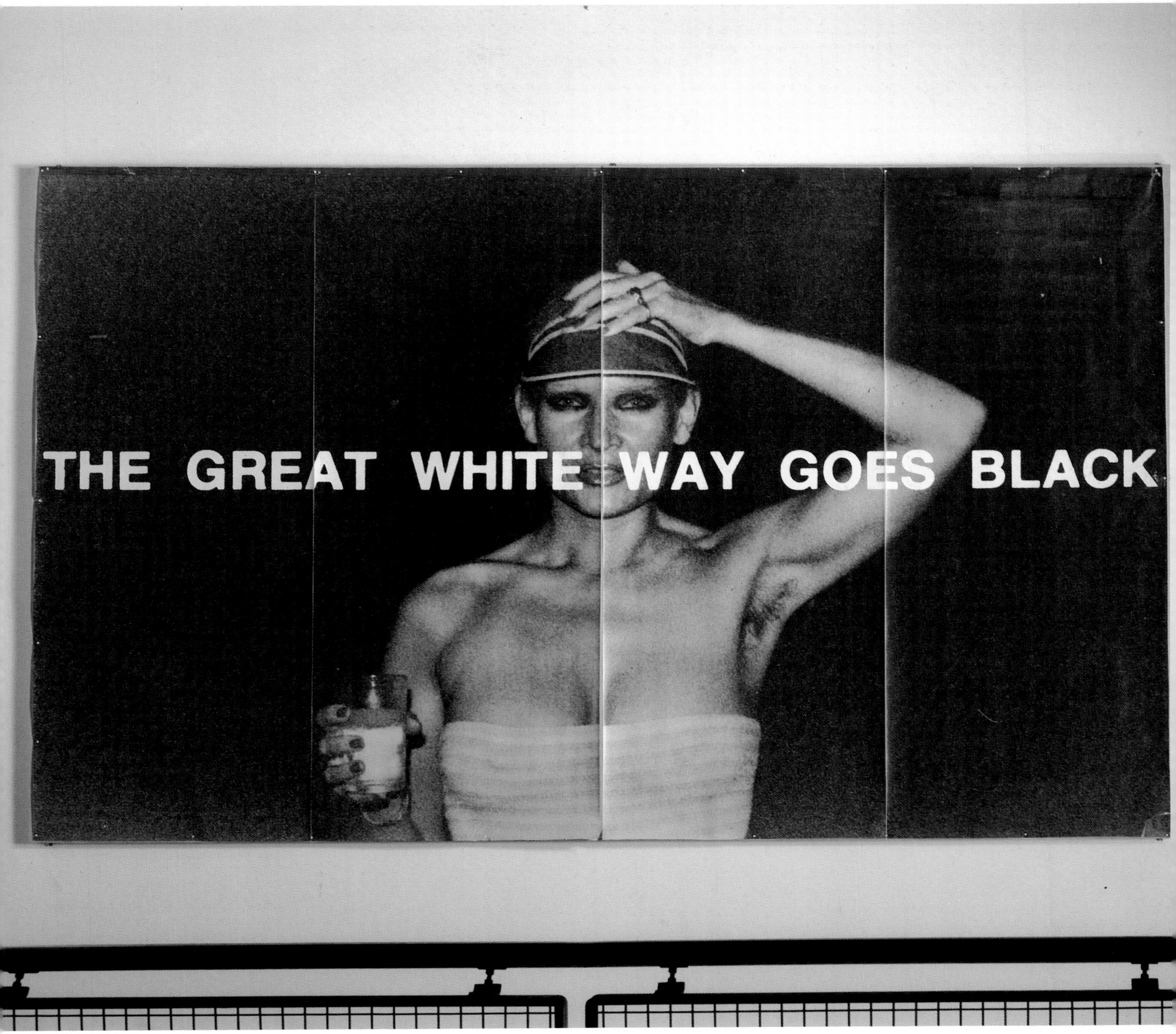
THE GREAT WHITE WAY GOES BLACK

Ettore Spalletti was born at Cappelle sul Tavo (Pescara) in 1940 and most of his works have been produced since 1975. His art vacillates between the different fields of painting and sculpture. One element common to both fields is colour, which the artist uses as a material. He mixes colours with plaster or impasto and spreads the results onto surfaces, which may be the planks of wood which he uses in his paintings, the walls of the exhibition environment or the pure forms which are his sculptures. The colour he uses is normally blue, which does not exist in nature, according to the artist, but assumes for us the symbolic meaning of infinity because we perceive it to be the colour of the sky. Apart from blue, he uses pink, grey and, more rarely, orange and yellow. The surfaces onto which he spreads his colours bear minimal but omnipresent signs of the brush-strokes which he uses to cover his various media with coloured material like a patina. Spalletti visualises primary forms, flat or solid geometrical figures, which are based on real, visible phenomena. He may take as his starting point the outline of mountains seen from his artist's studio, an iconographic part taken from an old painting, or the world of objects. In works such as *Vasi, anfora, bacile* (Vessels, amphor, basin) (1982) the image is subjected to an extreme process of synthesis which reduces it to a geometrical solids: an upturned truncated cone, cylinder or hemisphere. However, Spalletti's abstraction does not lose touch with the world of experience, as does the abstraction of earlier artists such as Mondrian or Malevic : his objects commemorate the world to which they belong, and which they transfigure through the intuitive sensitivity which produces them.

Dono (Gift) (1991) is a monochrome dyptic in pale pink mounted on the wall. The lower edge juts significantly from the flat surface. The monochrome surface is not simply painted, and the definition of "monochrome painting" is not, despite the work's appearance, the most appropriate. As in most of Spalletti's work, the colour is produced from a mixture of material built up in accordance with a complex process. The basic plaster is first mixed with adhesive, then spread onto the surface which the artist intends to cover: canvas, wood, marble or even the wall itself. Then coloured pigments are spread on, and absorbed by the soft plaster. When the treated surface has dried, the artist begins to smooth it with abrasive paper. In later works, his mixtures of plaster and colour are replaced with oil paints. This is therefore no ordinary painting process, but a new form designed to accentuate the manual and tactile values of the artistic language. The resulting colour is affected by its treatment. When bright pinks, greys or blues (the artist's preferred colours) are mixed with white plaster, they become subdued and the emotion conveyed by the colour is weakened. But Spalletti's work does not deal solely with emotional functions, designed to involve the spectator psychologically, but also conceptual functions. As we have already said, Spalletti's work is also a reflection on the relationship between work and space, and an exploration of the traditional distinctions between the various artistic forms: painting, sculpture and architecture. The resulting marriage between colour and craft indicates the way in which the artist sets out to examine the divide between painting and sculpture in order to overcome it. The work *Dono* is in this sense particularly relevant to the essentially ambiguous task the artist has set himself. It looks like a monochrome work, in other words one of the most typical icons of modernistic paintings. The opportunity for comparison with the absolute which the modern monochrome genre permits is nevertheless partly denied in this case. For the surface of the work reveals traces, albeit minimal, of the handiwork which has gone into it, the marks left by the abrasive paper, or the white appearing beneath the pink coat. All these signs link the work to the phenomenology of the body, its times and its biological rhythm. The work is thus relative, not absolute. The most relative aspect of the work is the relationship between itself and space: this concerns biological time and also the reality of the surrounding environment. The work's status as a monochrome work is also denied by its main premise: integrity. It is shown split in two, and projecting from the wall. The break is a harmonic projection, not caused by imposed laceration but an autonomous, interior opening motion. The work opens itself up to space and space enters the work without friction. This is illustrated by the longitudinal borders of the dyptic, which are flattened and painted silver, as though the pink were undergoing a process of sublimation to become pure light. Space is light, and colour (a sign of light) governs this transcendent route towards space as though toward a coherent achievement. This becomes apparent when we cease to see this work as a two-dimensional picture, but instead as an installation within the environment and/or as a sculpture.

Selected Bibliography

Spalletti, E. *Gruppo della Fonte*. Rome: AEIUO, 1989. Pasini, F. *Tra me e te*. Genoa: Locus Solus, 1990. *Ettore Spalletti*. Paris: Musée d'Art Moderne de la Ville de Paris, 1991. *Ettore Spalletti*. Valencia: IVAM Centre del Carme, 1992. *Osmosis. Ettore Spalletti - Haim Steinbach*. New York: The Solomon R. Guggenheim Museum, 1993. Celant, G. *Ettore Spalletti - Disegno*. Rome: Guida, 1993.

Dono (Gift), 1991
colour impasto on board, two units,
300 x 310 cm
Gift of Nuova Depositi S.p.A., 1992

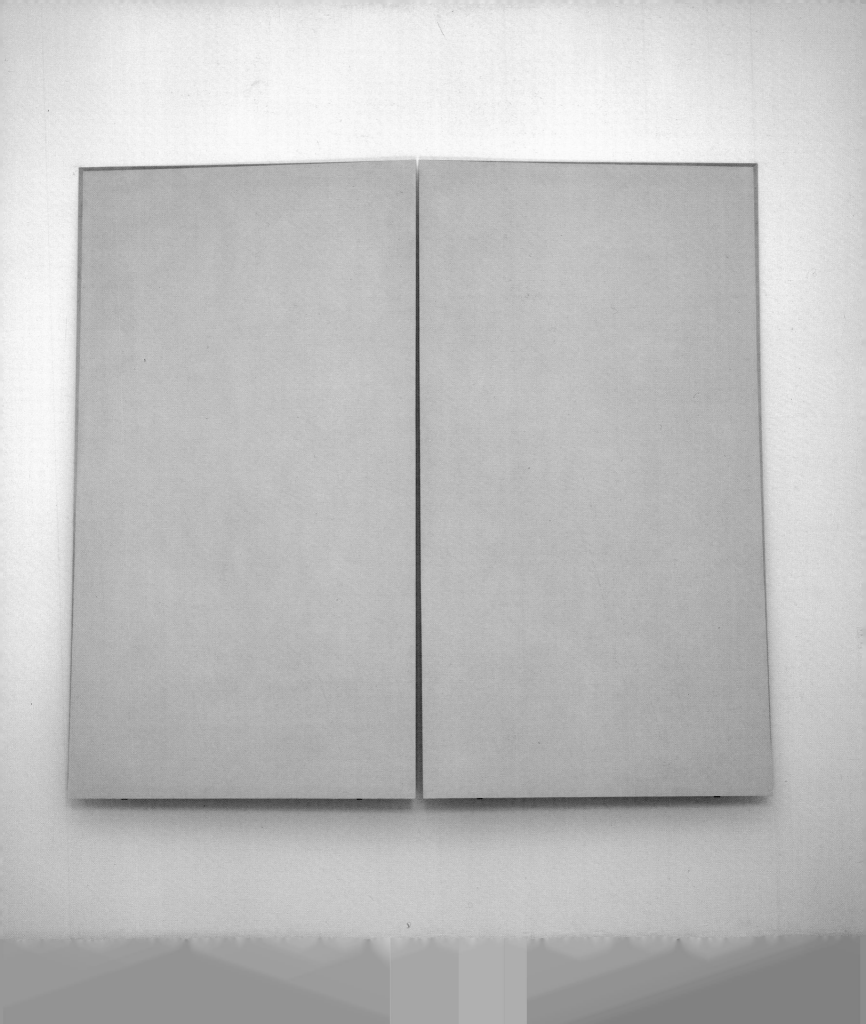

The first planned action carried out by Niele Toroni, born in Locarno Muralto in Switzerland in 1937, dates back to 3 January 1967. On that date, on the occasion of the "Salon de la Jeune Peinture" in Paris, the artist penned a declaration together with three other painters, Buren, Mosset and Parmentier, which set out his entire programme of work. The highly polemic statement listed the qualities and functions traditionally attributed to painting: "Puisque peindre c'est un jeu./ Puisque peindre c'est accorder our désaccorder des couleurs./ Puisque peindre c'est appliquer (consciemment ou non) des règles de composition…" and concluded with a laconic and decisive "Nous ne sommes pas peintres". This programme represented one of the most radical expression of the general reappraisal of painting typical of the Seventies, which was an outcome of the political ferment sparked throughout Europe by the cultural movements of 1968. Toroni, like Buren and the other signatories, and all other exponents of Conceptual Art, embarked on a critical examination of the expressive canons which govern the execution of art. He did not abandon specification in painting, but reduced his work to pre-ordained practices. The artist also decided to negate his work because he set out by refusing to do exactly what tradition expected of a painter. This position was based on his wish to re-assess the ideological and social role capitalist society attributes to the artist and his product. In our society, a work of art meets certain characteristics. We regard the distinctive features of this aesthetic object with unmistakable subjectivity and this contributes to create value. This value is measured in economic terms, because a work of art is an object which can be bought and sold in the same way as any other merchandise. In order to be competitive on the market, the work-merchandise cannot risk obsolescence, it must be appealing and thus variable, always different, so that appetites are never completely sated. Toroni turns these assumptions on their head. He does not adopt distinctive features but creates works based on a mechanical, anonymous process which anyone else could achieve. Instead of works which change in style, he embarks on a constant repetition of works which are "always the same", always based on the same linguistic rules. These rules are always connected with the basis of painting and do not deviate from this. They follow the basic premises of art to the letter and make use of an elementary, deliberately limited vocabulary. The title of the work by Toroni owned by the Castello di Rivoli is simply a description of the work, or the working method which produced it, like all other works by this painter. The work must be seen as one of the artist's many painting episodes which he inevitably terms "travail/peinture" (work/painting). It is based on the same rule always applied in his work: to apply fifty brush-strokes spaced exactly 30cm apart in order to fill the available surface in each case. This particular work is a square canvas, measuring 200 x 200 cm, fitted on a frame. The work could equally well be any other canvas of any size, a waxed canvas, a sheet of paper or newspaper, a pane of glass, the wall itself or the floor. The "work/painting" in Rivoli, for example, should be seen in the context of another work which the artist produced during the same year *in situ*, in other words by painting directly onto the walls of a room in the museum. The important thing is to be aware that the work of this painter consists entirely of mechanically applied brush-prints (a brush full of paint is held parallel to the surface). Toroni actually sets the entire painting system into action through the repetition of these elementary gestures, in the sense that he involves all the features of a work of art: canvas/backing, brush/tool, colour/expressive material - and the exhibition space. The spectator must be aware that his works consist simply of the marks of no. 50 brush applied every 30cm, because this is what the artist wishes to show us. If the spectator wishes, however, he may see in every work by Toroni all possible painted images, all possible painting, because this artist's work is avowedly metonymic: a part is designed to represent the whole. The artist reveals every last detail of the material bases of a complex system both of expression and ideology. The extreme, radical reduction undergone by the work obviously refers to the reasoning which underlies his work. This is no mere negation: not simply a statement of what the artist refuses to do. It is also an affirmation of the vitality of the pictorial language. Differences are apparent in the repetition, because no print is ever the same as another and each work deviates very slightly but very evidently from another. Each work is installed in the exhibition space with great freedom, without necessarily respecting the accepted canons of how paintings should be hung on a wall. This is even more true when the marks are applied with the same degree of freedom directly onto the walls or floor of the exhibition space. In this case the work operates as a device for revealing/sensitising and interpreting the space itself. The reduction to which Toroni subjects his specific pictorial language, his adoption of mechanical, easily learnt practices, also helps remove the myth surrounding the figure of the artist as creator by transforming his role into that of a cultural worker engaged in the socialisation of his expressive tools.

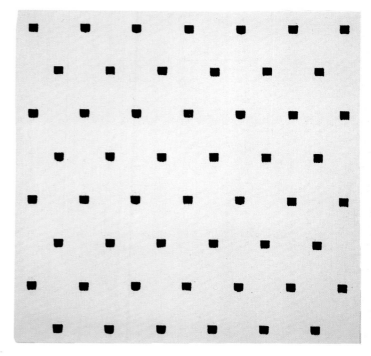

*Impronte di pennello n. 50 ripetute
a intervalli regolari di 30 cm
(Imprints of a n. 50 Paintbrush repeated
at Regular Intervals of 30 cm)*, 1984
acrylic on canvas, 200 x 200 cm
Castello di Rivoli Purchase, 1986

Selected Bibliography

Niele Toroni. 52 pages, 52 pagine, 52 Seiten.
Berne: Kunsthalle, 1978. *Niele Toroni.
Catalogue raisonnable 1967-1987. 20 ans
d'empreintes.* Nice: Villa Arson; Grenoble:
Musée de sculpture, 1987. *Niele Toroni.
Catalogue raisonnable - Suite n. 1.* Tourcoing:
Ecole Régionale Supérièure d'Expression
Plastique, 1989. *Niele Toroni.* Paris: Musée
National d'Art Moderne Centre Georges
Pompidou, 1991. *Niele Toroni. Catalogue
raisonnable - Suite n. 2.* The Hague:
Gemeente Museum; Amsterdam: Stedelijk
Museum, 1994.

*Impronte di pennello n. 50 ripetute a
intervalli regolari di 30 cm
(Imprints of a n. 50 Paintbrush repeated
at Regular Intervals of 30 cm)*, 1984
acrylic on wood, dimensions
determined by the environment
Castello di Rivoli Purchase, 1986

Emilio *Vedova*

Emilio Vedova was born in Venice in 1919. Since the Thirties, his work has been devoted to figurative painting and drawing which conveyed the emotional urgency typical of the artist's oeuvre. These sentiments are apparent in the oil paintings reminiscent of Goya, Daumier and Rouault he produced in the Thirties and Forties. In the Thirties, he was a member of the *Corrente* group, an important core of opposition to the official art of the period. After World War II, he became a leading member of the group of abstract painters opposed to realism. Emilio Vedova is one of the most important representatives of the pictorial movement known as *Informel* which arose during the Fifties in Europe and the United States. Since that time, the artist has always remained faithful to this extreme expressive choice which represents a radical rejection and transcendence of the idea of a defined image, and even of form itself, if form can be said to denote a statement of fixed identity. His choice also carries two ethical messages: a wish to refer to the state of constant emotional alarm experienced by historical man having to live in a society he feels at odds with: and the action of the conscious subject when faced with an ungovernable unconscious urge. To be true to these urges, Vedova chooses a form of painting based on pure gesture, free of impediments, and pure colour, free to express its own significant autonomous power. All Vedova's paintings hinge on this constantly fluctuating dialectic between gesture or sign and colour and between different functions of sign and colour, seen within the context of the real dialectic of struggle between the artist and his work. This conflictual relationship, apparent in all his work, nevertheless reveals a deeper knowledge: knowledge of composition, sense of space and pictorial sign, relationship between colours and sense of form. The work *Da dove…* (From where…) forms part of a pictorial cycle (common in the works of Emilio Vedova) which the artist painted between 1983 and 1984. The title is significant: not "towards where", towards where does this unruly painting lead, but "from where", from where does it draw the energy for the signs and colour which saturate the surface to create a single vital rhythm. Form for Vedova is a hypothesis which we see worked out before our eyes, and the title *Da dove…* actually emphasises an important feature of all his work: gesture sets out to delineate original hypotheses of form; it touches the original magma of language, like a senseless repetition where each element is confused with the others, not yet distinct, not yet existent in its own right. Each element is granted the time to make a momentary appearance, and each work is a sequence of different moments, where a differentiation of function is already apparent. These functions are attributed to colour and its relationship with gesture. While whites and yellows denote space, emptiness and light, red still conveys all the violent charge which we, even at unconscious level, associate with this colour. All these factors interact in accordance with an order which, albeit irrational, nevertheless designates a structure. The task of imposing structure is delegated to the strong colour: black. The weight and decision of the black brush strokes order the surface into spatial areas, or allude to a form simply as a latency. This is very apparent in the example owned by the Castello di Rivoli. Here the viscousness of black appears to stand out in the foreground and build up with difficulty, but resolutely, a vertical fluctuating body-like structure made up of big oblique signs which seem to be converging on the oval figure located at the top. Yet this relationship or slow movement may also be interpreted in the opposite sense, as a silent deflation of the figure from top to bottom. Vedova's hypotheses of form never work solely in one direction. Yet the relationships triggered on the surface between the various linguistic elements are unmistakable. This structure is strong even when broken up into sections and reveals an evident constrast with the background, or what appears to be the background, because for Vedova space is a dimension to be discovered intuitively. Here the background is defined with short, broad brush-strokes in yellow and white which lighten the entire composition with flowing movement and delicate colours.

Selected Bibliography

Vedova. Compresenze 1946-1981. San Marino: Palazzo dei Congressi, Electa, 1981. *Vedova 1935-1984*. Venice: Museo Correr, Electa, 1984. *Emilio Vedova*. Munich: Hirmer Verlag, 1986. Schulz-Hoffmann, C. *Vedova*. Munich: Hirmer Verlag, 1986. *Vedova uns Salzburg*. Salzburg: Internationale Sommerakademie für bildende Kunst, 1988. *Vedova. Absurdes Berliner Tagebuch '64*. Venice: Grafiche Veneziane, 1990. *Vedova…Continuum…* Milan: Padiglione d'Arte Contemporanea, Mazzotta, 1991. *Emilio Vedova*. Lugano: Museo d'Arte Moderna, Electa, 1993.

Da dove… (From Where), 1984
mixed media, 300 x 190 cm
Castello di Rivoli Purchase, 1989

Jan Vercruysse was born in Ostend in 1948. His background is that of a poet, but he devoted himself to visual art halfway through the Seventies. His first works consisted of sequences of black and white photographs, often depicting a self-portrait of the artist. They were designed to act as phrases in a conversation (or, in the words of the artist, like sonnets in a poetic composition) entirely expressed through image. In 1983, he began his series *Chambres* (Rooms). These imposing structures made out of rare wood take the form of rooms – lit by fluorescent lamps or openings in the walls – which the visitor is invited to enter. In 1985 he began to produce his *Atopies*, in other words sets of different elements such as frames, glass planes, mirrors and planks of wood. From the end of the Eighties, his works were entitled *Tombeaux*, as in the case of the constellation, as it is referred to by the artist, owned by the Castello di Rivoli. This work was exhibited at the museum initially in a personal exhibition held on the Belgian artist in 1991. The French term denotes a set of meanings which cannot simply be translated by the word "tomb". The word refers more to a "funerary monument" or "cenotaph": something erected in memory of someone no longer present, even as a corpse. Thus the monument serves only to call to mind or revitalise the thought or memory of the person. The French term also has another, different meaning: that of a poetic composition written in memory of a dead person, like the Italian "stanza". This term is also connected with poetry, because it describes the verse sung by a troubadour and was originally used to describe the actual room where the troubadour recited his compositions to the court of his lord. Two constants recur in this family of meanings: an examination of artistic language, its specificities and the way it can be used - and a sense of absence, in the name of which the language is created. The absence which Vercruysse speaks of is the absence of the reality Utopia sets out to transform, but inevitably fails. In art, Utopia has always represented a striving to overcome the specificity of art and make it more functional. Yet all artistic utopias fail to keep their appointment with reality: history always reveals their limits. Instead the artist must ask himself about the limits of his own reality, and make his art an arena for theoretical and mental reflection. Vercruysse therefore rejects the concept of utopia and prefers to speak of a-topia, a non-place, an absence conceived as a mental space and spiritual dimension, an allusion to the subjectivity with which reality is interpreted, by comparing the future against various categories of thought. Thought inhabits a dimension unfettered by physical phenomena, while reflection touches on the ontological. This, for Vercruysse, is the function of artistic activity.

The installation in the Castello di Rivoli shows two different types of objects: shelves and musical wind instruments (three cornets, three trombones, three tubas). Both types of object are made out of the same incongruous material, murano glass, and in the same colour, blue. The instruments do not stand on the shelves but are hung by leather straps from the wall. The shelves are applied to the adjacent wall, very high up, and not enough space is left between them and the ceiling to accommodate the objects which they are apparently designed to support. Here we see no allusion to functionality, but its disappearance: a space for reflection opens up when the world of function is eclipsed. The wind instruments made out of glass instead of brass are silenced sound machines: their original function has been reversed; they cannot make sound but only silence. This silence may be used to construct a non-place which transcends every other place and allows meditation.

Selected Bibliography

Jan Vercruysse. Paris: Musée d'Art Moderne de la Ville de Paris, 1986. *Jan Vercruysse*. Bruxelles: Société des Expositions Palais des Beaux-Arts, 1988. *Jan Vercruysse*. Eindhoven: Stedelijk Van Abbemuseum, 1990. *Jan Vercruysse Tombeaux "Stanza"*. Rivoli: Castello di Rivoli, 1992. *Jan Vercruysse*. Venice: La Biennale di Venezia, XLV International Art Exhibition, Belgian Pavilion, 1993. *Jan Vercruysse*. Toronto: The Power Plant, 1993.

Tombeaux, 1991
glass, iron, leather, dimensions
determined by the environment
Fractional gift of the Friends of the
Castello di Rivoli, 1993

Toon *Verhoef*

Toon Verhoef was born in Voorburg in Holland in 1946 and has been painting since the beginning of the Seventies. His interest has always been directed towards abstract painting, which the artist expresses in a rigorous language of his own. The sufaces of his compositions are organised in accordance with a precise relationship between background and figure. The form stands out starkly on the flat surface and colour relationships are distilled down to a choice of just two colours, usually primary. This approach was influenced by the working climate of the Seventies, which tended to make all elements of artistic language (whether relating to painting or sculpture) express a legible meaning of their own. Verhoef speaks of "thought" images, in other words a very precise mental direction is seen to be governing the creative act. This conception is the the opposite of the free flow of unconscious urges with which the idea of abstract painting is usually associated: a transcendence of real information. In this artist's work, this dimension of expressive immediacy takes the form of drawing, even sketches where, in the words of Verhoef, every formal idea has origin. Yet even this original moment often becomes the final act. It may be made concrete in a lightning flash and be taken from an idea of form whose origins lie in a visual experience, particularly a perceptive experience of colour, but not necessarily. For Verhoef, an image is something formed in the mind which may, in most cases, be defined in a painting without any other mediation than through the linguistic process. In many cases a drawing is used as a starting point for translating a formal idea into a painting, which thus mainly constitutes a transformation. When a pictorial image is subjected to rules of composition, determined by the size of the canvas and the choice of the two colours which define the figure and background, it may be modified in the act of being transposed from the drawing onto the canvas.

The work *Senza titolo* (Untitled) owned by the Castello di Rivoli collection, was painted in 1988. This painting displays the general traits of Verhoef's work. The image stands out starkly from the surface and the work is constructed on the basis of an elemental relationship between the figure in the foreground and the background. The flat surface is divided into two parts by a diagonal which cuts off a triangular section at the bottom left, coloured orange. The rest of the surface is white, and overlaid by a precisely described oval shape. This elongated figure is folded back on itself and rests on the orange area, from which it borrows its colour: both ends are pointed. The starkness of the figure and the sense of restraint which dominates the entire composition with its exact spatial divisions, serves to accentuate the dynamism suggested by the slash of the diagonal line and, above all, the bent oval band, which conveys a sense of potential energy poised for release.

Selected Bibliography

Toon Verhoef, Schilderijen en tekeningen 1968-1986. Eindhoven: Stedelijk Van Abbemuseum, 1987. *Toon Verhoef*. Amsterdam: Amsterdam Art Foundation, 1988. *Bianchi, Charlton, Förg, Kruger, Verhoef*. Rivoli: Castello di Rivoli, 1989.

Senza titolo (Untitled), 1988
oil on canvas, 290 x 190
Castello di Rivoli Purchase, 1990

Gilberto Zorio was born in Andorno Micca (Biella) in 1944. At the end of the Sixties, he began to locate industrially-manufactured materials in positions which revealed their latent potential energy. One such example was a cylinder made out of eternet resting on an inflated inner tube: *Senza titolo* (Untitled), (1967). Other works revealed the colour-light of a glowing wire. The relationship the artist assumes between creativity and energy is expressed by significant materials and images chosen to symbolise this idea: in the artist's cycle *Per purificare le parole* (To cleanse words) (from 1969), he constructs alcohol-filled containers without spouts, whereas his javelins held tautly in space and his image of a five-pointed star are expressions of energy. The star is made out of various materials: terracotta, copper, leather or laser beams, or is described on a wall using an oxy-acetylene blow lamp. The artist then moves on to examine the chemical changes which occur when metals come into contact with acids (copper sulphate, hydrochloric acid). Both components are placed within containers which allow the work to identify itself with an autonomous process of transmutation.

The title of the installation *Sogno in un sottotetto* (Dream under a roof) (1984) takes inspiration from its location in the area built above a great dome situated above a room in the castle, which is now used to connect the stairway and rooms on the third floor. In this extensive space, Gilberto Zorio has installed some of the objects which he uses most frequently in his work: canoes, javelins, crucibles and stills. The term "dream" is probably intended to emphasise the unusual location of these elements: a canoe suspended diagonally in mid-air, crucibles connected beneath a long slender bow of steel which extends through space and at whose opposite end rests a glass still containing alcohol. These objects seem to be gripped by movements of sliding and turning. Apart from the sensation of movement, a dream-like atmosphere may also be conjured up by the use to which these particular objects are put. Crucibles are used to melt metals and stills are objects used by alchemists, who employed their mysterious knowledge to combine elements in such containers with the aim of converting base material into gold. Gold is seen as a sublimation of material into spirituality, and as a metaphor for the cognitive process. This type of metaphorical use of material is present in all of Zorio's work. His attention is directed not at the mysterious, but at the revelation of truth, or rather, some of its secret properties. The installation of these objects does not so much transform the space into a dream but rather into an energy field. This is apparent in the systems of balance and the daring connections between the elements held in balance, connections which suggest the common action of a set of forces. Each element used is a potential force: in its structure, its balance and its individual substance. A canoe is a dynamic object, as is the javelin. They are objects designed for moving swiftly through water or air, just as the steel bow marks a transition and forms a line of progression. The still and crucibles are containers within which a process of transformation takes place. The material itself is a site of constant transformation because it is an energetic principle, whose effects escape empirical observation, but which science observes and art reveals to us. Acid solutions are placed into the crucibles; they come into contact with one another and metals to produce aggregations of crystals and salts as part of a constant, sometimes very slow process, which nevertheless produces tangible results. The artist provides the conditions for the process to take place, but may not govern it in its entirety. The completion of this process is dependent upon time and the nature of the materials used. The minuscule events which take place within the containers and the effects displayed by the materials are completely independent. For the artist, form is created by a dynamism inherent in the material, which is reflected and amplified in these installations, which all display forms of energy (whether kinetic or potential). The installation is also a process, a partly random form. Yet it is not mythical: it belongs to the real world, which may be the organic reality of living material or the reality of a technical tool constructed by man.

Selected Bibliography

Merz, B. and Zacharopoulos, D. *Gilberto Zorio*. Ravenna: Loggetta Lombardesca, Essegi Editrice, 1983. *Gilberto Zorio. Opere 1967-1984*. Modena: Galleria Civica, Panini, 1985. *Gilberto Zorio*. Stuttgart: Wurttembergischer Kunstverein, 1985. *Gilberto Zorio*. Eindhoven: Stedelijk Van Abbemuseum, 1987. *Gilberto Zorio*. Florence: Hopefulmonster,1987. *Gilberto Zorio*. Valencia: IVAM Centre del Carme, Hopefulmonster, 1992.

Sogno in un sottotetto
(Dream under a Roof), 1984
lead, leather, terracotta, glass, acid liquids,
dimensions given by the environments
Long-term loan of the artist

Mario Giacomelli was born in Senigallia (Ancona) in 1925. He is a completely self-taught photographer who started out by learning photography from international periodicals and exchanging pictures and ideas at camera-clubs. In the early Fifties his work earned him exhibitions and prizes at national and international amateur photographic competitions.

Even today, Giacomelli thinks of himself as a stubborn "amateur" photographer, passionately committed to the idea of photography as a form of visual art. His interests focus on experiments into the possibilities of the photographic medium. Since the early Sixties, Giacomelli has been recognised as the photographer who best exemplifies the idea of Italianness in contemporary photography. Indeed, for many years his pictures were the only works ever chosen to represent Italian photography in international photographic museum collections. The photographs by Giacomelli selected for the Castello di Rivoli's permanent Photography Collection document some of the key chapters in this photographer's prolific history.

Verrà la morte e avrà i tuoi occhi (Death will come and you will have your eyes), *1955; 1966-68; 1981-83*
This series includes photographs shot in three various periods and with different titles (*Vita d'ospizio* [Hospice life],1955-56); *Non fatemi domande* [Don't ask me questions], 1981-83), of which the most familiar title is *Verrà la morte e avrà i tuoi occhi*" which re-interprets the famous poem by Cesare Pavese. The subjects of the photographs, which depict episodes of life in a hospice in Senigallia, are treated with great conviction. The camera is pointed inexorably at suffering bodies, wrinkled skin and the spent eyes of the elderly. The photographer succeeds in documenting the removal of all dignity and absence of intimacy experienced by old people in the hospice. The photographs in this series tell of barely tolerable suffering and an emotional torment. Yet despite the discomfort and neglect, the mental and physical disarray, we see glimmerings of life and moments of great tenderness which affirm the will to live despite the spectre of death. Life goes on somehow, despite the purgatory of the hospice.

Scanno, 1955-59
The story of Giacomelli's Scanno is narrated in a series of photographs which describe the archaic religious conditions perpetuated by the inhabitants of this tiny village in Abruzzo. The place described in these images tells us of a universe inhabited by figures draped in black costumes, old people with faces that have no place in the present. The photographs describe the composed and ancient progress of women who appear to be engaged in a procession or ritual. This place is made to stick in the memory through the use of contrasting photographs. Here the distinction between tones is reduced to a division betweem unreal shades of white onto which burning blacks are imposed. This new technique proved an inexhaustible source of visual potential. It was also a formal innovation for its time, winning the acclaim of photographic critics.

La buona terra (The Good Earth)
The work of peasants forms the central theme of this series of reportage photographs. An entire family of peasants from the Italian region of Marche was followed throughout their working days in the fields. While the canons of the nineteenth-century pictorial tradition (particularly in Italy) would see the depiction of these peasants as secondary or complementary to more accepted genres such as portrait and landscape photography, Giacomelli manages not to let this subject fall into the usual mould adopted for this type of photography. His reportage documents important moments of everyday life and reflects on the daily toil of the peasants: the physical work of hoeing the fields, collecting the fruit and harvesting the grain.

Io non ho mani che mi accarezzino il viso (I have no hands to caress my face) *1962-63.*
These photographs are perhaps the most popular works by Mario Giacomelli, and their title is intended as a homage to the poet-priest David Maria Turaldo. First shown in the Italian magazine "L'Espresso", the photographs have since then constantly reappeared in the Italian press. They show a group of student priests at play, shown in delirious abandonment to childish games. But these are more than mere moments of uncontrollable hedonism because the photographs also make us involuntary witnesses of the unconfessed and tragic solitude of priests.

Paesaggi (Landscapes) *1956-60; 1970-76; 1984-1990; 1992*
The theme of landscapes has involved Mario Giacomelli is an extensive, unassuaged search, which has now lasted more than three decades. In his first photographs, which date back to 1955, his landscapes are represented from a viewpoint we could define as "terrestrial", captured from the highest point of a hill. The landscapes he produced during the Seventies, however, adopted an aerial viewpoint, with the line of the horizon irreparably lost. For Giacomelli, landscape is identified with and denotes the earth itself. All the furrows, lines and networks described by crops reveal a graphic fabric which can only be seen through the medium of photography.
Antonella Russo

Selected Bibliography

Quintavalle, A. C. *Mario Giacomelli*, Parma: Università di Parma - Centro Studi Archivio della Comunicazione, Feltrinelli, 1980. *I Grandi Fotografi: Mario Giacomelli*. Milan: Fabbri, 1983. Gianelli, I. and Russo, A. (edited by). *Mario Giacomelli*. Rivoli: Castello di Rivoli: Charta, 1992. Nori, C. *Mario Giacomelli*. Paris: Contrejour, 1992.

Autoritratto (Self-Portrait), 1955-56
gelatin silver print, 40.6 x 30.5 cm
Gift of BNL Banca Nazionale del Lavoro, 1993

Paesaggio (Landscape), 1956-60
gelatin silver print, 30.5 x 40.6 cm
Gift of BNL Banca Nazionale del
Lavoro, 1993

*"Io non ho mani che mi accarezzino
il viso" ("I do not Have Hands to
Caress My Face")*, 1962-63
gelatin silver print, 30.5 x 40.6 cm
Gift of BNL Banca Nazionale del
Lavoro, 1993

"Verrà la morte e avrà i tuoi occhi"
("Death Will Come and Will Have Your Eyes"), 1981-83
gelatin silver print, 40.6 x 30.5 cm
Gift of BNL Banca Nazionale del Lavoro, 1993

Mimmo Jodice

Mimmo Jodice was born in Sanita (Naples) in 1934 and began his photographic career in the mid-Sixties. His early photographs reveal a linguistic quest to investigate the ontology of the photographic image.

In the following decade Jodice committed himself to a form of documentary photography that reflects on ancient rooted social rituals and anthropological customs perpetuated within the Neapolitan hinterland. At the same time he also undertook a sort of archaeological tour throughout Naples as part of a mission to portray his city, which is both violent and surprising, a space where chaos and loneliness, ancient memories and present upheaval, coexist: where paradoxes are a way of life. Since the Eighties, Jodice has devoted his life and his photography to combing this city as part of a painstaking quest to reveal the identity of Neapolitans, who inhabit a city which even today, just as many centuries before, occupies a central position in the political attempt to solve social problems in Italy.

Mimmo Jodice's photographic work included in the Castello di Rivoli permanent Photographic Collection represents a partial but significant segment of Mimmo Jodice's photographic oeuvre and one which contributes to a wider recognition of the Italian photographic output both in Italy and abroad.

Suor Orsola 1985-86

The series of photographs entitled *Suor Orsola* is named after a Seventeenth-century monastery and evokes the memory, spaces and atmosphere of that ancient Neapolitan institute. A few centuries ago, the monastery exemplified the cultural and philosophical status of this great city, which was inhabited by Giambattista Vico, Gaetano Filangiere, and Benedetto Croce and which was the first true European capital. Jodice's photography takes us downstairs, through the cloisters and into the gardens of the monastery. We visit sacresties, and rooms for storing for works of art. His photographs revisit and frame the places and cultural fabric of a former Naples. These photographs show spaces inhabited by a past whose statues, frescoes and trusses sing of a glorious age.

La città invisibile (The Invisible City), *1985-90*

The photographs in this series, whose title refers to a famous novel by Italo Calvino, constitute a sort of review of the conventions of the Neapolitan "veduta" painting genre which was responsible for the city of Naples becoming the popular incarnation of southern Italy from the Fifteenth century onward. According to this genre, the city is typically represented as an open, clear and immediately accessible panorama, whose sites are exposed and offered up to the spectator: a Naples which generously offers itself up to view.

For travellers on an imaginary grand tour in our own day, these new views of the city of Naples are disorienting and defy categorisation. Deserted, maze-like alleyways, misty landscapes, solitary disquieting harbours, take the place of the trite painted themes reflected through the use (and abuse) of the "Vedutismo" genre. Instead, these photographs reveal an intriguing interior geography. Mimmo Jodice takes us through an itinerary which allows us to contemplate Naples as the capital of the Mediterranean world; a place lying at the threshold of history and mythology; a space between the formal and the fantastic. In his travels in search of this Mediterranean world, Jodice shows us the outline of bays and coasts, harbours and archaeological sites which stand out against open skies, marking and remarking the limits of a travel map which must ever be temporary.

Antonella Russo

Selected Bibliography

de Simone, R. and Jodice, M. *Chi è devoto - feste popolari in Campania*. Naples: Edizioni Scientifiche Italiane, 1974. Lemagny, J. - C. *Naples: une archeologie future*. Paris: Istituto Italiano di Cultura, 1982. Jodice, M. *Città invisibile*. Naples: Electa, 1990. Jodice, M. *Tempo interiore*. Milan: Federico Motta, 1993.

Castel Sant'Elmo, 1986
gelatin silver print, 19.5 x 43 cm
Gift of the photographer, 1993

Suor Orsola, 1987
gelatin silver print, 36 x 36 cm
Gift of the photographer, 1993

Arles, 1989
gelatin silver print, 35.5 x 36 cm
Gift of the photographer, 1993

Continued from page 118

Michelangelo
Pistoletto

over. The artist saw the looming nature of his works as a way of calling attention to the finished perfection of us, the onlookers, as we ponder the solidity (whether real or apparent) of these works and the enigmatic nature of the images portrayed.

The sense of disquiet which accompanies their appearance in closed or open spaces is similar to that determined by the disturbing power of mirrors to duplicate their environment. We are given an example of this in the work *L'Architettura dello specchio* (Mirror architecture). This consists of an enormous elegantly framed mirror which the artist has divided into four equal parts. There is a similarity between Pistolletto's long work on his mirror and his sculptures: the mirror reflects and thus potentially contains all possible images. Thus every mirror may reflect the entire world. Similarly, some of the infinite array of possible images may be hewn roughly out of material (the material of the world).

There exists an interior and exterior relationship between virtual space reflected by a mirror and real space: this reflection is designed by Pistoletto to act as a metaphor for reflection, the human ability to make conceptual relationships between real elements. Sculptures, on the other hand, inhabit a world of living and direct experience with things. The mirror/sculpture comparison is an example of the artist's dualism: his Apollonian side is expressed by images applied to mirrored surfaces while his Dionysian side is expressed by forays into Arte Povera or in theatrical animation. Now his mirrors no longer contain images of the world in their surfaces: any image could appear in the mirror and in one sense belong to it. His mirrors have had a frame since 1975-1978, when Pistoletto's work following the tenet "Art takes on Religion" the artist posited a mirror in a church in place of a sacred image on the altar. The place of reflection becomes a metaphor for reflection and an intellectual dimension. It also becomes a sign of spirituality and a place of the absolute. When considered as a metaphor for all that is possible, a mirror may also allude to transcendency and even contain itself, think itself up: mirror itself. A mirror reflects itself when it is divided and can generate an infinite series of self-reflections, in other words an image of infinity. Pistoletto's great work *Architettura dello specchio* shows us that division really means multiplication, and the artist pragmatically relates this concept to the world: a subject can be thought of as a fragment of a whole; a whole can divide and multiply to generate an infinite array of subjects; the subject forms a living part of this infinity. By reflecting us, the mirror refers us back to the totality of which we constitute an essential part, in the same way as sculpture refers us back to our history. This act of restoring our awareness of ourselves is done in a disturbing way, as occurs when we are brought face to face with a revelation. The looming sculpture produces the same effect as the perspective doubling brought about by the huge mirror which simply rests against a wall at a slight angle. The mirror interferes with our rational perception of the architecture in the exhibition site, which the mirror has always contained in itself.

the Castle

History

Maria Grazia Cerri

The Castello di Rivoli as it appears in a picture published by B. Debbene (Paris, 1609).

The village of Rivoli, the Castle and Carlo Emanuele I's long Pinacoteca (picture gallery) as shown in the Theatrum Sabaudiae (1683)

The present appearance of the Castello di Rivoli does not reveal its extremely ancient origins. Roman remains have been found in Rivoli, and evidence exists that a road once connected this region to the mountain passes leading to Gaul. We may therefore assume that this site, given its commanding position at the entrance to the Susa Valley, dominating the plain of Turin, was in those days used as a look-out or signalling point and played a part in the valley's defense.

A fortified centre certainly existed on this site during the medieval period. The castle was initially a stronghold of episcopal power, but then passed into the hands of the counts of Savoy. Although the castle's primary offensive function gave the building a somewhat forbidding appearance, it was nevertheless used to host ceremonies or meetings of particular importance. In 1350, the Green Count (Amedeus VI) celebrated the wedding of his sister Bianca of Savoy to Galeazzo Secondo Visconti with great pomp at the Castello di Rivoli. Charles of Anjou was a guest in 1382 and in 1414, Amedeus VIII welcomed the Emperor Sigismund at the castle with great ceremony when he stopped off on his way to Turin.

The remains of the medieval building are in the castle basement, where they are enclosed by later building work. But a medieval well can still be seen in a room on the first floor, while signs of ancient windows are apparent on the eastern front of the building.

A print dating back to 1606 reveals a compact stronghold, built up on high ground overlooking the village. The picture reveals the castle's eminently defensive origins and also shows how new parts were added onto a more ancient base. Extensive grounds slope down the sides of the hill towards the village of Rivoli.

This was how the castle looked after major work had been done by Emanuele Filiberto when he settled in Rivoli with his court after the Peace of Chateau Cambresis (1559). Under the terms of this agreement, the city of Turin was to be held by the French until the Duke produced a male child. The architect of the Sixteenth-century conversion was Paciotto da Urbino, who also planned the city of Turin. In 1560, Emanuele Filiberto had commissioned Paciotto da Urbino with Domenico Ponsello and other artists to give a new face to Rivoli Castle. A cistern discovered below the Manica Lunga during recent restoration work dates back to this stage of the work.

After the birth of Carlo Emanuele, the Savoys settled in Turin. The city remained their principal residence, but they continued to use Rivoli as an alternative home.

When Carlo Emanuele I came to power and developed Turin as the Savoy capital, he opened another important chapter in the history of architecture, for it now was devoted to creating an impression of consolidated power. The brief of the court architects entrusted with the task of conveying this impression was to show that the Savoy dynasty was a force to be reckoned with on the European scene. Rivoli was dear to the Duke because it was his birth place. He thus used the castle as an opportunity to try out the new architectural language and instigate a new architectural campaign throughout the territory. The result was a "corona delitiae" of sport and hunting residences for the monarchs and their court arranged around the capital. The first plans for the conversion of the old castle date from the final decades of the Sixteenth century. Ascanio Vitozzi and Carlo Castellamonte assisted with the plans, but building work did not start until the beginning of the next century under the guidance of Antonio Bertola.

A sumptuous printed version of *Theatrum Statuum Regiae Celsitudinis Sabaudiae Ducis*, produced by the publishers Bleau of Amsterdam in 1682, shows two images of the Castello di Rivoli based on a drawing by Carlo di Castellamonte. A picture of the south side shows large grounds sloping down the hillside as part of a more general view of Rivoli village with the mountainous slopes of the Susa Valley in the background. The compact bulk of the castle with its four angular towers is flanked by the long Pinacoteca (picture gallery) built by Carlo Emanuele I. This was designed to house antiques and works by renowned Italian and foreign artists acquired to expand collections already begun by Emanuele Filiberto.

French troops who invaded Piedmonte under the command of General Catinat between 1690 and 1693 caused great damage to the castle. A terrible fire destroyed furnishings and decorations together with certain vulnerable structural parts such as the roof and wooden floors. The building was left absolutely uninhabitable.

In the final years of the Seventeenth century, Vittorio Amedeo II undertook the task of restoring the castle to all the dignity of a court residence, and the Ducal architects were instructed accordingly. Repair work was carried out while plans were prepared in Turin and Paris. Despite his unresolved disputes with the French government, the Duke still regarded the Italian alpine capital an importance reference point in architectural terms. Building work was carried out at the Castello di Rivoli between 1711 and 1713, with Michelangelo Garove as architect.

Filippo Juvarra was appointed first architect of his Royal Highness Vittorio Amedeo of Savoy, on the 15th April 1714 and from that date took over the task of supervising building work and maintenance operations in the region governed by the Savoys. His plan for the rebuilding of the Castello di Rivoli dates back to 1718. Juvarra's grandiose plan incorporated Garove's idea for extending the castle but enlarged upon it to extend the range of the architectural construction. Only one third of the ambitious programme planned by Vittorio Amedeus II and Filippo Juvarra was completed: the rebuilding of the Seventeenth century castle. Political and financial difficulties intervened and building work was broken off just as the entrance pillars were erected. A plan to build a symmetrical structure on the site of the seventeenth century gallery was never started due to the suspension of building work.

Filippo Juvarra. Study for the entrance and grand staircase.

We can gain an idea of the grandiose nature of the design from drawings in the archives and architect's sketches and paintings that Juvarra himself commissioned from artists to show the sovereign how magnificent his new castle would be. Southern and eastern views of the new palace were painted by Giampaolo Pannini, while Andrea Lucatelli painted views from the north and west. Paintings by Massimo Teodoro Michela and Marco Ricci, inspired by Juvarra's sketches, revealed how the reception rooms would look when enlivened by colour.

A comparison between Juvarra's drawings and these paintings show how architect and painter worked together or, rather, how the architect tirelessly guided the artist's brush until he achieved exactly the appearance he required. Michela's painting in particular, with its cross-section view of the central entrance in the course of construction, with bricklayers and carpenters at work, gives an accurate picture of how the building work was planned. The results produced by this hive of industry remain a significant achievement, even though the architecture never reached its final form due to reasons beyond the control of the architect and the commissioner. The most complete picture of the construction designed by Juvarra is given to us by a modern model which Juvarra commissioned Carlo Maria Ugliengo to make in 1718. This was fortunately found in 1943 in the castle cellars by Vittorio Viale, director of the Turinese civic museums, during one of his pilgrimages to the castle. At that time he played a leading role in saving works of art threatened by bombardment and war-time attacks. Sadly, the model was severely damaged on one side because

M. T. Michela. Entrance to the Castello di Rivoli and grand staircase (detail).

G. P. Pannini. View of the Castello di Rivoli (detail).

M. Ricci, Reception room at the Castello di Rivoli (detail).

it had been used as firewood by soldiers staying in the castle. It was nevertheless saved from complete destruction and taken to Palazzo Madama. The missing part was the south slope, with its extensive parterres broken up by carriageways and a pedestrian stairway. This area was designed to act as a setting for future construction, but was never completed.

In 1730, Vittorio Amedeo II abdicated. His subsequent attempt to regain power was opposed by his son Carlo Emanuele III who decided to place his father in solitary confinement in Rivoli Castle. The sovereign's dreams of grandeur thus ended under these sorry circumstances.

During the last decade of the Eighteenth century, Vittorio Amadeo III commissioned Carlo Randoni to resume work at Rivoli. Changes in the political situation and the development of new republican trends had damped the ambitions of the House of Savoy. Randoni carried out as much work as was necessary to complete the castle up to the entrance area with the aim of restoring dignity to the building and making it as functional as possible. He even began to build a temporary stairway, but in 1798 this work was also broken off because the invasion of Napoleonic troops brought other more pressing problems for the Piedmontese state.

During the period of French occupation, Napoleon presented the Rivoli Castle to a marshall in his army as a prize for military merit. The building was returned to the Savoys after the Restoration, when it underwent further, minor building work. Soon it became a heavy financial burden and quite beyond the financial means of the far from rich Piedmontese state. As the other great Savoy palaces were gradually broken up or sold to the State to avoid the drain of maintenance costs on the family coffers, Rivoli Castle began to go into decline as well.

Throughout the Nineteenth century and until the first decade of the Twentieth century, the castle was used to house contingents of troops. They made themselves at home as best they could, but their presence led to a steady decline in the conditions of the furnishings with extremely severe loss of the artistic heritage.

In 1883, the town of Rivoli bought the castle from the Savoy heirs for the sum of 100,000 lire. Yet it continued to fall steadily into decline. Sporadic attempts to use the castle always resulted in more damage, as the castle was used for purposes for which it was not designed.

In 1906 and 1911, the castle housed two exhibitions which required adaptation work to be carried out on the ground floor. Juvarra's initial building work on the entrance was covered by a later form of architecture, intended solely for cosmetic purposes and thus destined to last only for a short time. No solid brick arches or stone columns; simply wooden vaults and fragile stucco columns.

After several decades of absolute abandonment, the rooms of Rivoli were reoccupied by the army, which returned in 1927 with a contingent of eight hundred soldiers. After all the castle's changes of ownership and different occupants, we must also add to the tally of destruction the damage caused by the German occupation during World War II; the damage caused by incendiary bombs; and subsequent damage which occurred during sporadic haphazard attempts to adapt the castle to various purposes.

Attitudes to the castle began to change after the war. The Rivoli complex was no longer seen as an inconveniently large presence to be used as a container for temporary purposes, but as a monument to be saved from certain ruin. Although this preoccupation lived on in the hearts of those who were aware of the importance of restoring the castle's lost dignity, this view was not favourably received at a time when the country's attention was taken up by the need for rebuilding rather than by a wish to preserve its historical and artistic heritage.

In 1961, the superintendent Umberto Chierici included the restoration of the Castello di Rivoli among other work planned for Piedmontese historical monuments to mark the Centenary of Italian Unification and commissioned Andrea Bruno to produce a plan, but the costs were found to be excessive and the attempt was not successful.

In the meantime, the rooms of the Manica Lunga had been adapted as emergency housing and provided refuge for thirty six homeless families. It also accommodated a timber mill, stabling for livestock and a mechanical workshop.

In May 1967, contributions from the Piedmont Historical Monument Committee and the town of Rivoli made it possible to begin building work. Although on a much smaller scale than originally planned in 1961, the work focused on a particularly significant point: the entrance designed by Juvarra. The cosmetic covering added to the Eighteenth-century structure at the beginning of this century was already in an advanced state of decay. When later elements and certain structures added by the army were removed, the original pillars and arches were revealed and an authentic appearance was restored to the incomplete entrance.

Ten more years went by before it was possible to tackle general restoration work on the castle. After a long period of abandonment, the building had been reduced to the brink of ruin. Water poured through the roof and unfastened windows, before going on to ruin floors, paintings and stuccoes. The structure began to give way. In the autumn of 1978 a vault on the second floor collapsed, while other parts of the Seventeenth century gallery now known as the Manica Lunga also collapsed.

Aid from the Piedmont Regional Authorities has finally made it possible to take on the restoration work so long overdue. The Castello di Rivoli's new role as a contemporary art museum has definitely given the building a living role which underscores its important cultural value.

Model by Carlo Maria Ugliengo opened to show entrance and grand staircase.

The drawing shows the actual Castle buildings, extended by Filippo Juvarra's plans.

Restoration

Andrea Bruno

The Rivoli complex seen from the air (Photo: Andrea Bruno Archive)

Panoramic look-out. (Photo: Andrea Bruno Archive)

Ten years have passed since the Castello di Rivoli was inaugurated by the "Ouverture" Exhibition held in December 1984. These years of far-sightedness and achievement have confirmed Turin as a force to be reckoned with within the world of contemporary art.

After years of abandonment to the ravages of time and unsympathetic men, the first glimmerings of interest and desire to care for this historical monument date back to the Sixties. Men such as Vittorio Viale, director of the Civic Museums of Turin, Luigi Carluccio, responsible for major exhibitions at the Turin Modern Art Gallery, and Umberto Chierici, superintendent of historical monuments in Piedmont, began to become concerned about the fate of the castle. These were the years of the building boom and proposals for restoring our architectural heritage received little consideration. The desire of these men to restore the monument to its former glory produced no immediate response because the cultural climate was not ready, but nevertheless set off a slow but steady chain reaction which led, in 1967, to a first result: restoration of the monumental entrance. When more recent superstructures added in recent times but now in dilapidated condition were removed, the work which Filippo Juvarra begun during the second decade of the Eighteenth century was bought to light and restored.

In 1978 the chairman of the Piedmont Regional Authority, Aldo Viglione, made a specific cultural decision to restore the castle in order to make it into a Museum of contemporary art.

The resulting building site became the dynamic and optimistic symbol of an idea which had seemed an impossible dream for many years. Human enterprise, skill, dreams and spirit of adventure were again engaged in the very place where, centuries before, other men with other dreams had been rudely interrupted in their work.

The history of the Savoy residence in Rivoli spans several centuries. During medieval times, a fortified castle was built on the site of a defensive stronghold dating from very ancient times. The castle later passed into the ownership of the Savoys, when it was rebuilt and adapted to form the residence of Emanuele Filiberto in the Sixteenth century. At the beginning of the Seventeenth century, extensive rebuilding work was undertaken by Carlo Emanuele I and his architect, Carlo di Castellamonte, to give the residence the appearance shown in the *Theatrum Sabaudiae*, with the compact castle centre separated from the "gallery" or long "sleeve" designed to house the Duke's picture gallery. In an overriding will to advertise their own presence, the Savoys made no scruple of wiping out signs of pre-existing presences. Furthermore, the Baroque culture prevalent at that time was based on a return to classical artistic canons and totally opposed to medieval architectural forms, which were considered barbarous and uncivilised.

The great building was burnt and severely damaged by French armies during the last decade of the Seventeenth century and rebuilding work was entrusted by Vittorio Amedeo II to Filippo Juvarra, an architect from Messina whom the duke called to Turin. In 1714, the same architect embarked upon projects for a third extension to the capital, the Basilica di Superga, the Chiesa di Santa Cristina, the military quarters of Porta Susina, the Palazzina di Caccia in Stupinigi, the Venaria Reale and Rivoli itself.

Juvarra's great idea of furnishing Vittorio Amedeo II with a palace able to stand on an equal footing with the great courts of Europe was achieved only in part. Building work was halted at the central point, which was destined to become a monumental entrance with grand staircases and reception rooms. This halt to building work saved the Seventeenth-century picture gallery building, which Juvarra had earmarked for total demolition.

Rivoli Castle is divided into two sections for specific historical reasons, which the restoration plan set out to respect and value. Juvarra's contribution still represents the pinnacle of the castle's architecture and, although incomplete, still reveals all the force of his original design. The recent restoration plan set out to emphasise these unfinished Juvarran features by avoiding attempts to complete his work or perform arbitrary reconstructions. The unfinished appearance has thus been maintained and the ancient structures preserved in full, while the equipment necessary for the castle's new function has been produced using the resources and technologies of today.

The Castle

Restoration work began in August 1979.

The disastrous condition of the roofing demanded that this aspect receive absolute priority. During the bombardments of 1943, some incendiary bombs destroyed part of the roof. Rainwater was thus able to penetrate the areas beneath the roofs and now the wood was rotting and infested with micro-organisms and cracks. Bushes flourished among the rubble in a surreal scene of decadence. Collapse appeared imminent for both the roof and its underlying vaults. The surviving structures were so unstable that they were dismantled and replaced by laminated wood trusses, which span a gap of twenty seven metres and leave the entire area under the roof exposed to view and available for exhibition purposes.

The entrance area most clearly reveals the break between the castle building, which was going up, and the Seventeenth-century gallery, which was due to come down in order to provide more space for the new palace. Here, the existence of pillars with joints for fitting arches and vaults which were never completed reveal how suddenly Juvarra's building work was halted. Everything that would ultimately have been hidden by subsequent decoration and finishing work is left exposed in its nakedness, like a sort of x-ray of building techniques, a lesson to be learnt by heart. The restoration work has preserved this sudden break. Stairways end in mid-air; column bases, niches where statues would have been housed, and bases for decorations never fitted have all been protected by taking simple steps to prevent further decay. Joints have been restored and filled, and flat surfaces have been protected with copper sheets and edging. A plan of the structure which was never completed has been reproduced on the ground. This is faithful to Juvarra's original drawings in every respect. Marble and stone slabs are used to mark the position of uprights and vault angles on the porphyry floor.

A lack of efficient links between floors made the castle ineffective as a court residence from the outset. At the end of the eighteenth century, Vittorio Amedeo III commissioned the architect Carlo Randoni to remedy this shortcoming by designing a temporary staircase in an area near the entrance. Yet this work was never completed either, for a variety of reasons. The form the vertical links would take was therefore a matter for the imagination. This problem had to be overcome, however, without interfering with the building's original and appealing air of incompletion. It would not be good enough to think of some over-clever solution or to mutilate the structure without cause.

The only possible site for a new stairway was the place suggested by Randoni at the end of the eighteenth century. This place was ideal because the compartment earmarked for the stairway was completely free from horizontal encumbrances and fixed structures throughout its entire height. The structure of the new stairway is mixed. The first floor is reached by walking along two ramps fitted against the perimeter walls. A central stairway supported by a steel structure then rises up into space from this height. This structure is divided into ten flights, each supported at one end by the walkways which

Part of south prospect "finished" in plaster (Photo: Andrea Bruno Archive)

Forecourt and exterior staircase of the Manica Lunga. (Photo: Andrea Bruno Archive).

Truncated head of the Manica Lunga (Photo: Andrea Bruno Archive)

Truncated head of the Manica Lunga as it appears today (Photo: Andrea Bruno Archive)

provide independent access to the various floors. The other end is suspended from two steel cables, which are in turn anchored to a cross-beam at the top. A preliminary survey carried out before work began revealed Randoni's original drawings of the stairway. They had been drawn in pencil on the walls of the stairwell and then coloured. These were duly restored.

A great roughly completed Eighteenth-century vault on the second floor of the castle bears witness to the boldness and technical skill of that age. The constructional layout of the vault can be seen in full from the area beneath the roof. After the war, the roof was rebuilt with reinforced concrete trusses by the Civil Engineering department. This design solution is one more example of how different approaches were adopted at different times to resolve the same problems. The great vault was consolidated and restored: a new metal walkway (the only route to the area beneath the roof) passes diagonally through the area so that visitors can see how it is constructed. The reinforced concrete roof has also been preserved because it reveals the stages this historical monument underwent during the destruction of the last war and marks the first contribution of modern technology to the body of the former building.

A steel and glass observatory window fitted at the top of the great unfinished wall juts out towards the Manica Lunga. This offers a vantage point from which to look out at the surrounding scenery and also affords vistors a close-up of the way Javarra's original structure would ideally have worked out. At one's feet lie the truncated entrance structures with a plan of the incomplete part drawn on the porphyry floor. Ahead stretches the Manica Lunga, its ancient form rebuilt and restored to new formal and functional dignity.

Decorations had been irreparably lost from castle rooms: furniture had disappeared completely while fixtures had been mutilated and damaged. The same was true of the paintings and stuccos. In this case too, we decided not to restore the rooms to a finished, uniform condition which would have evoked ancient splendours. We chose instead to preserve the rooms in their original state for now and the future. However damaged and fragmented this state may be, it is nevertheless a true reflection of the events experienced by the building during its long period of abandonment. We opted for completion only in two cases: a marble floor designed by Juvarra for a room on the first floor was completed with reference to archive documentation – and Carlo Emanuele I's room was restored to its original appearance on the basis of drawings left by Carlo Randoni.

The castle basement is not completely accessible. It contains small areas enclosed between very thick walls and spurs of rock jutting from the morainic base on which the ancient fortress was sited. Apart from the areas occupied by a small restaurant, present since the end of the Nineteenth century in the southeastern section, only one other room adjacent to the entrance area remains free and usable. This now contains a revolving stage and may be used as a small theatre for about one hundred people.

During the summer, the castle provides a backdrop for shows held in the open air, on the forecourt and in the entrance area. These events emphasise the relationship between the castle's specific function as a museum and the great cultural potential of the building.

The Manica Lunga

Once work on the castle was completed, building work began on the Manica Lunga. The building was still being used for purposes for which it had not been designed and was in a condition of advanced decay. Most of the roof and underlying roof space had collapsed and the fixtures had disappeared. Water was free to enter and cause damage to walls and vaults. The interior space was broken up by partition walls added to adapt the building for temporary housing. Three sections of a factory built before World War II were attached to the north facade.

Because the building had undergone so many changes, the line of great original windows was no longer recognisable because it had been concealed by an untidy series of openings of different sizes made at different levels. It took close examination of the dimensions and some probing around before the precise position could be established. It was then possible to see that the building really had looked like pictures of it published in the Seventeenth-century publication *Theatrum Sabaudiae*, and it became possible to restore the facades to their original dignity of composition.

Once the great building had been cleared of all the unsightly additions which had so marred its appearance, the Seventeenth-century Gallery was recovered in all its length. This exceptionally long and geometrically pure shape could not be diminished by the intrusion of other elements. For this reason, lifts and wash-rooms were located out of sight behind the outer wall. Light structures and mirrored glass were used to emphasise the formal and structural autonomy of old and new structures. The sloping stack of the steel chimney indicates its distinctive role as a technical and functional element.

The roof which covered the Manica Lunga was replaced by a structure designed for the Gallery's new role as an exhibition site. The roof slopes follow the outline of the original roof and are supported by a series of metal hoops. Two continuous slots allow light through but can be dimmed to adapt to exhibition requirements.

Mirrored windows along the side of the Gallery provide extensive views of the landscape. The gallery ends in a great window which frames a view of the opposite castle wall. The wall at the other end contains mirrored panels which appear to multiply the already great length of the Gallery, stretching as it does the entire length of the second floor. The Gallery is capable of housing large travelling exhibitions. Thus this building, which has been forced to suffer so many insults and so much mishandling during the course of the centuries, has been restored to its original function. This type of Gallery predated the concept of a museum and was designed to exhibit works of art selected from a great Lord's collection in sequence. The idea is obviously still of value today.

The main entrance to the Manica Lunga is Juvarra's original entrance, opposite the castle entrance. Only the outer walls of the entrance were built and this construction is still roofed in light material which reflects the pattern of the stairways designed by Juvarra but never built.

A large underground cistern commissioned by Emanuele Filiberto and now under the Manica Lunga was found intact. This structure makes an excellent caveau or temporary storage space for works of art.

The Manica Lunga is designed to house exhibitions put on by the Museum, and also scientific, teaching and accessory facilities for the public.

The ground floor houses offices, stores for exhibition materials and restoration workshops for wood and metals. A small cafeteria is directly accessible from the entrance, and rooms destined for information services and the presentation of cultural activities are also connected directly to the outside.

The first floor houses a library, reading room and video room. A space within the Museum has been set aside for the sale of books, catalogues and objects. An external balcony which runs along the south prospect is connected directly to the castle forecourt by a new stairway enclosed by brick walls. This was built to replace an old ruined room and provides a convenient alternative route.

Interior of the Manica Lunga (Photo: Andrea Bruno Archive)

Interior of the Manica Lunga as it appears today (Photo: Andrea Bruno Archive)

The Rivoli complex will become fully operational when the Manica Lunga is opened to the public and a new building designed to provide support services for the public and more Museum space is complete. This new one-storey building will be parallel to the south side of the Manica Lunga and separated from the Gallery by an extensive area which will be laid as a garden but may also be used for open-air exhibitions. The design of the new building will be uncluttered and economical and house washrooms, and restaurant with a spectacular view of the Alps. The building will be directly connected to the Manica Lunga by a tunnel with windows. Its flat roof is also designed to be used as a look-out, which can be reached by a small external stairway. This walkway will be about one hundred metres long and equipped with comfortable seats. Possible alternative uses for the walkway include temporary exhibitions (connected with the museum or completely independent), or exhibitions connected with meetings or shows planned by the Rivoli complex to complement and enhance its main function as a contemporary art museum.

The stairs seen from below (Photo Patrizia Mussa, Turin)

The work "Figure Nere" by Michelangelo Pistoletto in the Room of Bacchus and Ariadne with its original flooring designed by Juvarra. (Photo: Patrizia Mussa, Turin).

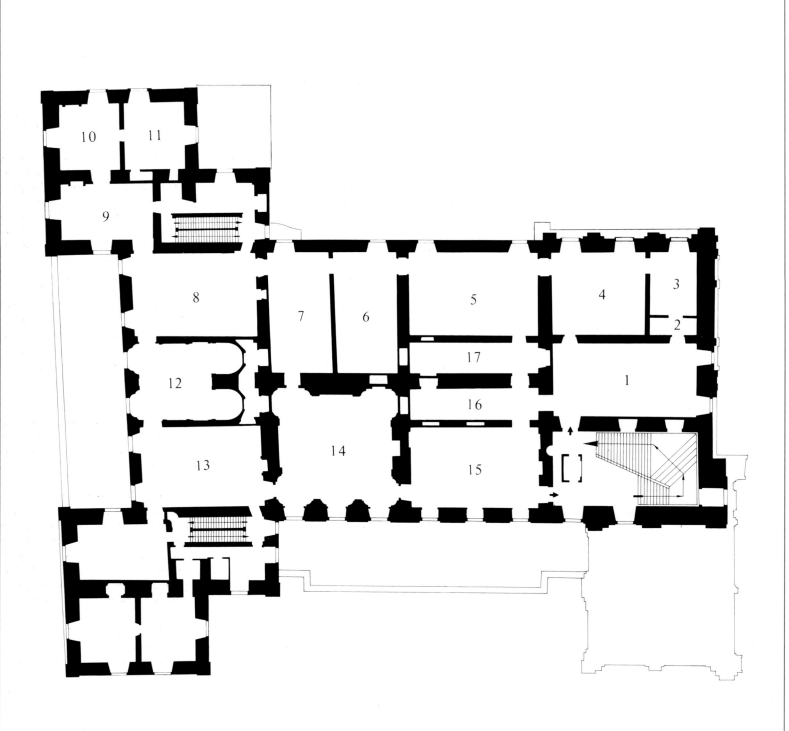

FIRST FLOOR

Guide to the Interior Decoration of Rivoli Castle

Gianfranco Gritella

First Floor
Staircase

The present metal staircase supported by steel tie-beams, completed in 1984, occupies a large stairwell that previously held a partially completed eighteenth-century staircase and a temporary nineteenth-century extension built during the period of military occupancy. When the construction work undertaken by Juvarra was definitively halted, all that had been built of the monumental double staircase with opposing ramps designed by the architect to flank the central hall, was the foundation and the first few steps, today outside the Castle, flanked by double columns.

When Carlo Randoni planned the completion of the building in the late Eighteenth century, the problem of quickly rendering the finished apartments accessible to the court made it indispensable to furnish the Castle with a temporary main staircase flanking Juvarra's, on which a great deal of work remained to be done.

On January 30, 1793 Randoni signed the plans for a brick staircase that was to connect the vestibule, located at the top of the first exterior ramp of Juvarra's staircase, with the first and second floors of the Castle. The new "temporary" staircase was to be built in place of the existing wood staircase, which Juvarra commissioned.

The new staircase was to be made up of five ramps borne by brick pillars. Only the first two, leading to the first floor of the Castle, were completed. The forms of the foundations of Randoni's staircase, demolished in 1981, are indicated in the floor of the interior atrium by slabs of white marble.

On the walls one can still see the grey painted marks indicating the placement of the supports of the staircase, which had been predisposed for the execution of the masonry work and for the positioning of the steps. Almost at the level of the second floor an exposed brick band around the perimeter of the stairwell marks the impost line of a ceiling vault that was to have been constructed in the place of the main staircase, creating the support for the additional room indicated in Juvarra's design.

Rooms 1, 2, 3, 4, 5, 6, 16, 17

These rooms, presently painted white, were not decorated during the building programmes directed by Juvarra (1717-1725) and Randoni (1792-1798).

Room 7. Parade Room, Room of the Grotesques with Procession of Bacchus, or Room of Orpheus and the Maenads

This is the last room on the first floor. The decoration was prepared in Juvarra's time and completed to the specifications of Randoni at the end of the century,

when the apartments were prepared to accommodate the courts of Vittorio Amedeo III and later, Vittorio Emanuele I.

Linked conceptually to Rooms 8, 9, 10, and 11 with which it shares the theme of grotesques, it preserves a fine ceiling fresco that can be attributed to the workshop of Filippo Minei and Nicolò Malatto.

In a mixtilinear frame at the centre of the ceiling appears a delicately executed scene enlivened by the dance of priestesses of Dionysus who, holding the verge crowned with ivy and vine leaves, give free play to their exaltation accompanied by musicians. At the sides, all around the vault, fantasy paintings – animals, winged figures, harpies, panels with zoomorphic scenes, mythological figures and curiosities – divide the surface of the ceiling into symmetrical fields. On the whole the scenes have maintained the sharp colours of the first painting, completed in 1726. The panels above the doors, with traces of a white and gold decoration that framed octagonal canvases, were installed after 1793. The two polychrome marble fireplaces date from the first half of the Eighteenth century.

Room 8. Parade Room or Room of the Cages

This room and the three rooms that follow, located in the southeast tower, were intended in Juvarra's plan to make up the private apartment of Vittorio Amedeo II. All four rooms are decorated with grotesques, which were executed by a large team of painters led by Francesco Fariano, Nicolò Malatto, Filippo Minei and Pietro Antonio Pozzo. The scheme as a whole is of high thematic and decorative quality. Its unique nature and controlled execution make it a singular expression of the pictorial repertory of the early Eighteenth century in Piedmont, a sign of a broadly based cultural renewal expressed in figurative motifs of antique ancestry and of Roman and Genoese derivation.

The suite was built between 1720 and 1727. The ceiling frescoes here represent, at the centre, Diana on a chariot pulled by deer and surrounded by plant and animal motifs, and fantastical subjects showing young girls with bows and arrows inside fragile pavilions borne by harpies; at the sides, trophies of weapons, animals, hunting equipment and filiform ornaments with hanging cages; in the corners, nymphs with deer and dogs seated on rectangular medallions with scenes of animals fighting and, at the centre, winged figures holding scrolls with landscapes.

The paintings, executed in bright colours on a white background, are among the most elegant decorations in the suite. Notwithstanding the contribution of numerous assistants, they are probably mainly the work of Nicolò Malatto (active at Rivoli from 1716), Michele Antonio Milocco and Filippo Minei. The decorative structure of the room was completed by the refined ornamentation of the doors, with mixtilinear panels by Domenico Olivero, Domenico Gambone and Michele Antonio Milocco representing landscapes with architecture, ruins, and small figures.

Rooms 9, 10, 11. Apartment of King Vittorio Amedeo II: first room or Room of the Trophies, second room or Room of the Labours of Hercules, bedroom or Room of the Grotesques

Formerly finished with damask wall coverings, the first room retains a grotesque ceiling with monochromatic rectangular panels showing battle scenes and two groups of three figures with trophies of weapons and flags. An ivy-shoot runs along the frieze of the lower moulding, which postdates the first decorations of the room (completed in Juvarra's time). The red breccia fireplace belongs to the earlier period.

The quality of the ceiling paintings and the theme of the subjects that accompany the principal scenes in the second room refer back to the preceding Room of the Cages. Around the central scene with Jupiter crowning the hero, appear four labours of Hercules: the struggle with the Nemean Lion, the killing of the Cretan Bull, the capture of the Erimantean Boar and the capture of the Cerinean Doe. Each scene is framed in a suspended temple with a tympanum borne by caryatids. In the corners are harpies with architectural motifs and filiform festoons, and putti and winged cherubim holding drapes. The cornice with stucchi and friezes in white and gold, is also well preserved. The decoration of the third room is qualitatively inferior to the preceding ones. The decorative elements are repeated with less expressive intensity, but in a similar thematic repertory. Grisaille figures stand out against gold-ground squares within oval panels enclosed by octagonal frames. The carved and gilded woodwork of the two small lateral doors (notably the oval panels at the top) which led to the private chapel and the service stair, belongs to Juvarra's period. A late eighteenth-century monochrome decoration adorns the walls, and *grisaille* floral motifs grace the panels above the doors and the older fireplace.

Room 12. Atrium or Room of Bacchus and Ariadne

The extraordinary decorations of this room, which are almost intact, were conceived and followed throughout their execution by Juvarra between 1718 and 1722. Located on the axis of two later, eighteenth-century corridors, this room had the function of con-necting the two first-floor apartments: that of King Vittorio Amedeo II, on the south side, and that of his queen, on the north.

The fine stucchi of the walls and vault frame frescoes are by the Florentine painter Sebastiano Galeotti: in the central tondo, the encounter of Bacchus and Ariadne; in the lunettes and wedges of the vaults, Bacchic scenes, in perfectly preserved bright colours. In the pendentives at the base of the vault are four oval fields framed by stucco scrolls with monochrome frescoes of two fauns and two Bacchantes. Contemporary documents place the date of execution of these frescoes at 1722. White marble columns with Corinthian capitals of refined design mark the corners of the room and the doors to the terrace. The Corinthian architectural order is taken up again in the pilasters that articulate the walls, with festoons of flowers and fruit in bas-relief and *rocaille* decorations in the region of the two false doors, which originally contained a pair of washstands. Niches at the centre of the lateral walls hold busts of Carlo Emanuele II, portrayed as Adonis, and his consort Maria Giovanna Battista di Savoia Nemours (mother of Vittorio Amedeo II, refined patron of the arts who commissioned Juvarra's façade for Palazzo Madama in Turin), here traditionally recognized as Diana. The two fine busts, made by the Luganese Bernardo Falconi in 1668-1669, were originally part of the selection of sculpture that the Duke of Savoy preserved in his apartments at the Royal Palace in Turin. The illusionistic floor, a geometric pattern in black Como, white Busca, and grey Valdieri marble, was designed by Juvarra in 1721 and executed by the stonecutter Carlo Berardo in 1725, for approximately 95 lire.

In the wall opposite the terrace are two large niches with shelves for glassware, graced by refined wood carvings that postdate Juvarra's period. The vaults of the niches are adorned with grotesques and arabesques by Francesco Fariano and Nicolò Malatto. The marble side tables and the pink colouring of the walls of the niches date from the time of the Duke of Aosta.

Room 13. Room of the Coats of Arms, originally Room of the Valets à Pieds

This room, which was remodeled in Juvarra's time, has a nineteenth-century geometric ceiling executed when the Castle was a barracks. It preserves fragments of the older decorative scheme at the bottom of the walls (originally covered with yellow fabric) and in the squinches of the windows, where one may glimpse a decoration with *rocaille* motifs that frame inner bays decorated with gold leaf, today virtually gone.

For a few years after 1724 this room hosted some of the large paintings, by Giovanni Paolo Pannini, Marco Ricci, Andrea Lucatelli and Massimo Teodoro Michela, showing Rivoli Castle as it would have appeared had Juvarra's design been completed. Today the paintings are preserved in the Museo Civico d'Arte Antica di Palazzo Madama in Turin and at Racconigi Castle. Through a hole in the floor made during the restoration one may view the medieval well which was the Castle's principal water source until the Eighteenth century. The water was drawn up by a system of winches worked from the lower opening, which communicated with the kitchens, located beneath the outside terrace.

Room 14. Room of the Stucchi or First Antechamber of the King's Apartment

This room, built to plans by Filippo Juvarra between 1718 and 1720, was obtained by demolishing the walls and ceilings of two earlier rooms and part of the seventeenth-century corridor designed by Castellamonte. The new volume was covered by the present baldachin vault, carried by buttresses from which volute-corbels that separate the four lunettes of the corners, emerge. Here a few fragments of a pictorial decoration with putti and military emblems, executed by Angelo Vacca and Giovanni Comandù in 1793-1794, remain. The polychrome false-marble decorations that cover the pillars and vaults date from roughly the same period. The stucchi were executed by Pietro Filippo Somasso under the direction of Juvarra. The central bay of the vault, divided into diminishing square coffers alluding to a false dome, is constructed around a medallion with the monogram of Vittorio Amedeo II. Four pendentives descending toward the corbels are decorated with rippled seashells that penetrate between the deep lunettes containing precious flowered garlands tied with ribbons. The theme of the seashell is taken up again at the base of the corbels that carry the vault and in the arched tympana over the doors, which postdate Juvarra's decorations. In the walls of the corner vaults, six circular niches contain antique marble busts from the collections of the Duke of Savoy, brought here in 1720. The military trophies in carved and painted wood, set on the moulding of the walls between the lunettes, date from the late eighteenth-century restructuring of the building.

The present floor in grey Valdieri, white Busca and green Alpine bardiglio, was executed during the recent restoration following instructions indicated in an autograph drawing by Juvarra dated June 1721. The late eighteenth-century fireplace contains an iron heat plate with the coat of arms of the Duke of Savoy and the initials of Vittorio Amedeo.

Room 15. Room of the Continents or Second Antechamber of the King's Apartment

This and the adjoining room were the antechambers that preceded the apartments of the sovereigns in Juvarra's design.

Built between 1718 and 1722 utilizing part of the walls erected by Amedeo di Castellamonte in the Seventeenth century, it opens toward the south onto one of the two seventeenth-century corridors that joined the reception room with the ducal apartments, facing east.

The walls and ceiling received a pictorial and polychrome stucco decoration between 1793 and 1795 under the direction of Carlo Randoni and Giuseppe Battista Piacenza, the architects commissioned to complete the building and "modernize" the apartments to accommodate the small court of Vittorio Emanuele, Duke of Aosta, to whom the Castle had been given in appanage by his father Vittorio Amedeo III.

Inside the framework of stucchi that graces the walls and ceiling with geometric profiles, festoons, and seashells, the painters Evangelista Torricelli and Giovanni Comandù and their assistants painted allegories of the four continents – Africa, America, Europe and Asia – in the lunettes of the corners; and the Chariot of Apollo with the rising sun in the central field. Two allegorical figures in sanguine monochrome, in the central panels, represent the Po and Dora Rivers. During the recent restoration coordinated by the Soprintendenza per i Beni Artistici e Storici del Piemonte, removal of the later repaintings that covered much of the ceiling revealed, in two lateral fields, the sketches executed in 1794 by Comandù for two of six allegories that were to represent six winds. As can be gleaned from a document in the painter's hand attached to the receipt of payment, the decorative scheme was abandoned: "The late Sig.e Intendente having ordered me to paint the six winds in low relief in the above-mentioned Chamber, and the cartoons, or large drawings, having been made earlier in Turin, I painted two of them, after which he had them rubbed out because they were too much for the Chamber. I [Comandù] spent seven days, cost L. 85".

The decorations of the walls, in pastel colours, embrace two elements in green marble designed by Randoni. The three doorways opening onto the corridor originally had glass doors in the same style as those leading to the outside terrace and to the staircase.

Second Floor
Rooms 18, 19, 20
These rooms, presently painted white, were not dec-

orated during the building programs directed by Juvarra (1717-1725) and Randoni (1792-1798).

Room 21. Audience Chamber or Room of the Putti
Adjacent to the duchess's bedroom (Room 21) was probably the bedroom of her eldest daughter Maria Beatrice, who in 1812 married Francesco IV of Austria, Duke of Modena, and whose children later inherited the Castle. A window on the south side opens onto an eighteenth-century balcony adorned with a forged-iron railing bearing the monogram of Vittorio Amedeo II. The railing was made between 1711 and 1713, at which time the reconstruction of the Castle, damaged in the war with the French, was directed by the architect Michelangelo Garove.

The room has an interesting decoration in the ceiling vault (partially ruined), a delicately colored and rapidly painted fresco of almost scenographic character. Eight groups of putti gazing out from behind a false balustrade pose playfully in alternation with four other groups in monochrome. Trompe-l'oeil architecture in pastel tones completes the scheme. The entire pictorial repertory of this room, including the temperas above the doors with pastoral scenes and peasant figures (today preserved at the Soprintendenza per i Beni Artistici e Storici del Piemonte), was executed in 1793-1794 by the Monregalese painter Giovenale Bongiovanni, who signed the ceiling at the bottom of the vault, above the moulding. This painter was particularly well known for his skill and imagination. He worked in various rooms of the Castle and, more extensively, in the Royal Palace of Turin during the last quarter of the eighteenth century.

The room was finished with floral-motif papier-peint wallpaper, of which a few small fragments are still visible. A mirror and wall console stood against the west wall, in front of the bed, which was located at the centre of the opposite wall. The room remained incomplete, as the wood plank floor was intended as a temporary substitute for inlaid parquets that were included in the cost estimate, but never executed.

Room 22. Room of the Sunrise or Bedroom
This room, also called the Room of Spring or Large Room, was the bedroom of the Duchess of Aosta, Maria Teresa d'Austria-Este, wife of Vittorio Amedeo I, King of Sardinia.

Its name derives from the ceiling decoration, with a brightly coloured allegory by Guglielmo Lévera and Pietro Cuniberti at the centre, and trompe-l'oeil caryatids painted by Angelo Vacca in the impost band of the vault. The paintings, approved by the architect Randoni, were completed in 1795. The pronunced

illusionism of the composition, with extensive parts in monochrome, shows a technique of execution derived from the scenographic and theatrical compositions in which Lévera, who had studied with Galliari and was active at the Teatro Regio in Turin, was specialized.

The distinct colour contrasts of the ceiling harmonize with the surrounding areas of the vault, containing volutes and garlands of flowers held by female figures in a trompe-l'oeil architectural compartmentation creating false corner lunettes, and these areas in turn tie in harmoniously with the wooden decorative structure applied to the walls. The gilt and lacquered wood carvings were executed by the sculptors Bozzelli, Gritella and Fumasi in 1793-94. The six panels above the doors probably held paintings by Angelo Vacca or Pietro Cuniberti. The white Pont Canavese marble fireplace, with fine carvings once fitted with gilt bronze inserts by Simone Doguet, was made in 1793 by the master stonecutter Giuseppe Marsaglia. The walls were covered with light blue fabric similar to the drapes of the bed, which stood at the centre of the room facing the fireplace. The parquet floor, with geometric designs in walnut, linden, and olive wood, has been removed for conservation.

Chapel. Entered from Room 21 and two lateral doors, this was the private oratory of the Duchess of Aosta and her daughter Beatrice
This small "court chapel" was built between 1794 and 1795 to a design by Carlo Randoni dated December 27, 1793. It occupies an earlier room whose wall structures date from Juvarra's period.

The decorative program, extensively damaged during the Second World War, preserves a false marble wall decoration with white and gold stucchi framing the ceiling. The latter contains a religious scene painted by Giovanni Comandù. The woodworking and sculpture workshop of Ghigo was assigned the execution of the details in wood, the decorative carvings, the glass doors that open on to the lateral rooms, and the two small bookcases in the jambs of the main doorway.

The polychrome wood altar and the sumptuous frame of the icon, carved and gilded with a glory of cherubim and the Savoy crown, have been lost. But the sixteenth-century wooden altarpiece with the Holy Family, painted by Gerolamo Giovenone, originally in the Savoy collections and re-used by Randoni in 1795, is now preserved at the Soprintendenza per i Beni Artistici e Storici del Piemonte.

Prie-dieus were placed near the lateral tribune in front

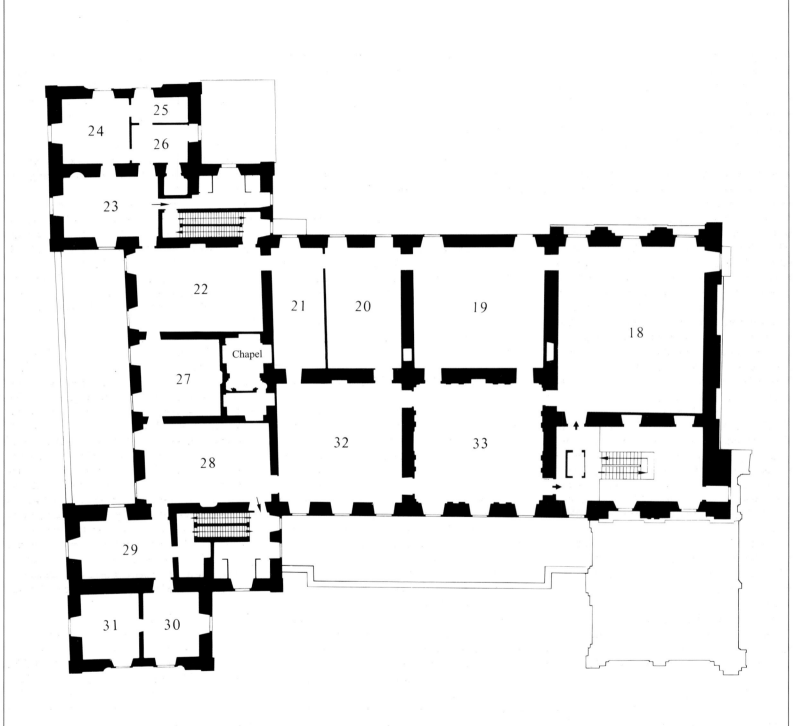

SECOND FLOOR

of the glass doors, and benches and a large prie-dieu by Giuseppe Gianotti and Vincenzo Spalla were located inside the chapel. Giovanni Comandù and Pietro Cuniberti made the paintings on wood with holy emblems and cherubim located on the splays of the doors, as well as the decorations, no longer in place, that completed the inside walls of the chapel.

Room 23. Room of Amedeo VIII or Room of the Incoronation
The fresco decoration of this room is the oldest in the entire building. It dates from 1623-28 and is a celebrated work by a team of painters from Lugano which included Isidoro, Francesco and Pompeo Bianchi.
The architecture of this room, like that of a few other rooms in the same tower and in the opposite one on the south side of the building, dates from the early decades of the seventeenth century, when the Castle was rebuilt under the architects Carlo and Amedeo di Castellamonte. The pictorial decoration survived the repeated wars fought by the Duchy of Savoy against France and was integrated into the renovation plan conceived by Filippo Juvarra in 1718.
The subjects of the frescoes are mentioned in numerous documents. They belong to a figurative program celebrating the political and military deeds of the principal representatives of the Counts of Savoy. Of the four rooms at Rivoli frescoed by the Bianchi (including the central Salone, where only a few fragments of the decoration discovered during the recent restoration remain), this is the only one in which the overall composition is virtually intact, despite the fact that the frescoes themselves have been repeatedly retouched.
The pictorial cycle represents the life of Amedeo VIII (1381-1451), the last Count and first Duke of Savoy. The description of the decorative scheme can be divided into two parts:
1) Ceiling.
The illusionistic architectural framework here consists of a group of corner columns bearing a series of arches surmounted by a balustrade surrounding an open space in which the Savoy coat of arms is held aloft by two allegorical figures symbolizing the virtues of Amedeo VIII. Four large panels located around the sides of the room represent the chief events in Amedeo's life: his investiture as Duke of Savoy (1391), his abdication (1439), his election to the papal throne at the Council of Basle (1439), and his subsequent renunciation (1449). The decorative complex is completed by allegorical personification of the Duke's theological, civil and military virtues, painted in the four corners in gold monochrome. Facts and events of the House of Savoy are narrated in the impost band of the vault, in small panels alternating with female figures in grisaille and the monogram of Vittorio Amedeo.
2) Walls.
Paintings representing allegories of the provinces annexed to the Duchy of Savoy or extended under the reign of Amedeo VIII occupy the walls, above a false marble inlay dado.
On the *Northeast Wall*: the left panel shows Savoy and the countryside of Nice with the Varo River; the right panel, the Iverdon River.
On the *Southeast Wall*: the left panel shows Savoy and the Duchy of Aosta with the Rhône River; the right panel, the Isére River.
On the *Southwest Wall*: the left panel shows the Duchy of Chiablese and the Rhône River, which in that Duchy becomes navigable; the right panel shows the Dora Baltea River and the city of Aosta.
On the *Northwest Wall*: the left panel shows the Po River; the right panel, the city of Cuneo and the Bormida River.

Room 24. Print Room or Room of the False Wood, originally Chamber of the Buffetto of the Duchess of Aosta
This room, included in Juvarra's extension of the southeast tower, was built between 1794 and 1795 under the direction of Randoni. It is characterized by a tempera decoration imitating fine wood veneer, which almost completely covers the walls and ceiling. This refined pictorial composition was executed by the brothers Pietro and Giovanni Torricelli, in collaboration with Pietro Palmieri, who made the paintings representing false etchings and drawings originally inserted in the octagonal frames above the doors and lost during the Napoleonic occupation. During the Restoration, before 1819, the missing paintings were replaced with allegorical subjects executed by Angelo Vacca. The few examples of extant woodwork – the frames of the doors, windows, and mirrors and the lateral panels – are the work of the woodcarver Ghigo. The decorative theme was in keeping with the new trends of "illuminated" decorativism of neoclassical derivation. It may still be seen to advantage today, thanks to preservation of the pictorial framework of the ceiling, the moulding and the walls. A central star-shaped space is surrounded by rhomboids containing "Pompeiian" figurines in tondos that imitate an intarsio of ebony wood. Other similar, brightly painted figurines revolve around the top of the vault. The cornice, partly carved with delicate bas-relief profiles, forms an ideal support for the band above, the Greek geometric pattern of which juts out illusionistically in trompe-l'oeil perspective. The room was also completed by neoclassical furniture (including three consoles beneath the mirrors, and benches with stools) and preparatory canvases for tapestries. The latter were placed in the vertical panels of the walls and of the double doors leading to the rooms at the sides.

Room 25. Bathroom or Room of the Veil
This may be the room that eighteenth-century documents indicate as the "Eastward-facing gauze cabinet".
It is a small room with wood trimming and a flat ceiling, the decoration of which, today badly ruined, dates from the time of the Duke of Aosta. The dominant theme of the ceiling fresco is a white veil with opulent festoons borne by gilt ribbons. The walls, today painted light blue, were once covered with wallpaper, furnished (like that of other rooms in the Castle) by the Turin bookseller Carlo Maria Toscanelli, in 1794.

Room 26. Room of the Falconers or Cabinet with Flowers, Animals and Putti
Built at the same time as the adjacent rooms, this room was decorated in 1793-94 by Angelo Vacca. The wall coverings have been lost, and the pictorial decoration, extensively damaged in the events that followed the armistice of 1943, does not appear to be of high quality. Qualitatively finer and better preserved is the dado, with hunting scenes and domestic animals, game, flowers and putti. The decorative theme, pertinent to the destination of the "villa" of Rivoli as a country residence, takes up a figurative repertory that was quite common in the monumental country palaces of the late Eighteenth and early Nineteenth centuries. The canvases that hung above the doors, with grisaille trompe-l'oeil bas-reliefs, flowers and animals, are preserved in the Palazzo Civico at Rivoli.

Room 27. Chinese Parlor
This is one of the most singular rooms in the whole Castle. Linking the apartments of the Duke and Duchess of Aosta, it was built between 1792 and 1794, when the building was granted in appanage by Vittorio Amedeo III to his son Vittorio Emanuele. The latter would become King of Sardinia in the post-Napoleonic Restoration.
The design is by Carlo Randoni, who also signed the decorative scheme on November 4, 1793. The artists Francesco and Giovanni Rebaudengo were charged with painting the wood details and the ceiling. The former was celebrated at the Savoy court as "specialist in several Chinese subjects".
The ornamentation takes the form of an illusory Ori-

ental garden pavilion on wooden columns over which a false fabric covering has been extended, hypothetically held up by a light trellis that gives rise to distinct trompe-l'oeil effects. Amidst a play of diamond-shapes, the fabric leaves an opening at the centre of the ceiling through which the sky may be glimpsed. A false red-and-gold brocade simulates Oriental wall-hangings that descend from a band with a Greek geometric decorative motif in wood. From the upper moulding emerged elements in papier-maché (some are still extant) in the form of dragon's heads. Stylized Oriental landscapes, in monochrome, alternate with scenes with exotic animals in gold on red in the band at the base of the vault. Numerous craftsmen worked, in 1793-94, on the wood carvings, the parquets, and the decoration at the bottom of the walls, an almost transparent wood trellis that creates a play of octagons. Giovanni Antonio Gritella and Giovanni Fumari are the wood sculptors who executed the sixteen wooden half-columns with flower-shoot reliefs, the decorations of the door and window frames, and the clusters of flowers above the doors. The same workshop of carpenters and sculptors made the furniture that completed the room, including the tables placed at the centre of the walls beneath the mirrors and the wooden fireplace with bronze detailing by Simone Doguet and carvings by Gianotti, Frotta and Raineri. The latter also made the mantelpiece with Chinese scene and the doors to the chapel and the adjacent rooms. Two false doors in the side walls reveal, beneath more recent paint, the original decoration with trompe-l'oeil drapes and wall-coverings. The panel with Oriental decoration located on the wall between the two windows, today contains an Oriental painting that is not part of the decorative scheme, instead of the original mirror.

Room 28. Audience Chamber or Room of the Crowns

This room adjoined the apartments of the Duke and Duchess of Aosta, on the right, and the group of rooms decorated by Juvarra and constituting the apartment of the Prince of Piedmont, to the north. Its decorations were extensively damaged during the period in which the Castle was abandoned, following the events of September 8, 1943. Only a few fragments of the wooden ornaments that surrounded the doors and the mirrors at the centre of the main walls, remain. The ceiling was never decorated. The double cornice is singular. The upper band, containing a fine stucco frieze with the initials of Vittorio Amedeo II surmounted by crowns, was executed in Juvarra's time by the stucco-workers directed by Somasso. The lower band, in monochrome lacquered wood with plant

motifs and festoons of flowers, belongs to the period of Randoni and shows decorative motifs similar to those that once occupied the wood dado at the bottom of the walls. The latter was surmounted by floral-motif wallpaper, some small fragments of which remain. The cabinet doors and panels above hosted carved and lacquered wood bas-reliefs of elegant workmanship with garlands of flowers, crowns, festoons of laurel, trophies of arms, geometric motifs, and the initials of Vittorio Amedeo III. On the walls were oil paintings with hunting scenes, classical ruins, seascapes, and rural subjects painted by Angelo Palanca and Francesco Antoniani and constituting the preparatory studies for tapestries by the eighteenth-century mills of Turin. Some of these "cartoons" are preserved in the Palazzo Civico at Rivoli and in the Palazzina di Caccia at Stupinigi, in the apartment of Carlo Felice.

Room 29. Room of the Stucchi or Antechamber of the Apartment of the Prince of Piedmont

This and the two following rooms were part of the suite that constituted the apartment of Vittorio Amedeo II's son, Prince Vittorio Amedeo Filippo, who died at the age of sixteen. The decorative program derives from Juvarra's project and was one of the first to be executed by the team of stucco-workers led by Pietro Somasso, to whom Juvarra entrusted the fine cornice with decorative elements in lacquered wood. A continuous festoon of oak and laurel leaves frames four trophies, in the corners, with crossed trumpets and the interwoven initials of Vittorio Amedeo. The scheme was completed by a high wood dado with curved pilasters in the corners that reached the cornice, supporting corbels. The walls, once covered with fabric, and, the ceiling do not show traces of decorations. Of the floor are preserved a few elements of a refined walnut and linden parquet (today removed), dating from the first decades of the Eighteenth century.

Room 30. Room of Pygmalion

Included, like the following room, in the extension of the north tower of the Castle carried out by Juvarra between 1718 and 1720, this was one of the more refined rooms of the apartment. The centre of the ceiling contained a fresco (still visible in 1930 and in 1936) by G .B . Van Loo with the myth of Pygmalion and Galatea. The scene, today completely destroyed by dampness from the roof, was painted between 1719 and 1720 and constituted one of the highest achievements of the decorative scheme imposed by Juvarra. The room nevertheless retains an extraordinary im-

portance today thanks to the band of stucchi around the base of the vault. The group of stucco-workers under Somasso developed Juvarra's basic idea around 1720-1721, in a tight sequence of motifs. Scrolls and wide volutes framing heraldic motifs and allegorical emblems alluding to the Savoy virtues and to absolute power, alternate between two mixtilinear cornices. Flowered garlands connect the central medallions with the royal symbols and the collar of the Order of the Annunziata. Composite allegorical groups with the sun, a green lizard and sheafs of grain; a temple with symbols of temporal power and horns of plenty; a brazier with its flame; and a quiver and bow, grace the corners.

Nothing remains of the decoration of the walls, which were papered over, except for a few fragments on the lintel of a window with two putti with a torch.

Room 31. Room of the Allegory of the Seasons or Bedroom of the Prince of Piedmont

Like the fresco cited above, this ceiling painting is also the work of G.B. Van Loo, whom Juvarra called from Rome to decorate the ceilings of these two rooms in 1719. Apollo appears at the centre of the vault, surrounded by Time, Abundance and Flora, with putti, flowers, vine-shoots and bundles of grain that allude to the four seasons, seated in the corners together with other divinities.

The fresco has recently been restored, having been repainted in the late Eighteenth century and in later epochs. Alterations have been made also to the cornice by Somasso, which now shows heavy polychrome repainting of the original pastel tones. The addition, at an unknown time, of stucco elements to the original text has changed certain ornaments and decorative details in the corners and in the central emblems, which allude to the mythological divinities of Mars, Jupiter, Neptune and Mercury.

Room 32. Music Room or Concert Room

In this room, too, the whole decoration was executed in the late Eighteenth century when the apartments were arranged to accommodate the Duke of Aosta's large family.

The pictorial decoration of the ceiling, today largely lost, was entrusted to a team of painters that included Guglielmo Lévera, Pietro Cuniberti, Ludovico Gioffrè and Angelo Vacca. The surviving paintings, of modest quality, represent a repertory of common forms in a simple geometric framework, a stylistically homogeneous work of repetitive, interwoven decoration. Coats of arms and festoons in grey and green monochrome mark the corners of the ceiling, alternating with trompe-l'oeil busts in red oval niches which originally included the idealized portraits of Counts Umberto I, Oddone, Berardo I and Amedeo I.

Other very fine works include the wooden decorations that surmount the doors and frame the mirrors at the centre of the walls. The bas-relief panels above the doors, with trophies of weapons and garlanded female heads, indulge in a neoclassical thematic repertory consonant with the historical period in which they were made, whereas the frames of the mirrors, showing an exuberant fantasy of decorative motifs carved with refined mastery, takes up the redundant manner of rococo and late baroque art.

This dualism of decorative forms was apparently amalgamated by the white and red lacquering of the woodwork, which originally alternated with fabrics in the wall panels today painted yellow.

The wood-carvers, carpenters and ebonists who worked in this room and in the following apartments from 1793 to 1796 are the same ones who were active at the time for the Savoy court in the palaces of Turin: Giovanni Battista Fortunati, Giuseppe Gianotti, Giovanni Antonio Gritella, Domenico Frolla, Giovanni Battista Pecors, Vittorio Viasco and Giovanni Orso.

Room 33. Room of Carlo Emanuele I

This room receives its name from Duke Carlo Emanuele I of Savoy, who was born in the pre-existing medieval castle in 1562. The distinctly neoclassical decorative scheme was prepared after Juvarra's time, between 1792 and 1795, by the architects Carlo Randoni and Giovanni Battista Piacenza.

The walls are punctuated by a sequence of Ionic pilasters bearing an elaborate trabeation on which rests the system of ribs and stucco profiles that divide up the ceiling, delimiting a central field originally frescoed by Giovenale Bongiovanni with an allegorical celebration of the Duke of Aosta.

The pictorial decoration has been almost completely lost, with the exception of a few fragments of a false coffered ceiling with rosettes in lozenges. In the corners, above the moulding, four stucco scrolls in high-relief carry the interlacing initials of Carlo Emanuele. The decoration of the door jambs and of the areas above was completed by sculptural elements in plaster, wood, and papier-maché. The stucchi of the ceiling and walls were made by the workshop of Giovanni Marmori, who completed the work in the autumn of 1793. The pair of console tables at the base of the lateral walls, executed to a design by Randoni in 1794, were realized in grey Valdieri marble by the stone-carver Giuseppe Marsaglia. The floor in Venetian seminato is a reconstruction – faithful in marble quality, colour and design of an earlier floor laid between the months of October 1793 and January 1794 by the Venetian craftsman Leopoldo Avoni.

Third Floor

The present third floor of the Castle took on its final architectural form in Juvarra's time and maintained it well into the Nineteenth century, when the assignment of the building for use by the military required radical changes. In the Eighteenth-century project thirteen small apartments occupied the large rectangular areas, which were covered with coffered wooden ceilings. Each apartment was made up of a main room, illuminated by one or two windows, preceded by two small rooms devoid of direct lighting: a dressing room, and an antechamber in which servants' beds were located. These apartments periodically accommodated members of the court or of the sovereigns' military entourage. Above this level, in the rooms of the attic and in the mezzanines of the corner pavilions, were the modest quarters of the palace servants.

The restoration of the Juvarran wing, the Manica Lunga and the interior of the Castello di Rivoli was carried out by the Regione Piemonte, which has turned the entire complex into a Museum of Contemporary Art.

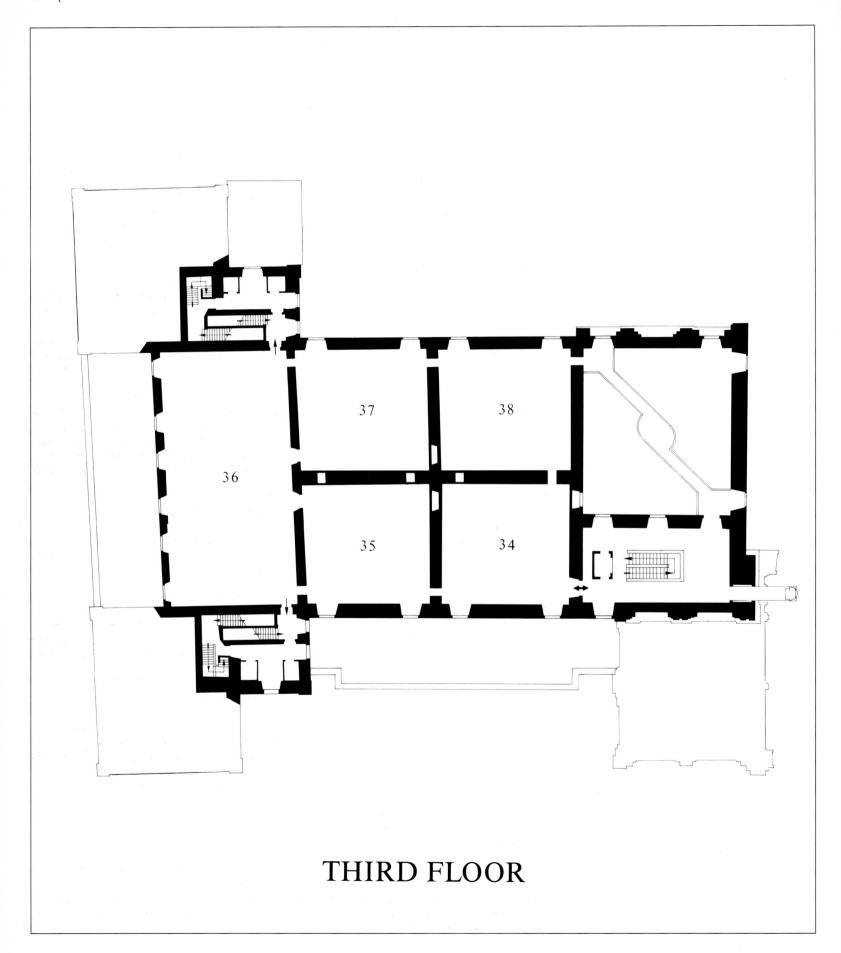

THIRD FLOOR

Exhibitions and catalogues 1984 - 1994

19 December 1984
Ouverture, curated by Rudi Fuchs.
Catalogue by Rudi Fuchs. Texts by Rudi Fuchs.

12 June - 25 August 1985
Bernd e Hilla Becher. Castelletti di estrazione, curated by Rudi Fuchs.
Catalogue by Zdenek Felix, Rudi Fuchs, Susanne Pagé, Marie-Madeleine Spehl-Robeyns. Texts by Bernd & Hilla Becher, Zdenek Felix, Rudi Fuchs, Susanne Pagé.

December 1984 - March 1985
Giovanni Anselmo, Per Kirkeby, Richard Long, group exhibition curated by Rudi Fuchs.
Catalogue by Rudi Fuchs.

25 October - 10 December 1985
Rennweg. Attersee, Brus, Nitsch, Pichler, Rainer, curated by Rudi Fuchs.
Catalogue by Rudi Fuchs. Texts by the artists.

24 October 1985
Gilbert & George. Life Death Hope Fear. Four images for one room of the Castello.
Pamphlet by Rudi Fuchs.

18 December 1985
Nicola De Maria. Cinque o sei lance spezzate a favore del coraggio e della virtù, curated by Rudi Fuchs.

December 1985 - February 1986
Il Museo Sperimentale di Torino. Arte italiana degli anni Sessanta nelle collezioni della Galleria Civica d'Arte Moderna, curated by Mirella Bandini and Rosanna Maggio Serra. Catalogue by Mirella Bandini and Rosanna Maggio Serra.

27 March - 11 May 1986
Frank O. Gehry, curated by Germano Celant.
Catalogue by Germano Celant. Text by Germano Celant. Castello di Rivoli.

19 April - 8 June 1986
Modus Vivendi. Ulay e Marina Abramovic, curated by Rudi Fuchs.
Catalogue by Thomas McEvilley. Text by Thomas McEvilley. Castello di Rivoli - Stedelijk van Abbemuseum, Eindhoven.

19 April - 8 June 1986
Camp Fire. Hamish Fulton, curated by Rudi Fuchs.
Catalogue by Jan Debbaut. Text by Michael Auping. Stedelijk van Abbemuseum, Eindhoven - Le Nouveau Musée, Lyons - Fruitmarket Gallery, Edinburgh.

June 1986
Ouverture II, curated by Rudi Fuchs and Johannes Gachnang.
Catalogue by Rudi Fuchs and Johannes Gachnang. Texts by Rudi Fuchs, Johannes Gachnang; interview by Francesco Poli to: Giovanni Anselmo, Georg Baselitz, Luciano Fabro, Donald Judd, Per Kirkeby. Umberto Allemandi & C., Turin.

21 June - 28 September 1986
Lucio Fontana. La cultura dell'occhio, curated by Rudi Fuchs, Johannes Gachnang, Cristina Mundici, Alessandra Santerini.
Catalogue by Rudi Fuchs, Johannes Gachnang, Cristina Mundici, Alessandra Santerini. Texts by Jole de Sanna, Rudi Fuchs, Johannes Gachnang. Castello di Rivoli.

19 December 1986 - 29 March 1987
Markus Lupertz, Giulio Paolini. Figure colonne finestre, curated by Rudi Fuchs and Johannes Gachnang.
Catalogue by Rudi Fuchs and Johannes Gachnang. Texts by Rudi Fuchs, Johannes Gachnang, Per Kirkeby, Markus Lupertz, Giulio Paolini. Castello di Rivoli.

May 1987
Ouverture, curated by Rudi Fuchs.

22 May - 6 September 1987
Carl Andre - Sculture, curated by Rudi Fuchs, Johannes Gachnang.

10 October - 29 November 1987
Karel Appel - Dipinti sculture e collages, curated by Rudi Fuchs, Johannes Gachnang, Alessandra Santerini.
Texts by Karel Appel, Wim Beeren, Hugo Claus, Rudi Fuchs, Sam Hunter, Rupert Martin. Castello di Rivoli.

17 December 1987 - 30 April 1988
Standing Sculpture, curated by Rudi Fuchs, Johannes Gachnang, Cristina Mundici.
Catalogue by Rudi Fuchs, Johannes Gachnang, Francesco Poli. Texts by Rudi Fuchs, Johannes Gachnang, Cristina Mundici, Francesco Poli. Castello di Rivoli.

17 June - 30 September 1988
Donald Judd
Richard Paul Lohse
Klaus Mettig, curated by Rudi Fuchs.

5 June - 18 September 1988
Joan Miró. Viaggio delle figure, curated by Rudi Fuchs, Johannes Gachnang, Cristina Mundici.
Catalogue by Rudi Fuchs, Johannes Gachnang, Cristina Mundici. Texts by Rudi Fuchs and Antoni Tàpies. Fabbri, Milan.

28 October - 12 February 1989
Jannis Kounellis, curated by Rudi Fuchs, Johannes Gachnang.
Catalogue by Rudi Fuchs, Johannes Gachnang, Cristina Mundici. Text by Rudi Fuchs. Fabbri, Milan.

December - 26 February 1989
Alberto Giacometti, curated by Rudi Fuchs, Johannes Gachnang, Cristina Mundici.
Catalogue by Rudi Fuchs, Johannes Gachnang, Cristina Mundici. Texts by Jole de Sanna, Johannes Gachnang, Jean Genet, Alberto Giacometti, Laszlo Glozer, Alessandra Lukinovich, Rudolf Schmitz, Christiane Meyer-Toss. Fabbri, Milan.

12 April - 17 June 1989
James Lee Byars: The Palace of Good Luck, curated by Rudi Fuchs, Johannes Gachnang, Cristina Mundici.
Catalogue by Rudi Fuchs, Johannes Gachnang, Cristina Mundici. Texts by Rudi Fuchs, James Lee Byars, Gianni Vattimo. Castello di Rivoli.

April - September 1989
Piano Nobile - Giuseppe Capogrossi, Enrico Castellani, Lucio Fontana, Francesco Lo Savio, Piero Manzoni, Fausto Melotti, Mimmo Rotella, Emilio Vedova, curated by Rudi Fuchs, Johannes Gachnang, Cristina Mundici.

28 June - 17 September 1989
Luciano Fabro, curated by Rudi Fuchs, Johannes Gachnang, Cristina Mundici.
Catalogue by Rudi Fuchs, Johannes Gachnang, Cristina Mundici. Texts by Jole de Sanna, Luciano Fabro, Mark Francis, Rudi Fuchs, Johannes Gachnang, John R. Lane, Daniel Soutif, Werner Oechslin. Fabbri, Milan.

6 October 1989 - 28 January 1990
Günther Förg, Alan Charlton, Domenico Bianchi, Barbara Kruger, Toon Verhoef, curated by Rudi Fuchs, Johannes Gachnang, Cristina Mundici.
Catalogue by Rudi Fuchs, Johannes Gachnang, Cristina Mundici. Texts by Jean Baudrillard, Bruno Corà, Rudi Fuchs, Johannes Gachnang, Donald Kuspit, Marcel Vos. Castello di Rivoli.

16 February - 29 April 1990
Arnulf Rainer, curated by Rudi Fuchs.
Catalogue by Rudi Fuchs, Johannes Gachnang, Cristina Mundici. Texts by Rudi Fuchs and Arnulf Rainer. Castello di Rivoli.

16 May - 23 September 1990
Mario Merz: Terra elevata o la storia del disegno, curated by Rudi Fuchs, Johannes Gachnang, Cristina Mundici.

Catalogue by Rudi Fuchs, Johannes Gachnang, Cristina Mundici. Texts by Rudi Fuchs, Johannes Gachnang, Beatrice Merz, Mario Merz. Castello di Rivoli.

21 September - 2 December 1990
Capolavori su carta. Opere espressioniste dal Museum Ludwig di Colonia: la Collezione Josef Haubrich, curated by Rudi Fuchs, Johannes Gachnang, Cristina Mundici. Catalogue by Rudi Fuchs, Johannes Gachnang, Cristina Mundici. Texts by Alfred M. Fischer, Peter Fuchs, Siegfried Gohr, Joseph Haubrich. Castello di Rivoli.

15 February - 31 May 1991
Arte & Arte. Dara Birnbaum, Rebecca Horn, Sol LeWitt, Philip Glass, Michelangelo Pistoletto, Cindy Sherman, Ettore Spalletti, Alberto Savinio, a cura di Ida Gianelli. "Alberto Savinio", curated by Maurizio Fagiolo dell'Arco. "La Manica Lunga e il Castello di Rivoli", curated by Andrea Bruno.
Catalogue by Ida Gianelli. Texts by Andrea Bruno, Maurizio Fagiolo dell'Arco, Ida Gianelli, Giorgio Verzotti. Fabbri, Milan.

5 April - 31 May 1991
Letteratura Artistica. Documenti del '900 in Italia, curated by Maurizio Fagiolo dell'Arco.
Catalogue by Maurizio Fagiolo dell'Arco. Text by Maurizio Fagiolo dell'Arco. Fabbri, Milan.

4 May - 30 July 1991
Anteprima 1: Giulio Paolini, curated by Ida Gianelli.
Catalogue by Ida Gianelli. Text by Giorgio Verzotti. Fabbri, Milan-Castello di Rivoli.

5 July - 27 September 1991
Sguardo di Medusa. Jean-Marc Bustamante, Clegg & Guttmann, Peter Fischli and David Weiss, Günther Förg, Andreas Gursky, Thomas Ruff, Andreas Serrano, Laurie Simmons, Thomas Struth, Jeff Wall, curated by Ida Gianelli.
Catalogue by Ida Gianelli. Texts by Ida Gianelli and Giorgio Verzotti. Fabbri, Milan.

2 October - 1 December 1991
Alberto Burri. Cellotex 1991, curated by Ida Gianelli. Catalogue by Ida Gianelli. Text by Ida Gianelli. Fabbri, Milan.

15 November - 9 February 1992
Giuseppe Penone, curated by Ida Gianelli and Giorgio Verzotti.
Catalogue by Ida Gianelli and Giorgio Verzotti. Texts by Johannes Cladders, Ida Gianelli, Remo Guidieri, Daniel Soutif, Giorgio Verzotti. Fabbri, Milan.

11 December 1992
Nuove acquisizioni: Carla Accardi, Pier Paolo Calzolari, Richard Long, Fausto Melotti.

13 December 1991 - 26 January 1992
Anteprima 2: Wim Delvoye, curated by Ida Gianelli. Catalogue by Ida Gianelli. Text by Giorgio Verzotti. Fabbri, Milan-Castello di Rivoli.

7 February - 3 May 1992
Piero Manzoni, curated by Germano Celant.
Catalogue by Germano Celant. Texts by Germano Celant, Jean Pierre Criqui, Jens Henrik Sandberg, Francisco Calvo Serraller, Nancy Spector. Electa, Milan.

27 March - 28 June 1992
Anteprima 3: Marco Bagnoli, curated by Ida Gianelli. Catalogue by Ida Gianelli. Text by Francesca Pasini. Fabbri, Milan-Castello di Rivoli.

27 March - 28 June 1992
Jan Vercruysse. Tombeaux (Stanza), curated by Ida Gianelli.
Catalogue by Ida Gianelli. Fabbri, Milan-Castello di Rivoli.

2 October - 22 November 1992
Post Human, curated by Jeffrey Deitch.
Catalogue by Jeffrey Deitch. Text by Jeffrey Deitch. Castello di Rivoli.

2 October - 22 November 1992
Anteprima 4: Guillaume Bijl, curated by Ida Gianelli and Giorgio Verzotti.
Catalogue by Ida Gianelli. Text by Giorgio Verzotti. Charta, Milan-Castello di Rivoli.

2 October 1992 - 10 January 1993
Mario Giacomelli, curated by Ida Gianelli and Antonella Russo.
Catalogue by Ida Gianelli and Antonella Russo. Texts by Charles-Henri Favrod, Mario Giacomelli, Ida Gianelli, Antonella Russo. Charta, Milan-Castello di Rivoli.

11 December 1992 - 10 January 1993
Anteprima 5: Annette Lemieux, curated by Ida Gianelli. Catalogue by Ida Gianelli. Text by Trevor Fairbrother. Charta, Milan-Castello di Rivoli.

5 February - 25 April 1993
Un'avventura internazionale. Torino e le arti 1950-1970, curated by Germano Celant, Paolo Fossati, Ida Gianelli. Architectural section curated by Roberto Gabetti and Aimaro Isola. Photography section curated by Cesare de Seta. Cinema section curated by Gian Piero Brunetta. Artistic Literature by Maurizio Fagiolo dell'Arco.

Activities 1985 - 1994

Catalogue by Ida Gianelli. Texts by Marella Agnelli, Giuseppe Bertasso, Guido Davico Bonino, Michel Bourel, Gian Piero Brunetta, Benedetto Camerana, Germano Celant, Pietro Derossi, Cesare de Seta, Maurizio Fagiolo dell'Arco, Paolo Fossati, Roberto Gabetti, Ida Gianelli, Aimaro Isola, Corrado Levi, Marcello Levi, Mario Messinis, Ada Minola, Alberto Papuzzi, Pier Luigi Pero, Paolo Pinamonti, Luciano Pistoi, Edoardo Sanguineti, Gian Enzo Sperone, Gianni Vattimo, Giorgio Verzotti. Charta, Milan.

2 October - 28 November 1993
Da Brancusi a Boltanski. Fotografie d'artista, curated by Alain Sayag and Agnès de Gouvion Saint-Cyr. Catalogue by Alain Sayag and Agnès de Gouvion Saint-Cyr. Texts by Alain Sayag and Agnès de Gouvion Saint-Cyr. Charta, Milan.

2 October - 31 December 1993
Enzo Cucchi, curated by Ida Gianelli and Giorgio Verzotti. Catalogue by Ida Gianelli. Texts by Achille Bonito Oliva, Ida Gianelli, Giorgio Verzotti. Charta, Milan.

4 February - 30 May 1994
Keith Haring, curated by Germano Celant. Catalogue by Germano Celant and Ida Gianelli. Texts by Germano Celant, Zdenek Felix, Ida Gianelli, Sune Nordgren, Giorgio Verzotti. Charta, Milan.

10 March - 24 April 1994
Gabetti e Isola. Architetture, curated by Roberto Gabetti and Aimaro Isola.

24 June - 28 August 1994
Carla Accardi, curated by Ida Gianelli and Giorgio Verzotti.
Catalogue by Ida Gianelli. Texts by Achille Bonito Oliva and Giorgio Verzotti. Charta, Milan.

24 June - 28 August 1994
Soggetto-Soggetto. Una nuova relazione nell'arte di oggi, curated by Francesca Pasini and Giorgio Verzotti. Catalogue by Francesca Pasini and Giorgio Verzotti. Texts by Francesca Pasini, Antonella Russo and Giorgio Verzotti. Charta, Milan.

24 September - 20 November 1994
Pier Paolo Calzolari, curated by Ida Gianelli. Catalogue by Ida Gianelli. Texts by Bruno Corà and Catherine David. Charta, Milan.

24 September - 20 November 1994
Helmut Newton, curated by Zdenek Felix. Catalogue by Zdenek Felix. Texts by Noemi Smolik and Urs Stahel. Schirmer/Mosel, Munich.

September 1985
Funerale, La montagna gialla, Il canto dell'usignolo, video shown on the "Zattera di Babele" by Carlo Quartucci and Anna Tatò, set design by Jannis Kounellis, Teatro del Castello, Rivoli.

3 October 1986
Videokunst, video-art in the German Federal Republic 1976-1986, in conjunction with the Goethe Institut Turin and Extrastudio, Turin, Castello di Rivoli.

3 October 1986
Arte e Mito, round table, speakers Germano Celant, Vittorio Fagone, Rudi Fuchs, Wulf Herzogenrath.

16-17 October 1987
Il restauro del contemporaneo., International Symposium, in conjunction with the Goethe Institut, Turin.

22 May 1990
Concerto per Rivoli, contemporary music performance: director Luca Pfaff, music by Wolfgang Rihm, Tomàs Marco, Gerard Grisey, Adriano Guarnieri, Lorenzo Ferrero, Teatro del Castello.

7 April 1991
Five Metamorphoses, concerto for pianoforte, music composed and performed by Philip Glass.

11 April 1992
Arte e Teatro. Michelangelo Pistoletto, lecture by Francesca Pasini, Teatro del Castello
Arte e Fotografia: Cindy Sherman, lecture by Giorgio Verzotti, Teatro del Castello.

18 April 1992
Arte e Musica: Sol LeWitt, lecture by Giorgio Verzotti.
Arte e Architettura: Ettore Spalletti, lecture by Francesca Pasini, Teatro del Castello.

24 April 1992
Arte e Cinema: Rebecca Horn, lecture by Giorgio Verzotti.
Arte e Video: Dara Birnbaum, lecture by Francesca Pasini, Teatro del Castello.

2 May 1992
Arte e Letteratura: Alberto Savinio, lecture by Maurizio Fagiolo dell'Arco, Teatro del Castello.

28-30 May 1991
Dall'Anno Uno ad oggi, play in four acts by Michelangelo Pistoletto.

20-21 June 1991
Il Canto del Drago, musical. Music by Giorgio Battistelli. Scores and texts by Bizhan Bassiri.

5 February 1992
Piero Manzoni, lecture by Germano Celant, Teatro del Castello.

23 April 1992
Marco Bagnoli, lecture by Bruno Corà and Francesca Pasini, Teatro del Castello.

21 May 1992
Jan Vercruysse, lecture by Alain Cueff, Teatro del Castello.

9 July 1992
Solo Concert per Due, violin concert, music written and performed by Michael Galasso.

October-December 1992
Corso teorico di storia e critica della fotografia 1910-1990, lecturer Antonella Russo, Teatro del Castello.
Corso di storia dell'arte contemporanea, lecturer Giorgio Verzotti, Teatro del Castello.

8 October 1992
Mario Giacomelli, lecture by Charles-Henri Favrod, Teatro del Castello.

21 October 1992
Il Viaggio dell'icononauta dalle lanterne magiche al cinema, lecture by Gian Piero Brunetta, Teatro del Castello.
La nascita del cinema, magic lantern show, directed by Museo Nazionale del Cinema di Torino, Teatro del Castello.
La fotografia nel cinema, film exhibition presented in conjunction with the Museo del Cinema and Centre Culturel Français di Torino, Teatro del Castello.

22 October 1992
Guillaume Bijl, lecture by Giorgio Verzotti, Teatro del Castello.

12 November 1992
Il post umano e l'esperienza artistica, lecture by Mario Perniola, Teatro del Castello.
L'opera d'arte e i suoi luoghi, lecture by Ann Van Sevenant, Teatro del Castello.

From 4 February - 25 April 1993
Torino Grigionera, directed by Francesco Conversano and Nene Grignaffini, for the Cinema section of the

exhibition "Un'avventura internazionale. Torino e le arti 1950-1970", Teatro del Castello.

6 March 1993
Lee Friedlander, meeting with the artist, co-ordinated by Antonella Russo, for the Photography section of the exhibition "Un'avventura internazionale. Torino e le arti 1950-1970", Teatro del Castello.

Sundays in March and April 1993
Un'avventura internazionale. Torino e le arti 1950-1970, lectures by Antonella Russo and Giorgio Verzotti, Teatro del Castello.

April - June 1993
Corso di storia della fotografia, lecturer Antonella Russo, Teatro del Castello
Corso di storia dell'arte contemporanea, lecturer Giorgio Verzotti, Teatro del Castello.

9-30 May 1993
Il teatro di Luca Ronconi, video in conjunction with the Centro Studi del Teatro Stabile di Torino, Teatro del Castello.

1-13 June 1993
Interviste a Pier Paolo Pasolini 1966-1975, video in conjunction with Fondo Pier Paolo Pasolini, Rome, Teatro del Castello.

From 1-13 June 1993
Pilade e Calderon, play directed by Luca Ronconi, in conjunction with Teatro Stabile di Torino.

18 September 1993
La Zattera di Babele e Tre pezzi di occasione, play, set design by Carlo Quartucci with Carla Tatò, in conjunction with the Festival del Nuovo Teatro-Festival di Chieri, Ivrea, Rivoli, Teatro del Castello.

From October - December 1993
Corso di storia e teoria della fotografia, lecturer Antonella Russo, Teatro del Castello.
Corso di storia dell'arte contemporanea, lecturer Giorgio Verzotti, Teatro del Castello
Sezione restauro, lecturers Luisa Mensi and Antonio Rava, Teatro del Castello.

12 November 1993
Incontro con Mario Botta e Enzo Cucchi, in conjunction with Accademia Albertina di Belle Arti di Torino and Ordine degli Architetti di Torino, Castello di Rivoli and Turin Architecture Faculty.

March - May 1994
Corso di storia della fotografia, lecturer Antonella Russo, Teatro del Castello.
Corso di storia dell'arte contemporanea, lecturer Giorgio Verzotti, Teatro del Castello.

30 February 1994
La luce nell'arte e nella fotografia, seminar, lecturers Giulio Paolini and Paolo Mussat Sartor in conjunction with Accademia di Belle Arti di Torino.

28 April 1994
Le Sirene di Haring, lecture by Germano Celant, Teatro del Castello.

8 June 1994
La luce nell'arte e nell'architettura, seminar, lecturers Gae Aulenti, Sandro Chia, Piero Castiglioni. Guest Carla Accardi, in conjunction with Accademia Albertina di Belle Arti di Torino, Teatro del Castello.

23 June 1994
Ars Ludi, concert performed by Officina Musicale, music by Giorgio Battistelli.

20 October 1994
Visione e perversione nella fotografia di Helmut Newton, lecture by Antonella Russo, Teatro del Castello.

17 November 1994
Pier Paolo Calzolari, lecture by Giorgio Verzotti, Teatro del Castello.